RECLAIMING PIETISM

Reclaiming Pietism

Retrieving an Evangelical Tradition

Roger E. Olson and Christian T. Collins Winn

WILLIAM B. EERDMANS PUBLISHING COMPANY
GRAND RAPIDS, MICHIGAN / CAMBRIDGE, U.K.

Published 2015 by
Wm. B. Eerdmans Publishing Co.
2140 Oak Industrial Drive N.E., Grand Rapids, Michigan 49505 /
P.O. Box 163, Cambridge CB3 9PU U.K.

Printed in the United States of America

21 20 19 18 17 16 15   7 6 5 4 3 2 1

Library of Congress Cataloging-in-Publication Data

ISBN 978-0-8028-6909-8

www.eerdmans.com

To our mutual friend and mentor, Donald W. Dayton

Contents

CONTENTS

Acknowledgments

This work has been helped along by the good efforts of others. Many thanks go to Sara Misgen, Robert Alexander Simpson, and Matthew Eddy for their editorial and organizational help at various stages of the project. We would also like to thank the editorial team at Eerdmans for their careful review of the manuscript and for helping us to bring the work to publication.

Introduction

"Pietism" is a bad word, or so claim common opinion and usage. We want to challenge and correct that. For us, "Pietism" is a good word; we are both Pietists without apology. Unfortunately, Pietism is often equated with a "holier-than-thou" spiritual attitude, with religious legalism, or with withdrawal from involvement in improving society. None of these images of Pietism holds up when examined historically; the Pietist movement and its aftermath, the Pietist ethos, required none of them. We acknowledge that some Pietists have earned a reputation, but that has been not for being good Pietists but for being bad ones. In this little book we hope to brush off, clean up, and reclaim our own Pietist heritage.

I (Roger) grew up in a Pentecostal home and church that were imbued with a Pietist spirituality. Deep — even emotional — devotion to Jesus Christ was a crucial part of our Christianity. For us, being "evangelical" meant being profoundly devoted to Jesus Christ and Holy Scripture. Our hymns and spiritual songs promoted this spirituality that I call "conversional piety." "Friendship with Jesus!/Fellowship divine!/Oh, what blessed, sweet communion!/ Jesus is a Friend of mine." Having a deep, personal relationship with Jesus Christ was not just a cliché for us; it was crucial to our spiritual lives. I attended a seminary founded by German Pietists that instilled in me a warm-hearted evangelicalism that replaced the emotional Pentecostalism of my youth. Later I taught at a Christian college founded by Swedish Pietists and discovered there a spiritual ethos that resonated with my warm-hearted evangelical faith.

In all of these settings I realized that the popular images of Pietism were largely incorrect.

I (Christian) came to know Pietism later in life through my Ph.D. work under theologian and historian Donald Dayton at Drew University. Dayton insisted that I needed to know and understand Pietism in order to make sense of modern Christianity, and it was at his suggestion that I took up my study of Johann Christoph and Christoph Friedrich Blumhardt, as well as the wider Württemberg Pietist tradition from which they came. Exposure to the primary texts of this tradition dispelled the negative caricatures of Pietism that I had harbored and also opened up for me a whole new way of seeing and understanding evangelicalism in North America. As a kind of happy by-product, I was deeply shaped by the spirituality of the two Blumhardts, a spirituality that focuses on the coming kingdom of God and the Christian commitment to hope as a form of witness and life. The Pietist emphasis on personal intimacy with Jesus was configured by the Blumhardts in such a way that it did not allow one to be overly introspective, but rather forced one to look outside oneself for signposts of the coming of the living God. With the Blumhardts' help I continue to learn what it means to pray, hope, and live the second petition of the Lord's Prayer: "Thy kingdom come!"

Pietism is undergoing a renaissance in scholarly historical and theological circles; recent years have seen numerous volumes published about Pietism, but most of them have been erudite treatments of the subject inaccessible to most laypeople and pastors. This has been especially the case in Germany, where Pietism began in the late seventeenth century and flourished in the early eighteenth century. In America, scholarly conferences about Pietism have produced a number of edited volumes of essays in the last decade, and recently both Roger and I contributed to such a conference and book.[1] Now our desire is to make the new Pietist research accessible to a wider audience of non-theologians and non-religious scholars.

But why? Why care about the reputation of Pietism? We believe that Pietism is an important element in evangelical Christianity[2] that still

1. See *The Pietist Impulse in Christianity,* ed. Christian T. Collins Winn et al. (Eugene, Ore.: Pickwick Press, 2011).

2. We realize, of course, that "evangelical" is an essentially contested concept, so a brief explanation of our use is in order. By "evangelical Christianity" we mean

has rich resources for spiritual renewal of individuals and communities. Rediscovering and recovering the impulses of original Pietism can contribute much to a contemporary understanding of evangelicalism and to spiritual revival. Those Pietist impulses are still at work in movements such as Renovaré and have influenced theologians such as Donald Bloesch and Stanley Grenz — two influential evangelical thinkers. A correct understanding of historical Pietism can help keep such spiritual movements and evangelical thinkers grounded in history — to help us learn from both its successes and its failures.

We believe that Pietism still has much to offer contemporary Christians who are interested in the spiritual life and in developing a theology that is grounded in experience while at the same time remaining biblically faithful. Our hope is that this book can be a contribution to the rediscovery and renewal of the original spirit of Pietism for those Christians. Above all, however, we offer this book to the glory of God and the renewal of the church of Jesus Christ.

A brief overview of the book may help those considering whether to read it or those who have already decided to read it but would like to know something about its content in advance. In Chapter 1 we discuss the various misconceptions of Pietism and correct them in terms of the actual history of the Pietist movement. In Chapter 2 we reveal the pre-history of historical Pietism in various Christian mystics and among devotionally minded Puritans. In Chapter 3 we turn to the beginning and progress of the Pietist movement of the seventeenth and eighteenth centuries, highlighting the contributions of two key Pietist founders, Philipp Jakob Spener and August Hermann Francke. In Chapter 4 we continue the discussion, offering a brief description of radical Pietism and then focusing on Nikolaus Ludwig von Zinzendorf and the Württemberg tradition of Pietism.

Chapter 5 is in many ways the heart of the book, because in it we explore the themes that define Pietism both past and present. In Chapter 6

Christianity that values and emphasizes the supreme authority of the Bible for faith and practice, reconciliation with God through the cross of Jesus Christ embraced in a personal decision of faith (conversion), the cross of Jesus Christ as the sole means by which people can be saved, and world transformation through evangelism and social action. As we see it, evangelical Christianity also places a high value on basic Christian orthodoxy — the incarnation of God in Christ and the Trinity.

we tell the story of how German Pietism moved onto British and North American soil through the evangelical awakenings led by John Wesley and others. In Chapter 7 we outline the reformulation of Pietism during the long nineteenth century in Europe and discuss how several leading modern theologians and philosophers took up elements of Pietism in their systems of thought. Chief among these are Friedrich Schleiermacher, the "father of modern theology," who called himself a Pietist "of a higher order," and the Danish "father of existentialism" Søren Kierkegaard. In our final chapter — Chapter 8 — we examine contemporary figures who have appropriated Pietism, looking especially at theologians such as Donald Bloesch, Richard Foster, Stanley Grenz, and Jürgen Moltmann. In conclusion, we call for a new and proper appreciation of historical Pietism especially among evangelicals who, apart from Pietism, tend to fall into dead orthodoxy.

We dedicate this book to a theologian who has influenced us both — Donald Dayton — Christian's *Doktorvater* and a major guide for Roger's thinking about the nature of evangelicalism.

CHAPTER ONE

Defining and Redefining Pietism

How a Good Word Got a Bad Reputation

Why a book about "reclaiming Pietism"? Why does Pietism need to be re-claimed? Like many good words, "Pietism" has taken on a life of its own that has little to do with its original meanings. This book is an attempt to reclaim the word by engaging the history of Pietism to understand the original motives and themes that energized the movement. This chapter offers a preview of the rest of the book because it will be necessary here to explain why Pietism is *not* what many people think it is. The main burden of this chapter, therefore, is simply to explain the many and sometimes widely varying views of Pietism that swirl around the term in contempo-rary culture — including Christian culture.

One of the most influential scholars of Pietism in the English-speaking world was F. Ernest Stoeffler (1911-2003), who famously wrote, "One of the least understood movements in the history of Christianity has un-doubtedly been that of Pietism."[1] In fact, most scholars of Pietism echo Stoeffler when they attempt to explain it. They usually begin with a brief account of misunderstandings and misrepresentations surrounding the movement. Another scholar of Pietism, Harry Yeide Jr., goes into great detail in exploding myths about Pietism. Contrary to its critics, he says, Pietism was and is "anything but individualistic, introverted, and emo-

---

1. F. Ernest Stoeffler, *The Rise of Evangelical Pietism* (Leiden: E. J. Brill, 1971), p. 1.

tional."[2] Paul Kuenning rightly notes that contemporary religious scholarship is revising its views of Pietism and that traditional and common accusations against it are turning out to be greatly exaggerated. Lutheran Pietism in America, which Kuenning studies, has often been accused of being "quietist" — a concept often confused with "Pietist." Quietism was a mystical form of Christianity that emphasized pure inwardness and detachment from social issues. According to Kuenning,

> German Lutheran Pietism has often been characterized as quietistic or otherworldly, as fostering a subjective spirituality that retreated into its own world of mystical asceticism or private piety. The inaccuracy of these descriptions when applied to the classical Lutheran Pietism of the Spener-Francke school [original Pietism] becomes apparent through even a cursory examination of its exuberant ethical activism.[3]

Pick up any book by a scholar of Pietism and you will find these kinds of adamant denials of common myths and misconceptions, accusations and charges, against Pietism. So far, however, they have failed to turn the tide of popular — and sometimes scholarly — negative opinion about Pietism. Though the tide may be turning in favor of a new and more positive perception of Pietism among historians and theologians, popular opinion is another matter. To a very large extent among the grassroots, "Pietist" is still, unfortunately, a pejorative epithet. Outside of a few Protestant denominations rooted in historical, classical Pietism, the label evokes images of super-spiritual otherworldliness, a "holier-than-thou" attitude, religious emotionalism and legalism, and many other undesirable religious attitudes and actions.

I (Roger) have had many unfortunate experiences with the label "Pietist" and the term "Pietism." I grew up in a family steeped in Pietism, even though the word was seldom used. My home churches, though nominally Pentecostal, were imbued with a Pietist ethos. While this book will elaborate on the content of the Pietist ethos in great detail below, theologian Ted

2. Harry Yeide Jr., *Studies in Classical Pietism: The Flowering of the Ecclesiola* (New York: Peter Lang, 1997), p. xi.

3. Paul P. Kuenning, *The Rise and Fall of American Lutheran Pietism* (Macon, Ga.: Mercer University Press, 1988), p. 13.

Campbell has expressed it vividly in a nutshell. Speaking of the original Pietist movement of the late seventeenth and early eighteenth centuries, he wrote,

> Pietism stressed personal religious experience, especially repentance (the experience of one's own unworthiness before God and of one's own need for grace) and sanctification (the experience of personal growth in holiness, involving progress towards complete or perfect fulfillment of God's intention).[4]

In other words, the Pietist ethos — stemming from the early and original Pietist movement, which we'll explain more in Chapters 3 and 4 — focused on *heart Christianity*. It was the "religion of the heart" or what early Pietist leader Philipp Jakob Spener (1635-1705) called "the inner man." Pietism was, and at its best is, about inward transformation by God through repentance and faith, which results in renewed affections, or feelings about God and the "things of God." My spiritual development was under the indirect influence of Pietism, and when I first encountered its history, theology, and spirituality as an academic study in college and seminary, I immediately recognized it as the ethos of my church and family. Imagine my surprise, then, when I began to hear my mentors insult and demean it.

Perhaps the first instance occurred after I stepped out of my own Christian tradition to pursue doctoral studies in theology at a major national research university. My main professor of theology, my first *Doktorvater*, often referred to Pietism in a profoundly negative tone and equated it with religious subjectivism, emotionalism, anti-intellectualism, and otherworldliness. I recognized these as very real dangers in the spirituality of my upbringing, but I also knew that they were not endemic to Pietism as a historical movement; I had learned that in the evangelical seminary with German Baptist and Pietist roots I had attended. At the same time, the pastor I worked under in a Presbyterian church called my spiritual-

---

4. Ted A. Campbell, *The Religion of the Heart: A Study of European Religious Life in the Seventeenth and Eighteenth Centuries* (Columbia: University of South Carolina Press, 1991), p. 71.

theological tradition "piousity" and firmly rejected it for the same reasons my mentor gave. Throughout my doctoral studies I felt I had to hide my Pietism; the walls against it were too high and too strong to breach.

During my doctoral studies I spent a year studying with Lutheran theologian Wolfhart Pannenberg (b. 1928) in Germany. Several times I heard him say, "Whatever I am, there is one thing I am *not* — a Pietist!" Later, during my tenure teaching theology at an evangelical Baptist college and seminary with Swedish-Pietist roots, I encountered a well-known pastor and critic of the institution who told me, "Pietism is just a mask for doctrinal indifference." Both of these men, astute and influential Christian thinkers and authors, viewed Pietism as a flight from reason and sound doctrinal belief into a private, inner, subjective realm of spiritual feelings where "anything goes" cognitively. Again, I realized that this is a danger surrounding Pietism, but I also knew that it was neither the essence of Pietism nor necessary to it. I recognized what these individuals were talking about as "Pietism gone to seed" — or Pietism allowed to lean deeply into its own pathologies, and perhaps even fall fully from its original intentions and best impulses. Original, essential, historical, classical Pietism, however, was not and, at its best, is not of that nature.

Previewing "Original Pietism"

These myths and misconceptions about, false impressions of, and accusations against Pietism persist and are common in evangelical Christian writings — in spite of the avalanche of recent scholarship showing that they are wrong. A 2002 article in a major evangelical publication by an evangelical philosopher-theologian asked in its title "What's wrong with Pietism?" The author trotted out some of the popular but false images of Pietism and concluded that it is a negative influence on American religious life because it "cuts itself loose from a doctrinally full and sound faith."[5] All one has to do to find popular, negative treatments of Pietism is search for the term using any Internet Web browser: most of what one finds includes

---

5. Mark R. Talbot, "What's Wrong with Pietism?," *Modern Reformation* 11, no. 4 (July/August 2002): 25.

and even emphasizes Pietism's alleged pernicious influences. A blogger on one Web site explains "how Pietism deceives Christians" and equates it with spiritual elitism, concluding that "Pietism cannot help but take people's minds off the gospel."[6]

Much of this book will be devoted to correcting these and other myths and misconceptions about Pietism. It will also recommend true Pietism, rooted in the original Pietist movement and faithful to its ethos, as a powerful resource for the renewal of contemporary Christianity. Here our main concern is to explain why this is necessary, why "reclaiming Pietism" must include dispelling popular and scholarly misconceptions of it. Here some of those major myths and misconceptions will be explored and, if not dismissed, at least countered. First, however, it will be helpful to readers to say something briefly about the Pietist movement and its ethos.

The origin of Pietism as a movement is much debated, but most scholars agree that a key figure in its early history was Spener and that his book *Pia Desideria* (1675) is a foundational text of the movement. The title means "pious desires." The book was originally intended as a new introduction to an older spiritual book entitled *True Christianity* (1605-1610) by Protestant mystic Johann Arndt (1555-1621), who could rightly be called a precursor of Pietism. *True Christianity* called for and expounded a deeper, more profound spiritual life than many Protestants experienced at the time. By the early seventeenth century, much European Protestantism had fallen into a dry scholasticism, "cheap grace" (to use Dietrich Bonhoeffer's twentieth-century term), and sacramental salvation devoid of any need for repentance or changes to daily living. Arndt's book sparked a new passion for inward spiritual renewal and experience of God beyond the intellectual and sacramental. Spener's *Pia Desideria* eclipsed *True Christianity* in influence as the author, a Lutheran pastor in Frankfurt, Germany, called for radical changes in church life to promote spiritual renewal. Above all, Spener emphasized the necessity of the "renewal of the inner man" for true Christianity: every individual ought to receive

---

6. Bob DeWay, "How Pietism Deceives Christians: The Errors of Elitist Teachings in the Church," at the "Critical Issues Commentary" blog at http://cicministry.org/commentary/issue101.htm.

the transforming grace of God within his or her own person, resulting in new affections for God and the "things of God" as well as an amended life moving toward holiness.

K. James Stein provides the context for understanding why Spener's proposals for individual and church renewal were needed and heeded by many European state-church Protestants in the late seventeenth and early eighteenth centuries:

> The scholastic spirit cast a pall of intellectualism over the Christian faith. Persons were left with the impression that Christianity consisted of the reception of God's saving Word through preaching and the sacraments along with loyal adherence to the Lutheran confessions. It was stated that with few exceptions, pastors avoided any stress upon inwardness.[7]

Thus, according to Stein, "Pietism was a plant grown up out of the soil of Lutheran Orthodoxy, which was becoming increasingly narrow as the century progressed."[8] By many accounts, Protestant state churches were spiritually stale spaces where sermons focused on hair-splitting theological controversies and salvation was offered based solely on participation in the sacraments and mental assent to correct doctrines.

Spener, and most Pietists after him, "distinguished between 'historical, dead faith' and 'true, living, divine, saving faith,'"[9] with the latter resulting from conversion or "new birth." For Spener, in conversion, or new birth,

> God creates a new manner and nature in the human soul. With their images restored through a birth out of God himself, reborn persons emulate their divine parent in manifesting pure holiness and righteousness, especially [in] a pure love and desire for everything that is right and good.[10]

7. K. James Stein, *Philipp Jakob Spener: Pietist Patriarch* (Chicago: Covenant Press, 1986), p. 21.
8. Stein, *Philipp Jakob Spener*, p. 28.
9. Stein, *Philipp Jakob Spener*, p. 171.
10. Stein, *Philipp Jakob Spener*, p. 193.

Traditional Protestant Orthodoxy had come to emphasize *justification* at the expense of *regeneration* and *sanctification* — the objective, "declaratory" aspect of salvation at the expense of the transforming, inwardly renewing aspect of salvation. Without in any way rejecting Martin Luther's doctrine of justification by grace through faith alone, Spener sought to add a new emphasis on the *response of faith* and *inward transformation* as crucial aspects of conversion to Christ. Again, Stein explains Spener's intentions well:

> Spener's appeal to his contemporaries was not necessarily that they undergo a dramatic and emotional conversion experience similar to those produced later in American revivalism, but that they understand themselves to be in a state or condition of new birth. It was the possession of the previously described "living faith" with its accompanying piety that would give these persons the assurance that, despite their continuing sin and weakness, they were in a right relationship with God.[11]

Spener's *Pia Desideria* was reviled and celebrated alike. It was especially odious to church leaders and theologians steeped in formalistic, nominal Christianity. But to make matters worse for them, and later for him, Spener began to set up what he called *collegia pietatis*, later called "conventicles" in English — small groups for Bible study, devotion, prayer, and discussion of faith outside the structures of the church. He began to preach against rulers and church leaders who lived immoral lives and absented themselves from devotion and worship. Eventually charges of heresy were brought against Spener, forcing him to leave Frankfurt and relocate several times. However, his reputation as a holy person and as a Christian reformer garnered him a large following. A new movement arose around him that came to be called Pietism. His student and protégé August Hermann Francke (1663-1727) became even more influential than Spener, an example of the student surpassing the teacher. Francke established a host of Pietist institutions in the German city of Halle and, through correspondence and some political machinations, became a powerful and influential figure in Prussian politics and world missions. Like

---

11. Stein, *Philipp Jakob Spener*, p. 197.

his mentor, Francke emphasized conversion and devotional life as well as evangelism and social transformation.

By the middle of the eighteenth century, Pietism had become what one church historian called "the second Reformation." According to Carter Lindberg of Boston University, "Lutheran Pietism became the dominant cultural force in the German states of the eighteenth century."[12] But Pietism was *not* primarily a political or secular cultural force; it was a spiritual movement. Lindberg defined it as "a Bible-centered movement concerned for holy living that flows from the regenerate heart."[13] Pietism gave rise to numerous individual Christian writers, ministers, new denominations, individual seekers, missionaries and mission agencies, publishing houses, and universities and seminaries. One religious commentator has gone so far as to claim that Pietism became *the* most influential spiritual movement since the Reformation, especially in America: "To meet the Pietists is to come home to what spawned not only many of us as religious believers, but almost all of us as citizens of contemporary America."[14]

What I have just presented is the briefest possible summary of the original Pietist movement — a summary that will be expanded into a fuller account in later chapters. The movement, however, is gone. To be sure, its influence is alive if not well. All movements have their time and die out; their lasting influence is through their ethos.[15] The Pietist movement was energized by a spiritual ethos that outlived it and can be seen in many sectors of contemporary Christianity. It is often the ethos that critics oppose — frequently based on misunderstandings. To fully understand the Pietist ethos, one *must* see it in relation to the movement that gave rise to it. One cannot point the finger at something completely unrelated to the Pietist movement and say, "There! That's what's wrong with Pietism!" And

12. Carter Lindberg, "Introduction," in *The Pietist Theologians*, ed. Carter Lindberg (Malden, Mass.: Blackwell, 2005), p. 9.

13. Lindberg, "Introduction," in *The Pietist Theologians*, p. 4.

14. Phyllis Tickle, "Foreword," in *The Pietists: Selected Writings*, ed. Emilie Griffin and Peter C. Erb (San Francisco: HarperSanFrancisco, 2006), p. ix.

15. This emphasis on Pietism as an ethos transcending the Pietist movement is indebted to Mary Fulbrook, who uses this rubric in *Piety and Politics: Religion and the Rise of Absolutism in England, Würrtemberg, and Prussia* (Cambridge: Cambridge University Press, 1983), pp. 31-36. Fulbrook calls Pietism (and Puritanism) "forms of religious aspiration and ethos" (p. 36).

yet that is exactly what many critics of Pietism do. "Pietism" has become a term loosely attached to many things foreign to the Pietist movement. Sometimes they are *distortions* of the ethos of the Pietist movement, even though critics fail to notice this.

The Pietist Ethos Previewed

So what is the *true* Pietist ethos?[16] There is bound to be less agreement about that than about the movement's history. Even the best and most widely acknowledged scholars of Pietism place the emphasis on different aspects of its ethos as central and crucial to its identity. However, the disagreements can be overemphasized to the detriment of general scholarly consensus.[17] Scholar of Pietism Jonathan Strom has rightly noted the *ecumenical* nature of the Pietist movement and the numerous networks to which it gave rise:

> Beyond geography, class, and even intellectual divisions, Pietists formed enduring networks among like-minded, spiritually awakened individuals, which did not prevent conflict but reinforces the idea of Pietist movements as an ecumenical expression of a religion of the heart.[18]

What we are here calling the "ethos of Pietism" is the distinctive set of emphases in this "ecumenical expression of a religion of the heart" — what it shares in common *not* widely emphasized in the same way elsewhere. This ethos transcends denominations and even traditions; it "pops up" in all kinds of Christian movements, organizations, and individuals. Some

16. By "true Pietist ethos" we do not mean to imply a homogeneity of Pietism past or present. We only mean that Pietism is not compatible with anything and everything and that the concept should not be identified with its distortions and misrepresentations.

17. For a lengthy, detailed account of contemporary scholarship of Pietism and its many flavors, see Jonathan Strom, "Problems and Promises of Pietism Research," *Church History* 71, no. 3 (September 2002): 536-54.

18. Jonathan Strom, "Introduction: Pietism in Two Worlds," in *Pietism in Germany and North America, 1680-1820*, ed. Jonathan Strom, Hartmut Lehmann, and James Van Horn Melton (Burlington, Vt.: Ashgate, 2009), p. 5.

take it for granted as "true Christianity," while others reject it as fanaticism and/or sectarianism.

Stoeffler boiled down the Pietist ethos to "experiential Protestantism"[19] — which is certainly not to say that that's all he said about it! But that is it in essence — also sometimes called simply "heart Christianity." Stoeffler provided a more detailed profile of what he called "historic Pietism," by which he meant a "spirit" and not a "socially perceptible form."[20] That's what we are calling its "ethos." For Stoeffler, Pietism's ethos has three equally weighty and interdependent characteristics. First, "The essence of Christianity is to be found in the personally meaningful relationship of the individual to God."[21] In other words, "formalism" is the "implacable enemy" of authentic Christianity. True Christianity cannot be found in a relationship to God that is wholly mediated by symbols, rituals, institutions, and the like. The true Christian relationship with God may include those, but it cannot be reduced to what they do. It is at its core unmediated, direct, and personal.

Second, the Pietist ethos thrives on "religious idealism" — belief in the possibility of total transformation of the individual and society by inwardly working grace.[22] Stoeffler opposed this to realism, which insists on limiting the transforming power of grace.

Third, Pietism's ethos places distinctive emphasis on the Bible.[23] Beyond recognizing the Bible's truth and authority, Pietism emphasizes love for the Bible and the Bible's ability to speak meaningfully and directly to untutored lay Christians. Pietism's "theory was . . . that the Spirit of God is able to commend the truth of the Bible to men's minds and hearts without the tortured interpretations of the professionals."[24]

Certainly, Stoeffler's three characteristics are not comprehensive or totalizing. The Pietist ethos contains other, perhaps equally important impulses, and these three, like others, are amenable to different flavors — a point we'll expound more in a later chapter. All that is intended here is the

---

19. Stoeffler, *The Rise of Evangelical Pietism*, p. 8.
20. Stoeffler, *The Rise of Evangelical Pietism*, p. 13.
21. Stoeffler, *The Rise of Evangelical Pietism*, pp. 13-15.
22. Stoeffler, *The Rise of Evangelical Pietism*, pp. 16-19.
23. Stoeffler, *The Rise of Evangelical Pietism*, pp. 20-23.
24. Stoeffler, *The Rise of Evangelical Pietism*, p. 21.

most essential exposition of "mere Pietism" — what all Pietists share in common. To Stoeffler's characteristics might be added the dimension of religious feelings as concomitant with the individual's personal relationship with God, which necessarily includes an experience of conversion, and the dimension of witness or testimony to the inwardly transforming grace of God. The original Pietists also emphasized what Spener called "hope for better times" — an eschatological vision of a transformed, "Christianized" social order — whether brought about by Christian mission or by Christ upon his return. Finally, Stoeffler mentions (but does not elevate to an essential characteristic) Pietism's "fundamentally irenical" nature: "Its interest was focused upon deepening and strengthening the devotional life of people rather than upon correctness of theological definition or liturgical form. Hence it has generally found polemic distasteful and has endeavored to avoid it wherever possible."[25]

This chapter is mainly about how and why Pietism came to be vilified and rejected, even demonized by many critics. To someone who grew up in the "thick" of Pietism, that's almost beyond comprehension — unless he or she has left it in disgust, shaking its experiential dust off his or her shoes (a not uncommon phenomenon!). And yet, from the very beginning both the movement and its ethos have been highly controversial — as already noted. How and why?

Albrecht Ritschl's Nineteenth-Century Critique of Pietism

Already during Spener's lifetime, critics of his ministry and renewal movement subjected him to scorn, and he became the target of heresy charges. One contemporaneous Lutheran theologian compiled a list of over fifty specific heresies of which he found Spener guilty. Perhaps the element of Spener's ministry that caused the most controversy was his emphasis on the priesthood of all believers, including ordinary believers' right and ability to read and interpret Scripture and meet to discuss it and pray outside the church. The conventicles that Spener initiated were illegal in many parts of Europe in the seventeenth and eighteenth centuries. Spener got

---

25. Stoeffler, *The Rise of Evangelical Pietism*, p. 2.

around laws prohibiting them by keeping them under his oversight so that they did not float away from or become independent of the state church. Ultimately, however, that was impossible, and one wing of the early Pietist movement did come to reject the state churches, while some radical Pietists rejected all formal, institutional churches. This led to tremendous criticism of Spener, even though he was also critical of radical Pietism.

One thing should be noted here. Like all movements, Pietism has had its extremes and extremists who attract disrepute. Much criticism of Pietism was (and still is) aimed at its fringe, which scholars label "radical" or "separatist" (sometimes also "spiritualist") Pietism.[26] There is no clear line between "mainstream" Pietists and radical Pietists, but some Pietists clearly departed far from Spener, Francke, and other mainstream Pietist founders by rejecting institutional Christianity altogether and even dabbling in esoteric, mystical religion. We believe *some* criticisms of Pietism are legitimate, but we do not think it is right to tar all Pietists with the same radical, separatist, "spiritualist" brush and dismiss the entire movement or ethos because some took its insights to extremes.

Several theologians and church historians have been especially instrumental in heaping scorn and disrepute upon the Pietist movement and its ethos. Some of their criticisms have been based on legitimate disagreement, and some on misunderstandings. One such person was the giant of nineteenth-century liberal Protestant theology, Albrecht Ritschl (1822-1889), who wrote a three-volume history of Pietism that included both specific criticism and an overall rejection of the movement. Ritschl was professor of dogmatics at the University of Göttingen and exercised greater influence on late nineteenth- and early twentieth-century Protestant theology than any other single individual. He was himself influenced by the philosophy of Immanuel Kant (1724-1804), in which religion was reduced to ethics. Ritschl regarded the kingdom of God — which he defined as "society organized by love" — as the central theme of Christian theology. He had no use for metaphysics or dogmas about God beyond ethical experience.

Ritschl's three-volume investigation and critique of Pietism was titled

26. On "radical Pietism," see Hans Schneider, *German Radical Pietism*, trans. Gerald T. MacDonald (Lanham, Md.: Scarecrow Press, 2007).

Die Geschichte des Pietismus (The History of Pietism) and was published between 1880 and 1886. It blasted both the movement and the ethos for a variety of alleged distortions of Protestant Christianity. Ritschl's complaint against Pietism was summed up in the second volume, where he described it as "non-Lutheran in character, more precisely expressed, an attempt to resurrect medieval monasticism outside the cloisters."[27] Ritschl's main accusation was that Pietism was more Catholic than Protestant in character. Specifically, he charged, it minimized grace and elevated works by aiming at spiritual perfection through performance. It was also, he argued, otherworldly and quietistic. Ritschl's virulent attack on Pietism stuck in Protestant scholarly circles; he did more damage to Pietism's reputation than any other single person before his own nemesis, Karl Barth (1886-1968).

To what extent were Ritschl's criticisms of Pietism valid? First, with regard to his accusation that Pietism was not authentically Protestant, Kuenning expresses a general consensus among contemporary Pietism scholars that early mainstream Pietism affirmed Luther's doctrine of justification — the doctrine with which, as Luther himself said, the church either stands or falls. Kuenning provides numerous quotes from Spener, Francke, and other early Pietist leaders affirming justification by grace through faith alone. He rightly concluded, "The genius of classical Pietism lay not in any rejection of justification by grace alone but in the revitalization and expansion of Martin Luther's original insights into the meaning of sanctification."[28]

As for Ritschl's charge of quietism — otherworldly detachment and lack of concern for social issues — Kuenning echoes most contemporary Pietism scholarship:

> German Lutheran pietism has often been characterized as quietistic or otherworldly, as fostering a subjective spirituality that retreated into its own world of mystical asceticism or private piety. The inaccuracy of these descriptions when applied to the classical Lutheran Pietism of

27. Albrecht Ritschl, *Die Geschichte des Pietismus*, vol. 2 (Bonn: Adolph Marcus, 1880-1886), p. 417; translation by author (Olson).

28. Kuenning, *The Rise and Fall of American Lutheran Pietism*, p. 20.

the Spener-Francke school becomes apparent through even a cursory examination of its exuberant ethical activism.[29]

Pietism's "exuberant ethical activism" has nowhere been expounded in greater detail and eloquence than in two recent volumes by Pietism scholars: *Spirituality and Social Liberation* by Frank D. Macchia (1993) and *Angels, Worms, and Bogeys: The Christian Ethic of Pietism* by Michelle A. Clifton-Soderstrom (2010). Both Macchia and Clifton-Soderstrom completely falsify Ritschl's (and other critics') accusations of Pietist quietism.

According to Clifton-Soderstrom, Spener, Francke, and their followers emphasized concern for the poor. Focusing on Spener, she notes,

> Wherever he ministered, Spener demonstrated his knowledge of and advocacy for the "least of these" — widows, orphans, peasants, unemployed, refugees, migrants, beggars, and invalids. He encouraged his parishes to work as Christians in partnership with the government to provide things like aid, jobs, relief, homes, and medical care.[30]

Drawing on Francke's sermon "The Duty to the Poor," she comments, "He framed all material goods by saying that God gives them to us so that we might use them to help our poor, suffering neighbor."[31] Francke's church, St. George's in Glaucha, a poor suburb of Halle, "became God's instrument of justice in the streets."[32]

Macchia uses a particular strain of Pietism to illustrate the error of Ritschl's and other critics' view of Pietism as essentially otherworldly and quietistic. He surveys "Württemberg Pietism" and concludes that it aimed not only at personal conversion but "toward world transformation."[33] Leading Pietists such as Johann Albrecht Bengel (1687-1752) and Christoph Blumhardt (1842-1919), and many Württembergers between them, used

---

29. Kuenning, *The Rise and Fall of American Lutheran Pietism*, p. 13.

30. Michelle A. Clifton-Soderstrom, *Angels, Worms, and Bogeys: The Christian Ethic of Pietism* (Eugene, Ore.: Cascade Books, 2010), p. 45.

31. Clifton-Soderstrom, *Angels, Worms, and Bogeys*, p. 80.

32. Clifton-Soderstrom, *Angels, Worms, and Bogeys*, p. 81.

33. Frank D. Macchia, *Spirituality and Social Liberation* (Metuchen, N.J.: Scarecrow Press, 1993), p. 31.

political activism to bring about Spener's hope for "better times" — an approximation of the kingdom of God on earth through a more just social order.

While some Pietists — especially those who were radical — may have fallen into spiritual perfectionism, works righteousness of a kind, otherworldly asceticism, and quietism, these are not endemic to Pietism as a whole. Pietism itself should not be blamed for those who distorted its original impulses in these directions.

Karl Barth's Twentieth-Century Critique of Pietism

After Ritschl, Karl Barth, a leading opponent of "Ritschlian" liberal theology, followed in his footsteps by attacking Pietism. So fraught with tension was Barth's relationship with Pietism that his biographer, Eberhard Busch, devoted an entire volume to it: *Karl Barth and the Pietists* (1978). The Swiss Barth was, by most accounts, the most influential Christian theologian of the twentieth century. He came to fame and acclaim with the publication of his *Der Römerbrief (The Epistle to the Romans)* in 1919. It was said to have fallen like a bombshell on the playground of the theologians — especially those under the influence of Ritschl and his modernized, liberal theology. And yet, early in his career Barth had one thing in common with Ritschl — a disdain for Pietism. He never wrote a three-volume — or even a one-volume — polemic against Pietism, but his scattered references to it reveal his ambivalence toward the remnants of the movement and its ethos in his time.

While acknowledging exceptions and even some positive contributions of Pietists to Protestant Christianity, Barth accused Pietism in general of being less than fully Protestant and of religious individualism.[34] Busch rightly notes that "Barth's position toward pietistic concerns and concepts is dialectical"[35] in *Der Römerbrief* and other early writings. In other words, he did not disagree with them entirely; he affirmed some of

34. Eberhard Busch, *Karl Barth and the Pietists: The Young Karl Barth's Critique of Pietism and Its Response*, trans. Daniel W. Bloesch (Downers Grove, Ill.: InterVarsity Press, 2004), pp. 216, 62.

35. Busch, *Karl Barth and the Pietists*, p. 101.

their contributions, while seeking to correct what he saw as distortions of Protestant doctrine in Pietism. However, at times Barth's approach to Pietism and Pietists could be aggressive and polemical. For example, he accused Pietism of giving rise to a "new Pharisaism" (and this is what he meant by Pietism being less than fully Protestant) by making the *possession of grace* visible and exclusive. According to Busch, Barth believed that "Pietism knows man is dependent on God's grace but does not know that man *remains* dependent on it, or does not know that grace *remains* free; instead it finally reestablishes a pious 'possession' of grace in the sight of God."[36]

In his early phase of theological reaction against liberal theology, Barth wanted to avoid any hint of subjectivism or anthropocentrism in theology. He emphasized the sovereignty of grace in perhaps a one-sided way.[37] At least that is how Pietists have seen it. When Barth looked at Pietism, he saw the seeds of liberal theology. After all, Friedrich Schleiermacher (1768-1834), the "father" of modern liberal theology and another of Barth's nemeses, had been raised Pietist and claimed to be a Pietist "of a higher order" after developing his liberal theology. Barth wanted to correct theology's course into anthropocentrism, whether conservative or liberal, by highlighting God's sovereignty in salvation to the exclusion of any human claim to "possess" grace — especially in a visible way.

Barth also accused Pietism, as he understood it, of excessive individualism. Pietism's "essence is *individual* conversion, *individual* sanctification, *individual* salvation, thus it is individualism, and it is especially so in the sense that it is individualistic consciously and intentionally."[38] Barth dismissed this emphasis on individual spirituality and individual relationship with God as "unredeemed . . . inwardness."[39] For him, election to salvation is corporate, and salvation takes place together with the people of God, in communion with them. Barth could be extremely harsh in his polemic against what he saw as Pietistic individualism: "I would rather be in hell

36. Busch, *Karl Barth and the Pietists*, p. 97.

37. Much later, in the 1970s, Pietist theologian Donald Bloesch criticized Barth for this one-sided emphasis on the sovereignty of grace and called it "objectivism" — excluding the human side of salvation. See *Jesus Is Victor! Karl Barth's Doctrine of Salvation* (Nashville: Abingdon Press, 1976).

38. Busch, *Karl Barth and the Pietists*, p. 43; italics added.

39. Busch, *Karl Barth and the Pietists*, p. 43.

with the world church than in heaven with Pietism, be it of a lower or higher order, of an older or more modern observance."[40]

Busch makes it clear that Barth was not entirely consistent in his attitude toward and treatment of Pietism. There were things about Pietism he appreciated; his horror at Pietism seemed to be conditioned by his encounters with certain Pietist groups active in Switzerland and Germany in the early twentieth century. Barth expressed agreement with and even dependence on *some* Pietists such as the Blumhardts, especially the younger, Christoph. But he did not seem to recognize Blumhardt as a Pietist — at least not as one of those to whom he was reacting.[41] Busch rightly points out in his book that Barth knew that different types of Pietism existed and that he had affinities with some historical types of Pietism; but when he criticized "Pietism," he was looking at an abstraction that was attached to a particular strain of Pietism with which he was most familiar.[42]

As we have already noted, extremes have arisen within Pietism; some Pietists have given Pietism a bad name. But we object to Ritschl, Barth, or anyone else tarring all Pietists with the same brush dipped in those extremes. We think that authentic Pietism — the historical Pietist movement launched by Spener, for example — and its genuine ethos have much to contribute to theologies influenced by Ritschl (modern liberalism) and Barth (neo-orthodoxy, dialectical theology), even by way of correction. We think that a sympathetic retrieval of *real* Pietism — Pietism as it originally was and always has been at its best — will show that it emphasizes an individual dimension to salvation that is not inherently individualistic; that many Pietists have leaned more in a synergistic rather than monergistic direction,[43] while not being inherently Pelagian or semi-Pelagian; and that it includes an emphasis on the vertical dimension of the Christian life while not becoming otherworldly.

---

40. Barth, quoted in Busch, *Karl Barth and the Pietists*, p. 43.

41. See Christian T. Collins Winn, *"Jesus Is Victor!": The Significance of the Blumhardts for the Theology of Karl Barth* (Eugene, Ore.: Pickwick Press, 2009), pp. 70-76.

42. Busch, *Karl Barth and the Pietists*, pp. 62-65.

43. "Monergism" is the view that in salvation God does everything and the human person being saved is passive; "synergism" is the view that salvation is a cooperation between God and the human person being saved even though God's grace is the only ground and basis of salvation.

It is unfortunate for Pietism that Ritschl's, Barth's, and others' polemics against its excesses and distortions — which did not sufficiently explain that they were aimed at excesses and distortions — have largely controlled popular and scholarly perceptions of Pietism. In our aim to retrieve key elements of an authentic Pietism for the renewal of contemporary Christianity, we now turn to the precursors of the Pietist movement.

CHAPTER TWO

Pietist Backgrounds

Precursors and Cousins of Pietism

Although Pietism arose among Lutherans in German-speaking lands in the latter half of the seventeenth century, the roots of Pietism are far more complex and ecumenical. A variety of figures and ideas emerging from late medieval mystics, Protestant radicals and reformers, reformist and Orthodox devotional writers in England and Germany, and spiritualist visionaries with an interest in alchemy all played a role in preparing the ground for the classical church Pietism of Spener and Francke, and the ecumenical Pietism of Zinzendorf. In addition, the social disruption and upheaval caused by the Thirty Years' War (1618-1648) played a key role in the "crisis of piety" in the latter half of the seventeenth century,[1] to which Pietism was certainly a response. Though the classical Pietism of Spener, Francke, and Zinzendorf should not be reduced to one or another of the figures discussed below, they all played an important role in contributing to the eclectic collage of the Pietist movement and ethos.

Late Medieval Precursors

Pietism's connection to earlier forms of Christian spirituality and devotion is evident in the role that late medieval mystical and devotional writings

---

1. See Johannes Wallmann, *Der Pietismus* (Göttingen: Vandenhoeck & Ruprecht, 2005), pp. 28-29.

played in the writing and thought of key figures like Johann Arndt and Philipp Jakob Spener. Of particular importance were the anonymous *Theologia Germanica*[2] and the classic devotional work of Thomas à Kempis (1380-1471), *The Imitation of Christ*.[3] Bearing the stamp of the tumultuous fourteenth century,[4] the *Theologia Germanica* was probably written sometime around 1350. In the eyes of the anonymous author, humanity's problem was one of self-will, or turning away from the source of all life: God. In agreement with classical theology, the *Theologia Germanica* argued that the only solution lay in God's becoming human: "He became humanized and man became divinized."[5] In becoming one with humanity in the Incarnation, God takes on humanity's plight, bears its sins, and turns it back toward God.

The objective event of the Incarnation notwithstanding, the author of the *Theologia Germanica* was keen to emphasize that salvation was God's work of taking up residence in the individual and turning her or him back toward God: "Even if God would take to himself all humans in the world and become humanized in them and they would become divinized in Him and this did not happen in me, my fall and my apostasy would never be amended."[6] What matters is the individual's experience of the living God, and as the *Theologia Germanica* maps out the spiritual and devotional itinerary of the disciplined Christian, it becomes clear that the experience of God and especially the love of God are superior to knowledge. The latter too often leads away from God back toward creaturely self-will, while the former lead toward the ultimate goal of Christian existence: union with God in Christ. This does not mean, however, that ethical issues and concern for the neighbor are of no account; rather, the *Theologia Germanica* lays great stress on the love of God that works its way out of the interior life toward the neighbor: "It follows from what we have said that love in the heart of a divinized person is undefiled and unadulterated, borne by good will toward

2. *The Theologia Germanica of Martin Luther*, translated and with an introduction and commentary by Bengt Hoffman (Mahwah, N.J.: Paulist Press, 1980).

3. Thomas à Kempis, *The Imitation of Christ* (Wheaton, Ill.: Christian Classics Ethereal Library, 1998).

4. For an excellent discussion of the upheavals of this time, see Barbara Tuchman, *A Distant Mirror: The Calamitous Fourteenth Century* (New York: Ballantine Books, 1978).

5. *The Theologia Germanica of Martin Luther*, p. 63.

6. *The Theologia Germanica of Martin Luther*, p. 63.

all humans and all created things. Therefore, from within this purity mankind and all created things must be sincerely loved, and one must will and wish and do what is best for them."[7] In the *Theologia Germanica*, the evolving encounter with God that occurs through repentance, poverty of spirit, humble imitation of Christ's suffering, and prayer not only leads to spiritual union with Christ, but also produces concrete acts of neighborly love.

Influenced by the Brethren of the Common Life, Thomas à Kempis was a member of the Augustinian Order in Zwolle, Holland. He was the author of a number of devotional writings, though the most famous was the immensely influential *Imitation of Christ*, first published in 1418. The text was probably intended as an instructional manual for young novices. In four different sections, Thomas counseled the spiritual novice toward repentance, devotion, and frequent participation in the Eucharist. Thomas was especially concerned with the transformation of the inner life of the monk, counseling the novice not to concentrate on outward appearances, but to live inwardly toward God.[8] Both Arndt and Spener published multiple editions of the *Theologia Germanica* and *The Imitation of Christ*, providing laudatory prefaces for the two works.[9] In the case of Arndt, the publication of his seminal *True Christianity* in 1605 was accompanied by a new edition of the *Theologia Germanica* in that same year, and according to Martin Brecht, *True Christianity* was significantly influenced by the *Theologia Germanica*.[10]

Reformation Era Precursors

Of course, early Protestant impulses, both radical and more mainstream, also played a role in the development of Pietism. Though different in

---

7. *The Theologia Germanica of Martin Luther*, p. 104.

8. See, for instance, *The Imitation of Christ*, pp. 84-86.

9. See Martin Brecht, "Das Aufkommen der neuen Frömmigkeitsbewegung in Deutschland," in *Geschichte des Pietismus*, vol. 1: *Der Pietismus vom siebzehnten bis zum frühen achtzehnten Jahrhundert*, ed. Martin Brecht (Göttingen: Vandenhoeck & Ruprecht, 1993), pp. 132-33.

10. Brecht, "Das Aufkommen der neuen Frömmigkeitsbewegung in Deutschland," p. 136.

their approach and concern, Caspar Schwenckfeld (1489-1561) and Paracelsus (1493-1541) are usually placed on the radical side of the Reformation. Each emphasized a component that would become important in the Pietist vision of Spener and others. Schwenckfeld, who was from an aristocratic Silesian family, experienced a conversion in 1519.[11] He was a devoted proponent of the reforms of Luther, visiting Wittenberg on at least three occasions, until he fell out of favor with Luther due to his Spiritualist interpretation of the Eucharist.[12] Schwenckfeld argued that only that which was spiritual could feed the spirit, and so he advocated a spiritual feeding on the body and blood of Christ through the inner contemplation of the celestial body of Christ.[13] Faith, which Schwenckfeld understood as a process, was feeding on Christ. For spiritual feeding to happen, external trappings would have to be laid aside, though not necessarily rejected. Schwenckfeld was concerned that the external signs of religious devotion and authority — such as the sacraments, the clerical order, and to some extent the Bible — could hamper direct spiritual union with Christ, and so he encouraged his followers to gather together in small groups for study, prayer, admonition, and contemplation.[14] These groups became the school of Christ, through which faith was nurtured in the individual.

Although clearly containing problematic elements — not least the bifurcation of the external and the internal aspects of faith and the Christian life — Schwenckfeld's emphasis on encounter with Christ in the context of a small group would become an important emphasis in later Pietism.[15] In addition, Schwenckfeld and his co-laborer, Valentin Krautwald (1465-1545), held to a form of millennialism in which a restored church figured prominently. Flowing out of the apocalyptic thought of Joachim of Fiore (1135-1202), these expectations emphasized a coming age of the Spirit

---

11. See Douglas H. Shantz, *An Introduction to German Pietism: Protestant Renewal at the Dawn of Modern Europe* (Baltimore: Johns Hopkins University Press, 2013), p. 16.

12. See George H. Williams, *The Radical Reformation* (Philadelphia: Westminster Press, 1962), pp. 106-7.

13. Williams, *The Radical Reformation*, pp. 111-15.

14. See Brecht, "Das Aufkommen der neuen Frömmigkeitsbewegung in Deutschland," pp. 120-21.

15. Williams, *The Radical Reformation*, p. 115.

in which a true church of the truly reborn — which was often called the church of Philadelphia, after Revelation 2:7-13 — would appear on the stage of history.[16] Though these eschatological expectations would prove to be far more influential in radical Pietist circles, Spener's "hopes for better times" did receive some impetus from these ideas.

Paracelsus, or Philippus Theophrastus, is another important figure from among the Protestant radicals. A peripatetic doctor whose search for medical wisdom took him throughout Europe, Asia Minor, and into Egypt and Ethiopia, Paracelsus never fully found a religious home, though his thought bears strong affinities with that of Anabaptist and Spiritualist figures like Schwenckfeld. He was intensely critical of both the Roman Catholic Church and Lutheran Protestantism because of their moral failures, but he was too much concerned with nature, the body, and alchemical models of spirituality to fit fully into the Spiritualist camp.[17] Martin Brecht has called him a "spiritualistic realist."[18] As W. R. Ward has noted, Paracelsus' vitalism — his emphasis on the all-pervasive presence of life — was of great interest for later Pietists, particularly Johann Arndt.[19]

Our discussion of Pietist precursors would be incomplete if we did not include brief mention of elements in Martin Luther (1483-1546) — particularly during the early phase of his development — that were important for later Pietist figures. A number of scholars have pointed out the profound influence that late medieval mysticism had on Luther, especially the writings of Johann Tauler and the *Theologia Germanica* discussed above.[20] The stamp of mysticism — in particular, the importance of religious experience and the union of the soul with Christ — is palpable in the 1520 tract *The Freedom of a Christian*. In referring to Ephesians 5:31-33, Luther

---

16. See Shantz, *An Introduction to German Pietism*, p. 17.

17. See Shantz, *An Introduction to German Pietism*, p. 23.

18. See Brecht, "Das Aufkommen der neuen Frömmigkeitsbewegung in Deutschland," p. 124.

19. See W. R. Ward, *Early Evangelicalism: A Global Intellectual History, 1670-1789* (Cambridge: Cambridge University Press, 2006), p. 11.

20. See Brecht, "Das Aufkommen der neuen Frömmigkeitsbewegung in Deutschland," pp. 116-17; and F. Ernest Stoeffler, *The Rise of Evangelical Pietism* (Leiden: E. J. Brill, 1971), pp. 190-93.

remarks, "The third incomparable benefit of faith is that it unites the soul with Christ as a bride is united with her bridegroom. By this mystery, as the Apostle teaches, Christ and the soul become one flesh."[21] The language and categories of mystical union and the profoundly important role of religious experience evident in the early Luther were also important elements in later Pietism, and Spener in particular showed a deep knowledge of and affection for Luther's conception of the transformative power of faith as outlined in his preface to Romans.[22]

Johann Arndt

Of all the figures discussed in this chapter, by far the most significant is Johann Arndt (1555-1621). Arndt is widely considered one of the most important figures of the post-Reformation era. Scholars debate whether Arndt should be considered the father or grandfather of Pietism. They do not, however, debate his significance for the post-Reformation period, as Douglas Shantz's estimation makes clear: "His [Arndt's] successful devotional writings have made him the most important figure in the history of modern Protestantism, even surpassing Luther."[23] A key figure in what has come to be called the "piety movement" by scholars of the seventeenth century,[24] Arndt's reputation rises or falls — depending on one's perspective — with his influential text, *True Christianity*.[25]

Arndt was born in the small village of Edderitz in the duchy of Anhalt. He spent his formative years in the village of Ballenstädt, where his father, Jakob Arndt, served as pastor. From 1575 to 1579, he studied the liberal arts and medicine — including the medical writings of Paracelsus — at Helmstedt, Strasbourg, and Basel. Though Arndt never completed

---

21. *Martin Luther: Selections from His Writings*, ed. John Dillenberger (New York: Doubleday, 1961), p. 60.

22. See Martin Brecht, "Ansätze einer Reform — die Collegia Pietatis — die Hoffnung besserer Zeiten," in *Geschichte des Pietismus*, vol. 1, p. 293.

23. Shantz, *An Introduction to German Pietism*, p. 25.

24. See Ward, *Early Evangelicalism*, p. 7.

25. Johann Arndt, *True Christianity*, translated and with an introduction by Peter Erb (Mahwah, N.J.: Paulist Press, 1979).

a theological degree, there is evidence that he read widely in the field, and he was ordained to the pastorate in 1583.[26] Arndt served as pastor in Badeborn, Quedlinburg, Braunschweig, and Eisleben — all located in central Germany between modern-day Hannover and Leipzig — and was eventually appointed general superintendent in Celle in 1611, where he served until his death in 1621. Arndt was praised for the medical service he rendered in the communities where he pastored, twice having to deal with outbreaks of plague.[27]

Arndt took a great interest in the medieval mystics in the 1590s, publishing a new edition of *Theologia Germanica* in 1597. According to Martin Brecht, the preface that Arndt provided for this mystical text already contained many of the key themes that would be central to the later *True Christianity*: true repentance, a concern with the reform of life, and the distinction between true and false Christianity.[28]

Book I of *True Christianity* first appeared at the Frankfurt Easter book fair in 1605. A revised edition was published in 1606, and in 1610 Arndt published a new edition which included three new sections, substantially increasing the size of the treatise. In posthumous printings, two additional sections were added; they were comprised of shorter writings, letters, and Arndt's answers to critics. Because Book I, also called the "Book of Scripture," was the first book published by Arndt, it is the least derivative in terms of content — though it does contain quite a bit of internal repetition.[29] The book consists of 42 chapters. Arndt's concern is stated clearly in the introduction:

> Dear Christian reader, that the holy Gospel is subjected, in our time, to a great and shameful abuse is fully proved by the impenitent life of the ungodly who praise Christ and his word with their mouths and yet lead an unchristian life that is like that of persons who dwell in heathendom, not in the Christian world. Such ungodly conduct gave me cause to write this book to show simple readers wherein true Christianity con-

---

26. See Shantz, *An Introduction to German Pietism*, pp. 25-26.
27. See Shantz, *An Introduction to German Pietism*, p. 26.
28. See Brecht, "Das Aufkommen der neuen Frömmigkeitsbewegung in Deutschland," p. 133.
29. See Stoeffler, *The Rise of Evangelical Pietism*, p. 205.

sists, namely, in the exhibition of a true, living faith, active in genuine godliness and the fruits of righteousness.[30]

The renewal of Christian life is what motivates Arndt from beginning to end. After discussing the fall of humanity (chaps. 1-2), Arndt highlights God's choosing to bring about a new birth in humanity in and through Jesus Christ. The new birth results in the presence of a "new inner person" who lives side by side with the old person, locked in a deadly struggle. In order for the "new inner person" to ultimately replace the old, an amendment of life must be forthcoming. The new birth then calls for true repentance and love of neighbor.

Arndt articulates a vision of repentance that is largely fueled by divine initiative and action, but which elicits human cooperation:

> Repentance or true conversion is a work of God the Holy Spirit, by which man understands his sins and the wrath of God against sins from the law. . . . This is true repentance when the heart internally through sorrow and regret is broken down, destroyed, laid low, and by faith and forgiveness of sins is made holy, consoled, purified, changed and made better so that an external improvement in life follows.[31]

Repentance is a battle with the desires of the flesh, by which Arndt means love of the world, and especially self-love. Importantly, repentance — or conversion, as Arndt also calls it — is not a one-time event. Rather, it is a process that is to mark the whole of the Christian life.[32]

The life of repentance ultimately gives way to the true end of Arndt's concern: love of God and neighbor. The emphasis on love in the latter half of the book (chaps. 22-42), and especially love of neighbor, is so strong that one is forced to concede that Arndt should probably not be interpreted as a mystic, despite his use of mystical categories like "union with Christ." "God is to be served with nothing else except service given to neighbor with love and pleasure."[33] The experience of "new birth" or "conversion" or

30. Arndt, *True Christianity*, p. 21.
31. Arndt, *True Christianity*, p. 41.
32. See Arndt, *True Christianity*, pp. 64-89.
33. Arndt, *True Christianity*, p. 133.

even "union with Christ" are all subordinate to the love of neighbor, which is also love of God. "Thus, God has bound us to the love of our neighbors. He does not wish to be loved by us, aside from the love of our neighbors. Insofar as we look to the love of our neighbors, so far also we look to the love of God."[34] Lack of love places one in grave danger of God's judgment; thus ongoing repentance and the cultivation of the devotional life, especially prayer, are means by which to grow into the grace of God, which Arndt also described as "the kingdom of God."[35]

Books II-III filled out Arndt's vision of the renewed Christian life, drawing especially on the writings of Johann Tauler in Book III, while Book IV, the "Book of Nature," offered a cosmically oriented natural theology based on the writings of Paracelsus and a symbolic reading of the first chapter of Genesis.[36] *True Christianity* would become the most widely read and disseminated devotional book of the seventeenth and eighteenth centuries, with no less than 240 German-language editions appearing by the end of the eighteenth century; additional editions appeared in translations in twenty-eight different languages.[37]

Given the popularity of *True Christianity* and of Arndt's prayer book, *The Garden of Paradise*,[38] it is little wonder that Arndt's work fell under suspicion in the context of post–Reformation Lutheranism, where his emphasis on the constitutive necessity of living a godly Christian life sounded far too Roman Catholic for some Orthodox readers. His use of medieval mystics and the affinities that he shared with more radical Protestants and Spiritualists did not help, either. Arndt came under attack from clergy in Braunschweig fairly soon after the publication of *True Christianity*, and he decided to relocate in 1608.

Nevertheless, Arndt received considerable widespread support from

34. Arndt, *True Christianity*, p. 130.

35. See Johannes Wallmann, "Johann Arndt (1555-1621)," in *The Pietist Theologians*, ed. Carter Lindberg (Oxford: Blackwell Publishing, 2005), pp. 29-30.

36. For a discussion of Book IV, see Anne-Charlott Trepp, "Natural Order and Divine Salvation: Protestant Conceptions in Early Modern Germany (1550-1750)," in *Natural Laws and Laws of Nature in Early Modern Europe: Jurisprudence, Theology, and Moral and Natural Philosophy*, ed. Lorraine Daston and Michael Stolleis (Burlington, Vt.: Ashgate Publishing, 2008), pp. 126-31.

37. See Shantz, *An Introduction to German Pietism*, p. 29.

38. Johann Arndt, *The Garden of Paradise* (London: J. Downing, 1716).

clergy and laity alike, which is evident from the letters that he received from across the German-speaking world.[39] As Douglas Shantz notes, "Readers of Arndt's book covered a wide spectrum, from Orthodox Lutherans to radical separatists. The first category included people such as Johann Gerhard, Heinrich Varenius, Johann Valentin Andreae, and Paul Egard, all of whom came out in support of Arndt."[40] However, because of the appropriation of Arndt by more radical and Spiritualist writers, his writings often came under suspicion.[41] His description of salvation as a process; his emphasis on repentance and love as defining characteristics of a transformed Christian life; his fondness for mystical categories like "union with Christ"; his incorporation of the vitalism of Paracelsus and his disciple, Valentin Weigel (1533-1588); his use of symbols — all these things made Arndt appealing to more radical writers and thinkers, and therefore more susceptible to critique from Orthodox theologians and clergy. Arndt's final writings in 1620, the result of a conflict which originated in the city of Danzig, were aimed primarily at vindicating the orthodoxy of his cause.[42] And though Ernest Stoeffler's estimation that "the majority of interpreters within his own communion have felt that classical Lutheranism and Arndtian piety are not entirely the same"[43] rings true, Arndt's vision of a revitalized Christian life and community would go on to inspire not only later Pietism, but also major reformers in Lutheran Orthodox circles, like Johann Valentin Andreae (1586-1654).[44]

Jakob Böhme

Jakob Böhme (1575-1624), our next figure, did not enjoy such support from the Orthodox, though his influence on later Pietism can also be detected.

---

39. See Brecht, "Das Aufkommen der neuen Frömmigkeitsbewegung in Deutschland," p. 142.

40. Shantz, *An Introduction to German Pietism*, p. 29.

41. See Wallmann, "Johann Arndt (1555-1621)," p. 35.

42. See Brecht, "Das Aufkommen der neuen Frömmigkeitsbewegung in Deutschland," p. 144.

43. Stoeffler, *The Rise of Evangelical Pietism*, p. 205.

44. See Carter Lindberg, "Introduction," in *The Pietist Theologians*, p. 7.

In fact, Böhme, the "shoemaker from Görlitz," is widely regarded as one of the most significant speculative mystics of the post-Reformation period, influencing not only Pietism but also later Romanticism, Idealism, and Existentialism.[45]

Böhme was born in 1575 near the town of Görlitz, located southeast of Berlin on the modern-day border between Germany and Poland. In his youth, Böhme received a minimal education, though he appears to have picked up some Latin later in life, and he was working as a shoemaker in Görlitz by 1599. Shoemaking brought Böhme into contact with a diverse group of people from various strata of society, and the village of Görlitz as well as the surrounding region was a hotbed for radical Spiritualist groups, especially those influenced by Caspar Schwenckfeld and Paracelsus.[46] In addition, the Lutheran minister Martin Moller, who came to Görlitz in 1600, was instrumental in Böhme's development, introducing him to the German mystical tradition.[47]

In 1595 and 1600, Böhme purportedly had powerful visionary experiences in which he was given insight into the structure and heart of the natural world. The first experience lasted seven days, while the second and far more important experience lasted only fifteen minutes. Böhme was working at his bench when he was distracted by a beam of light reflecting off a pewter vessel. Probably to escape the distraction, Böhme went for a walk, ending up in a field where he saw a vision: "In this light my spirit came to recognize God in everything and in all creatures, even plants and grass — who he is and how he is and what his will is. In this light I grew in my ability to describe the being of God."[48]

Some twelve years later, in 1612, Böhme published his first work, *Aurora: The Root or Mother of Philosophy, Astrology, and Theology from the True*

---

45. See Andrew Weeks, *Boehme: An Intellectual Biography of the Seventeenth-Century Philosopher and Mystic* (Albany, N.Y.: State University of New York Press, 1991), pp. 2-3; see also, Cyril O'Regan, *Gnostic Apocalypse: Jacob Boehme's Haunted Narrative* (Albany, N.Y.: State University of New York Press, 2002).

46. Weeks, *Boehme*, pp. 26-31.

47. Peter Erb, "Introduction," in Jacob Boehme, *The Way to Christ*, trans. Peter Erb (New York: Paulist Press, 1979), pp. 5-6.

48. Jakob Böhme, *Aurora, oder Morgenröte im Ausgang*, ed. Gerhard Wehr (Frankfurt: Insel Verlag, 1992), p. 362, as quoted in Shantz, *An Introduction to German Pietism*, p. 31.

Foundation. Heavily influenced by Paracelsus and cabbalistic, alchemical, and Neoplatonic gnostic ideas, Böhme offers a speculative and mystical vision in which all of life, both the material and the immaterial, is simultaneously united and yet also caught up in a dualism between God's love and God's wrath. According to Douglas Shantz, "He offered readers a true philosophy, describing the origin of all things in God; a true astrology, explaining the struggle of good and evil in all things; and a true theology, discussing the kingdom of Christ and how, by faith, humanity can triumph over evil and gain eternal salvation."[49] Gregor Richter, the local Lutheran minister and successor of Moller, accused Böhme of being a false prophet, and through his efforts convinced the city magistrates and clergy to have Böhme silenced. From 1612 to 1618, Böhme abided by the order, all the while deepening his knowledge of Paracelsus, Schwenckfeld, and other mystical sources. Then, in 1619, he broke his silence.

From 1619 until his death in 1624, Böhme was remarkably productive, publishing at least twenty-four different titles, including his most widely read book, *The Way to Christ* (1622). The work shared much in common with Arndt's concern for the renewal of the individual's inner spiritual life, repentance, and true and false Christianity:

> Now we are to consider man, what and how he is; that a true Christian is not only a historical new man; that it is not enough that we believe in Christ and confess that He is God's Son and paid for us. No externally imputed righteousness that we only believe has happened [has any value]; only an inborn, a childlike [righteousness] counts. . . . So too a Christian's will must enter completely into its mother, as into the Spirit of Christ and into self, and become a child of self-willing and abilities. There will and desire are only ordered to the mother, and it must rise out of death with a new will and obedience in the Spirit of Christ in righteousness and no longer will sin.[50]

The work was designed to lead the reader into a closer union with God: "Whichever man desires to attain to divine contemplation within himself

49. Shantz, *An Introduction to German Pietism*, p. 33.
50. Boehme, *The Way to Christ*, pp. 139-40.

and speak with God in Christ must follow this way and then he will achieve it."[51] However, the work was far more clearly shaped by alchemical, cabbalistic, and gnostic influences than Arndt's work. Nevertheless, though filled with speculative passages, it also included practical spiritual exercises like confessions and short prayers that readers could use as they took the way to union with the heavenly Sophia, or Christ.

Although controversial, Böhme's intense concern with describing a "reborn" Christianity in which the secrets of the universe were unveiled proved to be a source of much fascination for Pietist figures like August Hermann Francke and Nikolaus Ludwig von Zinzendorf, and especially Friedrich Oetinger. Böhme's chiliastic (referring to the literal thousand-year reign of Christ on earth before history's end) and millennialist eschatology was also very influential among radical Pietists. At the same time, Spener was more reserved toward the mystical philosopher. Although appreciative of Böhme's call for repentance and an authentic Christian life marked by intimate communion with Christ, he was less interested in Böhme's speculative theories.[52] Notwithstanding the interest in Böhme's speculative side by men like Francke, Zinzendorf, and Oetinger, Spener's attitude carried the day among most Pietists: Böhme was joined to Arndt, and together they formed a single call for a more authentic Christian life marked by genuine piety and love of neighbor.

The Thirty Years' War, the Era of Confessionalization, and Orthodox Piety Movements

Perhaps the most significant world-historical event for Pietism overlapped with the lives of Arndt and Böhme — the Thirty Years' War (1618-1648). Ending with the Peace of Westphalia in 1648, the Thirty Years' War is widely considered the most destructive conflict to take place on German soil prior to the Second World War. The irony was that the conflict which devastated German lands — most scholars agree that the population de-

---

51. Boehme, *The Way to Christ*, p. 65.
52. See Hans Schneider, *German Radical Pietism* (Lanham, Md.: Scarecrow Press, 2007), p. 6.

creased by almost a third in the Holy Roman Empire, with some regions losing as much as 50 percent of their populace[53] — was fueled by political interests emanating out of Spain, Austria, France, Denmark, and Sweden. The constant disruption and devastation caused by warfare, which was particularly brutal for civilians, especially the rural peasantry, was accompanied by recurring cycles of famine and outbreaks of plague. And although the war was largely about political and dynastic politics, it was experienced by many as a war fueled by religious divisions. Needless to say, the war wreaked havoc on the collective psyche of German-speaking peoples within the Holy Roman Empire.

In the context of German Lutheranism, the war exacerbated what were already bad conditions in the churches. Scholars have dubbed the period from the late sixteenth through much of the seventeenth century the Age of Orthodoxy or the Era of Confessionalization. Confessionalization refers to a broad social strategy deployed by church and government officials for internalizing religious and political identity through the use of public confessional documents which not only prescribed belief but also laid out guidelines for worship. Lutheran Orthodoxy, which was the theological correlate of Confessionalization, refers to the development of the Lutheran scholastic theological method, in which Lutheran theologians developed highly refined and detailed theological systems whose aim was to promote doctrinal clarity and to critique the views of opposing Christian communities. Due to the abstract and impersonal nature of much Orthodox confessionalism, as well as the vitriolic character of intra-Christian relations, this was also a period marked by a "crisis of piety." Johann Arndt's judgment echoes a widespread assessment of the times: "Everyone now endeavors to be eminent and distinguished in the world, but no one is willing to learn to be pious. . . . It is as if Christianity consisted only in disputations and the production of polemical books, and not far more in seeing to it that the Holy Gospel and the teaching of Christ [are] practiced in a holy life."[54]

A number of strategies developed after the Thirty Years' War seeking

53. See Shantz, *An Introduction to German Pietism*, pp. 42-47.

54. Arndt, *True Christianity*, pp. 21, 174, as quoted in Eric Lund, "Introduction," in *Seventeenth-Century Lutheran Meditations and Hymns*, ed. Eric Lund (Mahwah, N.J.: Paulist Press, 2011), p. 9.

to respond to the conditions created by the war and the broader "crisis of piety."[55] One important response was efforts on the part of church leaders to restore basic Christian moral standards in the broader public through religious instruction and the broader dissemination of devotional literature. Arndt's work was characteristic of the type of devotional literature published during this time, but he was not alone. Key Orthodox theologians, like Arndt's lifelong friend Johann Gerhard, were part of a reform movement within Orthodox circles which both preceded and followed the Thirty Years' War. These reformers shared many of the concerns of later Pietists, even though they were committed to a Lutheran scholastic theological method.[56]

In addition to the writings of reform-minded Orthodox clergy, large numbers of Puritan devotional writings were also published in Germany during this time, particularly after 1660. Devotional classics from Puritans like William Perkins, Lewis Bayly, John Bunyan, and Richard Baxter made their way into the hands of German readers.[57] Bayly's devotional book, *The Practice of Piety: Directing a Christian How to Walk, That He May Please God*, was discussed in a conventicle group that met in the home of Philipp Jakob Spener in Frankfurt.[58] These works shared the same basic emphases of Arndt: the call for a more robust Christian devotional life in search of greater intimacy with God; a more fervent commitment to and practice of prayer; and a genuine desire to instruct and inspire Christians to love their neighbors and to avoid controversy.

---

55. For a discussion of these responses, see Shantz, *An Introduction to German Pietism*, pp. 45-47.

56. For a discussion of Gerhard and others, as well as a representative selection of primary texts from this period, see Lund, *Seventeenth-Century Lutheran Meditations and Hymns*. For a discussion of other reform efforts within Orthodox circles, see Jonathan Strom, *Orthodoxy and Reform: The Clergy in Seventeenth-Century Rostock* (Tübingen: Mohr Siebeck, 1999); and Mary Noll Venables, "Pietist Fruits from Orthodox Seeds: The Case of Ernst the Pious of Saxe-Gotha-Altenburg," in *Confessionalism and Pietism: Religious Reform in Early Modern Europe*, ed. Fred Van Lieburg (Mainz: Verlag Philipp von Zabern, 2006), pp. 91-109.

57. For a discussion of the relationship between Pietism and Puritanism, see Stoeffler, *The Rise of Evangelical Pietism*, pp. 24-108.

58. See Shantz, *An Introduction to German Pietism*, p. 47.

Jean de Labadie

In the postwar period, by far the most important figure for the later rise of Pietism is the enigmatic figure Jean de Labadie (1610-1674). "A spirit in search of a place," as Michel de Certeau described him, Labadie lived a life of continual migration.[59] Moving from Catholicism to Reformed Protestantism to sectarianism in the form of "Labadism," Labadie also wandered from France to Switzerland, Holland, Germany, and Denmark. Although a restless spirit, Labadie nevertheless managed to exert considerable influence on figures and movements concerned with "authentic Christianity."

Born in southern France, Labadie joined the Jesuit Order in 1625 in Bordeaux. During his fourteen years in the society, Labadie garnered a following due to his spiritual visions and to the exemplary nature of his spiritual life. In 1639, Labadie left the order due to failing health, as well as tensions with other brothers in the society. After spending some time in Jansenist circles in Paris, Amiens, and Port Royal, in 1650 Labadie converted to the Reformed faith.[60] Jansenism and Calvinism bore some peculiar similarities: both emphasized total depravity and the overwhelming power of divine grace as well as the call for the individual to live an upright life. Of some importance for later developments, Jansenists were also given to gathering in small groups to discuss religious topics and edifying literature of various kinds and held communitarian social arrangements in high regard.[61]

After his conversion, Labadie was eventually ordained to the pastorate and served congregations in Montaubon and Geneva, among other cities. Ever the polarizing figure, Labadie managed to run afoul of authorities in Geneva and its leading theologian, François Turretini, over his chiliastic views and his practice of holding devotional meetings in his home.[62] Drawing on a combination of spiritual visions and exegesis of the book of Revelation, Labadie held that the final appearing of the kingdom of God

---

59. See Michel de Certeau, *The Mystic Fable*, vol. 1: *The Sixteenth and Seventeenth Century*, trans. Michael B. Smith (Chicago: University of Chicago Press, 1992), pp. 271-93.

60. See Trevor J. Saxby, *The Quest for the New Jerusalem: Jean de Labadie and the Labadists, 1610-1744* (Dordrecht: Martinus Nijhoff Publishers, 1987), pp. 1-57.

61. See Stoeffler, *The Rise of Evangelical Pietism*, p. 163.

62. See Saxby, *The Quest for the New Jerusalem*, p. 116.

would not simply be a spiritual event, outside of time and history. Rather, the kingdom would appear as a physical reality on earth and would be preceded by a general time of renewal for the church and the conversion of the Jewish people.

These expectations are clear in his 1667 pamphlet, "The Reformation of the Church by the Pastorate." In this work, Labadie offers a diagnosis of the ills that beset the Christian church and a call to repentance and faith on the part of the faithful. Labadie's call for a "further reformation" is undergirded by the general eschatological conviction that God calls the church to participate in the hastening of God's kingdom through "preparing the way of the Lord" by doing good works:

> If there are signs that the reign of God is approaching and if we can think and say with good reason that our time is not far away from the one of that great and final good, that divine manifestation of power, virtue, grace, and judgment, as may easily be proved, do we not also have reason to hope for a fairly considerable period of conspicuous mercy which will reform us in order to prepare us for it and put us in a suitable state of mind for such an excellent good?[63]

The parallels to Spener's call for reform in the *Pia Desideria* — the manifesto of Pietism — are striking. The reasons to reform the church are, first, that the final appearing of Christ is near; second, that God gives us reason to hope that things can and will get better in the life of the church before the coming of Christ; and third, that the calling of the church is to prepare itself for the coming of the Lord through repentance and a deepened faith expressed in communal and individual righteousness and holiness. In Labadie, the call to repentance and faith — the central hallmarks of his piety — was tied to concrete manifestations of God's holiness, righteousness, and justice in the life of the community, but also fit within a larger chiliastic framework which hoped for the final appearing of the kingdom of God on earth.

63. Jean de Labadie, "The Reformation of the Church by the Pastorate," in *European Pietism Reviewed*, ed. Frederick Herzog (San Jose, Calif.: Pickwick Publications, 2003), p. 73.

These ideas were certainly not within the norm of confessional Protestantism, but what got Labadie into even more trouble in Geneva, and later in Holland, was the practice of hosting conventicles in his home. The purpose of these meetings was to cultivate Bible reading, prayer, and mutual edification. The description of one of these conventicles is illuminating:

> The leader offers a short address followed with a prayer. Then those gathered sing and a challenging passage of Scripture is read and introduced. Then the exercise of prophecy begins, with discussion concerning the Scripture text or especially important Christian truths, done concisely and clearly, in a way that is practical and not obscure. Anyone — meaning only the men, not women as among the Quakers — can speak and raise questions, ideas, objections, always keeping edification in view. Then follows a short summary and prayer (or silent prayer) and a blessing.[64]

Such conventicles eventually became a hallmark of Pietism. Spener, who used conventicles in his reforming program in Frankfurt in 1670, had himself attended meetings like the one described above at Labadie's home in 1661 in Geneva.[65] Religious and civil authorities, however, were deeply suspicious of this practice, both in Labadie's case and in the case of later Pietism.

Chiliasm and the use of conventicles would also land Labadie in trouble in Middleburg, Holland, where he had migrated in 1666 from Geneva. By 1669, Labadie and his small group of well-connected followers no longer had a place in the Reformed communion in Holland, and they eventually became a self-constituted sect in the final stage of Labadie's career; they were known as Labadists. In keeping with Labadie's former practice, the Labadists roamed from Amsterdam to Herford, Germany, and later to Altona, Denmark, where Labadie died in 1674, though Labadism lasted well into the eighteenth century.[66]

---

64. Max Goebel, *Geschichte des christlichen Lebens in der rheinisch-westphälischen evangelischen Kirche* (Koblenz: Karl Bädeker, 1852), pp. 208-9, as quoted in Shantz, *An Introduction to German Pietism*, p. 51.

65. Saxby, *The Quest for the New Jerusalem*, p. 116.

66. For a discussion of the later years, see Saxby, *The Quest for the New Jerusalem*, pp. 241-336.

Labadie's contribution to Pietism is significant, with both thematic affinities and historical connections. Regarding the latter, Spener heard Labadie preach several times during 1660-1661, attended conventicles at Labadie's home in Geneva (as mentioned above), and later translated and published a short devotional by Labadie in 1667. His close associate, Johann Jakob Schütz (1640-1690), carried on a lengthy correspondence with the Labadists, particularly Anna Maria van Schurman, one of Labadie's most important followers, and was one of the biggest proponents of the use of conventicles for Pietism. In addition to these historical connections, a number of scholars have pointed out that Labadie anticipated key themes in Spener's program of reform, most notably in the use of conventicles and in the chiliastic "hope for better times for the church."[67] A key influence, Labadie deserves to be put alongside Arndt and Böhme as a major precursor of Pietism.

Conclusion

As we have seen, from the late medieval to the early modern era, there were a number of important voices who were calling for a deeper practice of devotion to God and a more fervent love of neighbor — voices that longed for a renewal of the Christian church and potentially of society as a whole. Many of these precursors contributed in significant ways to the rise of Pietism, which was also concerned with the renewal of Christian communal life. It is to this story, and the key figures of Spener and Francke, that we now turn.

---

67. See Shantz, *An Introduction to German Pietism*, p. 55.

CHAPTER THREE

Reforming the Reformation

Classical Pietism's Beginnings, Part I

As our last chapter showed, the precursors of Pietism are varied and complex. Ranging from Protestant radicals and separatists to medieval mystics, all of the figures were united in their concern to pursue and encourage a more authentic form of Christian life and discipleship. It was this concern for a deeper commitment to the love of God and neighbor that eventuated in the appearance of Pietism in the late seventeenth century. The Pietist movement itself was from its beginnings an internally diverse phenomenon, with separatist and church-focused wings that mutually influenced one another. The movement spanned multiple Protestant communions, and as later chapters will show, was also a trans-Atlantic occurrence.

Notwithstanding this diversity, our focus in this and the following chapter will be on the ecclesial Pietism of Spener and Francke, as well as the remarkable history of Nikolaus Ludwig von Zinzendorf and the Moravian movement. Though not representative of every form of Pietism, Spener, Francke, and Zinzendorf — and the movements, ministries, and writings that they were responsible for — were nevertheless central in the development of classical Pietism. To round out our picture of Pietism as it developed in the seventeenth and eighteenth centuries, in Chapter 4 we will also briefly consider the radical separatist wing of Pietism, as well as the Württemberg tradition represented by figures like Johann Albrecht Bengel and Friedrich Christoph Oetinger.

Philipp Jakob Spener

Undoubtedly the key figure in any telling of the story of Pietism is Philipp Jakob Spener (1635-1705). A Lutheran minister, Spener is widely regarded as the father of ecclesial Pietism and, along with his close associate, Johann Jakob Schütz (1640-1690), one of the principal architects of the Pietist ethos and vision which began in Frankfurt and quickly spread to other German-speaking centers, most notably Leipzig.[1] Author of the *Pia Desideria* — the programmatic text of Pietism — Spener articulated a program of educational and church reform meant to renew and revitalize both church and society. Calling for a more heartfelt commitment to Christ, Spener championed the "priesthood of all believers" and called for the creation of conventicles for the purpose of communal Bible reading, prayer, mutual support, and admonition. He deplored the contentious and controversial tone of contemporary church life, and urged Christians to commit themselves to the practice of love of neighbor, though without sacrificing a commitment to truth. His confidence that the Christian community could in fact experience genuine renewal, which was striking in the context of his times, was undergirded by a modified form of the hopeful chiliastic eschatology of Jean de Labadie and others. Although Spener's ministry and thought does not encompass all of the expressions of the Pietist impulse, he did articulate a path toward church renewal which was taken up by contemporaries and followers alike and which eventually took hold in large portions of the Protestant world.

Spener was born in 1635 in Rappoltsweiler, in the upper Alsace region in what is today eastern France. (Rappoltsweiler was spared much of the destruction of the Thirty Years' War.) The region was under the jurisdiction of the Lutheran Count of Rappoltstein, Johann Jakob von Rappoltstein (1598-1673), who was an avid collector of devotional literature. The Spener family enjoyed good relations with the House of Rappoltstein, and apparently Spener's parents had their own sizeable collection of devotional

---

1. For a discussion that focuses especially on Frankfurt and Leipzig, see Douglas H. Shantz, *An Introduction to German Pietism: Protestant Renewal at the Dawn of Modern Europe* (Baltimore: Johns Hopkins University Press, 2013), pp. 71-116.

literature which the young Spener would come to prize highly, such as Lewis Bayly's *Practice of Piety* and Johann Arndt's *True Christianity.*[2]

At the age of sixteen, only three years after the signing of the Peace of Westphalia in 1648, Spener enrolled at the University of Strasbourg. He completed a master's thesis on Thomas Hobbes in 1653, and studied theology at Strasbourg from 1654 to 1659. Spener would come to revere his teachers, Johann Schmidt, Johann Conrad Dannhauer, and Sebastian Schmidt, all leading figures in the theological faculty at Strasbourg. Johann Schmidt, who was devoted to the writings of Johann Arndt, left a lasting impression on Spener, while Sebastian Schmidt was significant for emphasizing that dogmatic assumptions should not overdetermine biblical exegesis.[3]

In keeping with the academic custom of the time, from 1659 to 1662 Spener traveled to visit other universities and study with scholars in Basel, Geneva, Lyon, and Tübingen.[4] In 1660-1661, during his visit to Geneva, Spener met Jean de Labadie, the charismatic reformer and convert to Protestantism discussed in the previous chapter. Spener heard Labadie preach on several occasions, visited with him at least once, and participated in a conventicle held at Labadie's home. He was also introduced to Labadie's writings by his French tutor, a convinced Labadist, Monsieur Tridon.[5] Spener would eventually translate and publish one of Labadie's tracts in 1667: "The Practice of Christian Prayer and Meditation." Though Spener was critical of the separatist impulse — one which would eventually claim Spener's close associate, Johann Jakob Schütz[6] — he was nevertheless influenced by the deep commitment to church reform that Labadie espoused.

June 23, 1664, was one of the most important days of Spener's life. In the morning he was married to Suzanna Erhardt, and in the afternoon he was awarded a doctorate in theology. By all accounts, the Speners' marriage was a happy one, and Suzanna bore Philipp eleven children,

---

2. See K. James Stein, *Philipp Jakob Spener: Pietist Patriarch* (Chicago: Covenant Press, 1986), pp. 33-35, 37-39.

3. See Shantz, *An Introduction to German Pietism*, pp. 76-77.

4. See Stein, *Philipp Jakob Spener*, pp. 57-63.

5. See Stein, *Philipp Jakob Spener*, pp. 60-61.

6. Stein, *Philipp Jakob Spener*, p. 92.

though three of them died young. The doctoral dissertation for which Spener was awarded his degree was an exegesis of Revelation 9:13-21, foreshadowing Spener's lifelong — and controversial — interest in eschatology. Spener's interpretation followed the traditional Lutheran Orthodox reading of the passage, arguing that the sixth angel which blew the trumpet to release the avenging armies from the east was a prophetic reference to the rise of Islam, specifically the Turks.[7] This reading, though traditional, was also timely, given that in 1663 the Turks had invaded Hungary. The work is marked by careful consideration of the field of interpretation, as Spener consulted between fifty and sixty different commentaries and provided a table with no less than thirty-eight interpretations, though it does not yet bear the marks of Spener's own unique eschatological conceptions.[8]

In 1666 Spener was appointed senior minister in Frankfurt am Main, where he would oversee the city's Lutheran clergy and minister among its fifteen thousand inhabitants for the next twenty years.[9] Frankfurt was a major trading center, with a Lutheran majority which controlled the city council. There were, however, sizeable Reformed, Roman Catholic, and Jewish minorities in the city, as well as a thriving subculture of religious nonconformity fueled by the writings of Jakob Böhme, Caspar Schwenckfeld, and Paracelsus, made possible in large measure by the printing and publishing industry for which Frankfurt was famous.[10]

From the start, Spener's ministry was marked by a desire to encourage a deeper sense of religious commitment among Frankfurters. As W. R. Ward notes, in the years prior to 1670, Spener's approach to reform was much in keeping with the reforming programs of other Orthodox Lutheran figures, most notably Ernest the Pious in Saxe-Gotha, who "had

7. See W. R. Ward, *Early Evangelicalism: A Global Intellectual History, 1670-1789* (Cambridge: Cambridge University Press, 2006), p. 26.

8. See Martin Brecht, "Philipp Jakob Spener, sein Programm und dessen Auswirkungen," in *Geschichte des Pietismus*, vol. 1: *Der Pietismus vom siebzehnten bis zum frühen achtzehnten Jahrhundert*, ed. Martin Brecht (Göttingen: Vandenhoeck & Ruprecht, 1993), pp. 284-85.

9. Brecht, "Philipp Jakob Spener, sein Programm und dessen Auswirkungen," p. 286.

10. See Shantz, *An Introduction to German Pietism*, pp. 72-73.

sought to tighten up religious observance and discipline, and to reinforce the operation of church, state, and law by education."[11] This strategy, which relied more on external enforcement of civic statutes for Sunday observance and so on, gave way in 1670 through the urging of congregants in Spener's St. Nicholas Church, among whom was the lawyer Johann Jakob Schütz. Schütz had experienced a dramatic conversion in 1668 through reading the Bible and the works of Johann Tauler, and would become an important figure in the early formation of the Pietist movement in Frankfurt. It was through the suggestion of Schütz and others that Spener's reform program turned to the use of conventicles.

Although there is some indication that Spener may have been hinting at establishing conventicles in the autumn of 1669, it was not until the summer of 1670 that these meetings became a reality.[12] The meetings were meant to satisfy a longing expressed by Spener's congregants to "have the opportunity where godly-minded people could come together and confer with each other in simplicity and love."[13] Originally held on Sunday and Wednesday evenings,[14] the meetings were intended to deepen Christian fellowship through prayer, study, and mutual edification. These meetings, which were held in the parsonage, started with only six in attendance, but by 1677 had to be moved to a small church because the attendance had swelled to over one hundred. Until 1674, meetings were organized around prayer, edification, and the reading and discussion of devotional literature or sermons. In 1674, the Bible became the primary focus of discussion. Other changes also occurred. The demographic of the meetings shifted from largely educated to uneducated laity. As Schütz noted, "We are all one, and call one another brother or sister, for there is neither male nor

11. Ward, *Early Evangelicalism*, pp. 26-27. See also Mary Noll Venables, "Pietist Fruit from Orthodox Seeds: The Case of Ernst the Pious of Saxe-Gotha-Altenburg," in *Confessionalism and Pietism: Religious Reform in Early Modern Europe*, ed. Fred Van Lieburg (Mainz: Verlag Philipp von Zabern, 2006), pp. 91-110.

12. See Stein, *Philipp Jakob Spener*, pp. 86-87.

13. Philipp Jakob Spener, "Bericht über die Motivation der Anreger der *Collegia pietatis*," in Ph. J. Spener, *Schriften*, ed. Erich Beyreuther and Dietrich Blaufuâ (New York: Olms Verlag, 1979), 1:44-46, as quoted in Shantz, *An Introduction to German Pietism*, p. 78.

14. Brecht, "Philipp Jakob Spener, sein Programm und dessen Auswirkungen," p. 297.

female but we are all one in Christ."[15] Women also attended, though they were not allowed to speak — a fact which would lead to the formation of the Saalhof conventicle, led by Juliana Baur von Eyseneck and Johanna Eleonora von Merlau (Petersen). This group would eventually separate itself from the church — and some Reformed and Roman Catholic participants would also attend.[16]

One of the theological tenets which underlay the conventicle movement was the "priesthood of all believers" or "spiritual priesthood," as Spener called it. His 1677 tract "The Spiritual Priesthood" offered a nuanced defense of the leveling dynamic that conventicles invariably would bring into the church:

10. Who then are such spiritual priests? All Christians without distinction (1 Pet. 2:9), old and young, male and female, bond and free (Gal. 3:28).

11. Does not the name "priest" belong only to ministers? No. Ministers, according to their office, are not properly priests, nor are they so called anywhere in the New Testament, but they are servants of Christ, stewards of the mysteries of God, bishops, elders, servants of the Gospel, of the Word, and so forth. Rather, the name "priest" is a general name for all Christians and applies to ministers not otherwise than to other Christians (1 Cor. 4:1, 3:5; 1 Tim. 3:1, 2, 5:17; Eph. 3:7; Acts 26:16; Luke 1:2).[17]

Although there was a decidedly egalitarian impulse in his conception, Spener's vision was meant to reform — not overthrow — the current arrangements within German Lutheranism. All Christians must diligently search the Scriptures to test and approve what they hear from the minister; however, not all Christians are meant to preach.[18] Women were also

---

15. Andreas Deppermann, *Johann Jakob Schütz und die Anfänge des Pietismus*, 2nd ed. (Tübingen: J. C. B. Mohr, 1986), p. 88, as quoted in Shantz, *An Introduction to German Pietism*, p. 79.

16. See Stein, *Philipp Jakob Spener*, p. 89.

17. Philipp Jakob Spener, "The Spiritual Priesthood," in *The Pietists: Selected Writings*, ed. Emilie Griffin and Peter C. Erb (San Francisco: HarperSanFrancisco, 2006), p. 3.

18. Spener, "The Spiritual Priesthood," pp. 7-13.

heirs of the spiritual priesthood, but under no circumstances were they to teach publicly[19] — and as we noted above, Spener did not even allow them to speak during the early conventicle gatherings! The liturgical forms and social roles of the seventeenth century were to be retained, but redirected toward service to others and a vital Christian faith. Believers were not only to read the Bible, but to allow it to reshape their lives, especially in regard to care for others, so that the *collegia pietatis* were ultimately not just for mutual edification, but for the renewal of the whole church.[20] These small group meetings were meant to be a kind of "church within the church" — *ecclesiola in ecclesia* — an instrument by which church and society could be revived.[21]

The *Pia Desideria*

Community renewal as the *raison d'être* of conventicles is nowhere more clearly expressed than in Spener's 1675 *Pia Desideria: Or, Heartfelt Desires for a God-pleasing Improvement of the True Protestant Church.*[22] Originally published as the preface for a re-issue of Johann Arndt's *True Christianity,* the *Pia Desideria* is widely regarded as the programmatic expression of Pietism, with its publication date in 1675 sometimes used as the official beginning of Pietism as a movement. Arguments about precisely when Pietism begins and ends aside, the *Pia Desideria* signals a change in the original conception of conventicles.[23] No longer would they simply be voluntary societies with some loose connection to the established church; now they would be cultivated by the clergy for the purpose of renewing church and society. The *Pia Desideria,* however, offered far more than a

19. Spener, "The Spiritual Priesthood," pp. 17-18.

20. See Johannes Wallmann, "Geistliche Erneuerung der Kirche nach Philipp Jakob Spener," *Pietismus und Neuzeit* 12 (1986): 12-37; see also Stein, *Philipp Jakob Spener,* pp. 205-28.

21. See Moonkee Kim, *Gemeinde der Widergeborenen: Das Kirchenverständnis in Speners Evangelischer Glaubenslehre* (München: Herbert Utz Verlag, 2003), pp. 161-78.

22. Philipp Jakob Spener, *Pia Desideria: Or, Heartfelt Desires for a God-pleasing Improvement of the True Protestant Church,* trans. Theodore G. Tappert (Philadelphia: Fortress Press, 1964).

23. See Stein, *Philipp Jakob Spener,* p. 90.

barometer reading of Spener's thoughts on the purpose of the Frankfurt conventicles. The short document also offered a broad program of reform, undergirded by key theological emphases that would become hallmarks of many forms of Pietism.

The *Pia Desideria* is divided into three sections. The first section details the awful conditions in the church. Offering an assessment of all three estates — civil authorities, ecclesiastical authorities, and common people — the *Pia Desideria* paints the picture of a lax, coarse, and generally decaying Christian society. "The precious spiritual body of Christ is now afflicted with distress and sickness."[24] The civil authorities abuse their power, and church officials are too busy seeking the best positions in the church, arguing and engaging in polemics, and generally neglecting their duties to care for the body of the church. Particularly regrettable is the way in which controversies and debate are handled within the church. "They think that everything has turned out well if only they know how to give answer to the errors of the papists, the Reformed, the Anabaptists, etc. They pay no attention to the fruits of those articles of faith which we presumably still hold in common with them or of those rules of morality which are acknowledged by us all."[25] In short, being proved right in doctrinal dispute superseded love for others and devotion to the way of Jesus, a fact that Spener found doubly scandalous because many of the arguments over finer points of doctrine were the result of scholastic method being re-introduced into Protestant theology. Such controversies certainly produce knowledge, but only the kind that "puffs up," not the kind that "builds up."[26]

This situation is responsible for the conditions among the laity. Lack of love, unwillingness to share with those in need, drunkenness, and sacramental formalism are among the many problems identified. The larger picture painted is of a Christian church that, if it is still alive, is on life support. And this state of affairs is bad not only because it raises the question of whether or not the vast majority of Christians are truly saved, but also because it discredits the gospel in the eyes of unbelievers, particularly the Jews.[27] In all of this, Spener is careful not to exempt himself from crit-

24. Spener, *Pia Desideria*, p. 31.
25. Spener, *Pia Desideria*, p. 49.
26. See Spener, *Pia Desideria*, p. 56.
27. Spener, *Pia Desideria*, pp. 68-75.

icism. "I do not exclude myself from the number of those in our estate who are lacking in the reputation we ought to have before God and the church. On the contrary, I recognize more and more how deficient I myself am, and I am prepared to be fraternally corrected by others. Indeed, nothing grieves me more than this: that I can hardly see how, in the face of such frightful corruption, such a one as I am can possibly recover a good conscience."[28]

The second, very brief section outlines Spener's "hopes for better times" for the church — a key theological rationale for why reform and renewal should be pursued and better conditions in the church expected. The last section details Spener's proposals for reform. The second and third sections contain the kernel of the unique Pietist agenda; we will describe them in reverse order.

Spener offers six proposals to deal with the deplorable conditions in the church. The proposals can be broken into two tables: the first dealing with practices that empower and include the laity; the second dealing with the reform of theological education and pastoral practice. The first proposal is a call for more extensive exposure to the Word of God through household and personal reading of Scripture and most importantly through the use of conventicles. As noted above, conventicles are envisioned as the vehicle through which believers find genuine Christian fellowship, exposure to the Word of God, mutual admonition, and prayer.[29]

The second is the need to cultivate the practice of the spiritual priesthood, already described above. The third proposal is for a more intentional emphasis on orthopraxy, or right practice. The fourth proposal deals with transforming the way that religious controversies are conducted. The fifth is a call for the reform of how church offices are allocated, Spener's aim being to move away from patronage and connection being the deciding factor, toward something more in keeping with the motif of calling — only those who are truly called by God should be permitted to enter the ordained ministry. "It is certain that a young man who fervently loves God, although adorned with limited gifts, will be more useful to the church of God with his meager talent and academic achievement than a vain and

28. Spener, *Pia Desideria*, p. 45.
29. See Spener, *Pia Desideria*, pp. 89-92.

worldly fool with double doctor's degrees who is very clever but has not been taught by God."[30] In other words, Spener was calling for a regenerate clergy.

To this end, a thorough overhaul of theological education is also envisioned, such that professors of theology "would pay attention to the life as well as the studies of the students entrusted to them and would from time to time speak to those who need to be spoken to."[31] As Martin Brecht describes it, "Pious existence and theological science have to form a unit."[32] Finally, Spener calls for a reform of preaching in a time when sermons tended to be heavy on doctrinal exposition and learning, and too light on simple and accessible preaching that promoted godly living. As he says, "Our whole Christian religion consists of the inner man or the new man, whose soul is faith and whose expressions are the fruits of life, and all sermons should be aimed at this."[33]

The reform proposals of the *Pia Desideria* are cast within a larger eschatological framework, one that has come to be termed Spener's "hope for better times for the church." Influenced by Labadist ideas, Spener's expectations for reform were fueled by a conviction that the millennium described in Revelation 20:1-10 did not mark the end of history, but rather referred to a period within history in which God would renew the church in order that Christ might work *through* the community to prepare the world for the final coming of the Lord. Though Spener worked out his chiliasm in more explicit terms in his 1693 *Assertion of the Hope of Better Future Times*,[34] the basic outlines can already be detected in the *Pia*.

The final coming of the Lord was to be preceded by at least two things: the conversion of the Jews and the renewal of the church. Though God

---

30. Spener, *Pia Desideria*, p. 108.

31. Spener, *Pia Desideria*, p. 107.

32. Brecht, "Philipp Jakob Spener, sein Programm und dessen Auswirkungen," p. 305.

33. Spener, *Pia Desideria*, p. 116.

34. Philipp Jakob Spener, *Assertion of the Hope of Better Future Times*, reprinted in *Philipp Jakob Spener Schriften*, vol. 6, ed. Erich Beyreuther (Hildesheim: Olms, 2001); as noted in K. James Stein, "Philipp Jakob Spener (1635-1705)," in *The Pietist Theologians*, ed. Carter Lindberg (Oxford: Blackwell Publishing, 2005), p. 95.

was the primary actor in these events, the church and individual Christians were not thereby free to be lazy.[35] "While hoping for such fruit, however, it is not enough idly to wait for it and be killed by the desire. . . . Even if it may be evident that we cannot achieve the whole and complete purpose, we can at least do as much as possible."[36] The church is called to action within its own life for the sake of its witness and in cooperation with the wider cosmic purpose of God's kingdom. This approach places Spener's eschatology closer to postmillennial eschatology than premillennial, because the work of Christ in and through the church is meant to prepare the world for the final, cosmic appearing of Christ.[37] Answering objections that his call was too optimistic and arrogant, Spener argued that the pursuit of reform was a task laid upon the community, though this did not mean that human effort was responsible for bringing in the kingdom of God.

The "hope for better times" was the eschatological correlate of what many consider the central tenet of Pietism: *Wiedergeburt*, or "new birth."[38] Although the *Pia Desideria* does not have a section dedicated to this theme, it is, along with Spener's eschatology, the presupposition of the whole. The term, whose origins are more deeply rooted in the radical reformation theology of Böhme and others,[39] refers to the event wherein God acts to bring about a radical transformation in the believer. It is the initiating event which founds the Christian life and which produces faith, justification, and sanctification. In this event, a new nature is born in the heart

35. For an outstanding discussion of this, see Kevin Ray Baxter, "From Cooperative Orthodox Optimism to Passive Chiliasm: The Effects of the Evolution of Spener's *Zunkunftshoffnung* on His Expectations, Ideas, Methods, and Efforts in Church Renewal," Ph.D. dissertation, Northwestern University, 1993, pp. 163-208.

36. Spener, *Pia Desideria*, p. 78.

37. Stein, "Philipp Jakob Spener (1635-1705)," p. 95.

38. See Manfred Kohl, "*Wiedergeburt* as the Central Theme in Pietism," *The Covenant Quarterly* 32, no. 4 (November 1974): 15-35.

39. See Douglas H. Shantz, "The Origin of Pietist Notions of New Birth and the New Man: Alchemy and Alchemists in Gottfried Arnold and Johann Henrich Reitz," in *The Pietist Impulse in Christianity*, ed. Christian T. Collins Winn et al. (Eugene, Ore.: Pickwick Press, 2011), pp. 29-41; see also Martin Schmidt, *Wiedergeburt und Neuer Mensch: Gesammelte Studien zur Geschichte des Pietismus* (Witten-Rhur: Luther Verlag, 1969), pp. 169-94.

of the believer.[40] Spener, in traditional Lutheran style, associated this event with baptism, though not necessarily with the waters of baptism, nor through any kind of sacramental formalism. Rather, it is through the Word spoken at baptism that one is born anew. Of significant importance for Spener's reforming program, however, was the fact that this new birth could be lost if left unattended. Thus, as Stein says, "He believed that virtually all baptized people needed 'to be born again again.'"[41]

Other features of Spener's theology of new birth included an emphasis on the passivity of the human person in the initial event of rebirth (only God can bring about the new birth) and an expected growth in grace or a renewal of life through the cooperation of the individual with God. Though Spener did not teach the same kind of perfectionism that one finds in John Wesley, he nevertheless expected that reborn Christians would show marked outward change and transformation in their lives. New birth and renewal, which are largely biological metaphors, functioned almost like similes for justification and sanctification, though Spener was quick to emphasize that justification occurred as a subset of the event of new birth. In a necessary consequence of rebirth, the newly born person learns over time to love God and neighbor — this is the new person, which Spener was most deeply concerned to cultivate in the *Pia Desideria:* "Our whole Christian religion consists of the inner man or the new man, whose soul is faith and whose expressions are the fruits of life...."[42]

The Early Pietist Movement Begins to Grow

Spener's *Pia Desideria* would offer a useful template for later forms of Pietism and, in many ways, is the quintessential expression of the Pietist ethos. The fruits of Spener's practice and his short tract resulted in conventicles spreading to other cities as well, while in Frankfurt itself additional conventicles were organized without clerical supervision or Spener's knowledge.[43] These developments proved to be a mixed blessing. On

40. See Stein, "Philipp Jakob Spener (1635-1705)," pp. 89-93.
41. Stein, "Philipp Jakob Spener (1635-1705)," p. 91.
42. Spener, *Pia Desideria*, p. 116.
43. See Stein, *Philipp Jakob Spener*, p. 88.

the one hand, Spener welcomed the spread of conventicles to other cities, viewing the development as positive and ultimately good for the health of the church. On the other hand, the central weakness of the conventicles (their separatist tendencies) became a real problem for Spener, as his close associate, Schütz, as well as Johanna Eleonora Petersen (1644-1724) — an important Pietist in her own right[44] — eventually separated from the state church. Spener was forced to distance himself from this group after 1682, and when he moved to Dresden in 1686, he did not implement conventicles.

Spener's Dresden period (1686-1691), where he served as preacher to the Saxon Court, was undoubtedly the most difficult of his ministry. Nevertheless, two events were of great importance. The first was the enthusiastic embrace of Spener's reform program in nearby Leipzig, and the second was his budding relationship with August Hermann Francke (1663-1727), who would become Spener's most important follower.

The Leipzig movement was begun by students at the University of Leipzig who began holding conventicles for the purpose of Bible study. These meetings were started at the instigation of Professor Johann Benedict Carpzov, a leading Orthodox theologian and, later, a bitter opponent of Pietism. He suggested that Francke and his friend Paul Anton begin holding meetings to study the Bible more carefully. Spener visited the group in 1687, after he had suggested they redirect their meetings away from academics and more toward devotional edification.[45] These meetings, and the tireless efforts of Francke and others, resulted in a revival in the town in 1689-1690. The revival was especially shaped by students and commoners, and eventually ran afoul of the authorities. The subsequent dispersal in 1690 of a large number of Pietist students from the university certainly quelled the revival, but ultimately led to the spread of Pietism throughout Germany.[46]

---

44. See Johanna Eleonora Petersen, *The Life of Lady Johanna Eleonora Petersen, Written by Herself,* edited and translated by Barbara Becker-Cantarino (Chicago: University of Chicago Press, 2005).

45. See Shantz, *An Introduction to German Pietism,* pp. 102-6.

46. See Shantz, *An Introduction to German Pietism,* pp. 109-11.

August Hermann Francke and Hallensian Pietism

Of perhaps even greater significance for the future of Pietism was the relationship which formed between August Hermann Francke and Spener. Francke was born in 1663 in Lübeck on the Baltic coast. His father, Johannes Francke, a lawyer, was called to take up a position as court advisor to Ernest the Pious, Duke of Saxe-Gotha, to assist with social and ecclesial reconstruction after the Thirty Years' War.[47] The public and private atmosphere in which Francke grew up was imbued with the spirit of a reform-minded Orthodoxy, in which Johann Arndt's call for an authentic Christianity mingled with a serious devotion to Lutheran Orthodoxy. After his father's death in 1670, Francke was provided for by the Duke. He matriculated at the University of Erfurt in 1679, but after one semester transferred to the University of Kiel and remained there until 1682. After a short stint in Hamburg studying Hebrew, Francke entered the University of Leipzig in 1684. He had been at Leipzig for two years when he and Paul Anton began hosting their *collegium philobiblicum*, which was devoted to biblical exegesis.

October of 1687 was especially important for Francke, as he had left Leipzig to pursue further studies in Lüneberg, located southeast of Hamburg. When he arrived, Francke was asked to preach a sermon to the local congregation. Since Francke was already deeply committed to Spener's vision of a living faith, this event created a kind of crisis of conscience for him. He recounts the event in his *Autobiography* (1692):

> My mind was in such a state that I was not only concerned with the mere preaching of a sermon but chiefly with the upbuilding of the congregation. Thinking on this, the text came to me; "this is written that you may believe that Jesus is the Christ, the Son of God, and that believing, you may have life in his name" (John 20:31). With this text I had particular opportunity to discuss true living faith, and how this faith is distinguished from a mere human and imaginary foolish faith. Earnestly

47. See Gary R. Sattler, *God's Glory, Neighbor's Good: A Brief Introduction to the Life and Writings of August Hermann Francke* (Chicago: Covenant Press, 1982), pp. 19-20.

considering this matter, the thought came to me that I did not find the faith in myself that I was to demand in the sermon.[48]

Francke goes on to recount in great detail the inner spiritual turmoil this realization caused him for the next week, until finally, he experienced a breakthrough:

In such great dread I went once more upon my knees on the evening before the Sunday on which I was to preach. I cried to God, whom I still did not know nor trust, for salvation from such a miserable state [asking him to save me], if indeed he was a true God. The Lord, the living God, heard me from his throne while I yet knelt. So great was his fatherly love that he wished to take me finally, after such doubts and unrest of my heart, so that I might be more convinced that he could satisfy me well, and that my erring reason might be tamed, so as not to move against his power and faithfulness. He immediately heard me. My doubt vanished as quickly as one turns one's hand: I was assured in my heart of the grace of God in Christ Jesus and I knew God not only as God but as my Father.[49]

Francke's conversion, a visceral and life-altering event, became something of a model for later Hallensian Pietism,[50] and Francke himself repeatedly looked back to this event as defining his own calling.

Although working largely within Spener's notion of new birth, Francke brought out the psychological experience which marked the movement of the individual from a life controlled by sin to a life in fellowship with God. The contrast between life before and life after conversion was stark: the first marked by fear, doubt, addiction to sin, lovelessness, and indifference to others; the other marked by peace, joy, faith, hope, and love. This blatant difference between an unregenerate life and a re-

48. August Hermann Francke, *Autobiography*, in *Pietists: Selected Writings*, ed. Peter C. Erb (Ramsey, N.J.: Paulist Press, 1983), p. 102.

49. Francke, *Autobiography*, p. 105.

50. See Hans-Martin Kirn, "The Penitential Struggle ('Busskampf') of August Hermann Francke (1663-1727): A Model of Pietistic Conversion?" in *Paradigms, Poetics, and Politics of Conversion*, ed. Jan N. Bremmer, Wout Jac van Bekkum, and Arie L. Molendjik (Leuven: Peeters, 2006), pp. 123-32.

generate life, which Francke had existentially experienced himself, was the underlying impetus for his desire to guide others toward conversion. Even Francke's educational philosophy had conversion in view, though both as end and as presupposition.

A subtle but important difference from Spener lay in his preference for the use of the word *Bekehrung* or conversion to describe the new birth.[51] Spener's notion of "new birth" was primarily a passive experience in which the principal actor was God, whereas *Bekehrung* carried a more activist orientation, in which the initiating work of God must be grasped by the individual. Though conversion is, "initially, exclusively the work of God," God nevertheless "wants man to willingly take hold of it. If he does not [and therefore is not converted], it is man's own fault."[52] Because of Francke's concern for a true Christianity, his theology of conversion highlighted the empirical psychological states that the individual passed through as he or she moved from damnation to salvation, thereby verifying his or her salvation.[53] Of particular importance was the trial of struggle or *Busskampf* which preceded conversion, an experience that mirrored Francke's own. During these trials, individuals became acutely aware of their sins and of the need to call out for God. After passing through a variety of stages, individuals arrived at an emotional *Durchbruch*, or "breakthrough," in which they grasped hold of God's grace and were pulled out of darkness and into the light.

To be sure, though Francke was concerned with the process and event of conversion, his real concern was with the Christian life which lay on the other side. His conviction that only the reborn were able to truly hear and profit from the guidance of the Scriptures and to live lives that were aimed at loving God and neighbor was what lay behind his concern with conversion. Without a genuine conversion as the presupposition of the life of the church and the individual, a true and living Christianity, such as Arndt, Spener, and others were hoping for, would never be possible.

When Francke returned to Leipzig in 1689, he was literally a new man.

51. See Kohl, "*Wiedergeburt* as the Central Theme in Pietism," p. 21.
52. Martin Brecht, "August Hermann Francke und der Hallische Pietismus," in *Geschichte des Pietismus*, vol. 1, p. 463.
53. See Markus Matthias, "August Hermann Francke (1663-1727)," in *The Pietist Theologians*, pp. 107-8.

His lectures on Scripture under the auspices of the *collegia philobiblicum* were the primary catalyst for the revival that erupted in Leipzig. Because of the opposition of the Orthodox faculty at Leipzig, Francke eventually left to minister in Erfurt. There too he met with suspicion and opposition, and was eventually forced to leave that city in September 1691. In the meantime, Spener had moved in June of that year to a new position in Berlin because opposition to his ministry had made work in Dresden untenable. This move, though made under clouds of controversy, proved to be fortuitous for Spener, who immediately won the confidence of the Elector of Brandenburg-Prussia.[54] This gave him incredible influence at the Prussian court, which he used to promote the Pietist cause. Of great importance were his suggestions that Joachim Justus Breithaupt (1658-1732) and Francke be given positions at the newly formed University of Halle. In 1692 Francke became professor of Greek and Oriental languages at Halle, where he made theological contributions in biblical exegesis, hermeneutics, and philology.[55] That same year, he was also installed as pastor in the town of Glaucha, a suburb of Halle.

Francke's ministry in Glaucha/Halle would be defining for the future of Pietism. His ministry in Glaucha included work among the city's poor, to whom Francke was especially committed. He noted, "I will believe that there is a true Christianity among us when I see that one uses the temporal goods among us not for pleasure and luxury, but rather in sincere love toward the poor."[56] Francke's commitment to the poor was above all embodied in the famous Halle *Stiftungen*, or institutions, which began in 1695.

Beginning in the summer of 1694, Francke hosted educational classes for poor children in his home. By Easter of 1695, because of an anonymous donation, Francke managed to found a school for poor children. Francke's pedagogical philosophy was largely driven by a desire that "children be instructed aright unto a true, unblemished piety which may bring fruit in their old age,"[57] such that education was put in service of the

---

54. See Stein, *Philipp Jakob Spener*, pp. 127-30.

55. For a discussion of these, see Matthias, "August Hermann Francke (1663-1727)," pp. 104-10.

56. August Hermann Francke, "The Duty to the Poor," in Sattler, *God's Glory, Neighbor's Good*, p. 171.

57. *A. H. Francke's Pädagogische Schriften*, ed. G. Kramer (Langensalza: Verlags-

reform of both church and state. Poor children — and, eventually, really, all children — should have Christian character and wisdom cultivated in them so that they could be productive members of society;[58] to that end, schools should create a learning environment that does not hamper but rather facilitates conversion and growth in godliness. From 1695 to 1702 a variety of schools were founded, "including schools for orphans and the poor, a Latin school, and the exclusive Pädagogium Regium, an elector's school. Francke's foundations in Halle were justly described as 'a school city.'"[59] By the time of Francke's death in 1727, the Halle schools employed 175 teachers with some 2,000 students enrolled, including children from every level of society, both boys and girls.[60] Halle's educational methods, as well as the students and teachers trained in the institutions, influenced institutions in "England, Denmark, Hungary, Estonia, Siberia, and India."[61]

More important than Francke's educational work, however, was his work with orphans. In 1698 construction began on an orphanage, the largest of all the buildings in the sprawling complex at Halle. Inspired by Dutch models, the Halle orphanage was a progressive institution for its time, offering orphans an education and making use of modern hygienic methods. Through association, the various Halle institutions — including the schools, the publishing ventures, the medical dispensary, the bakery, the brewery, and so on — eventually came to be subsumed under the orphanage.[62] According to Douglas Shantz, 25 percent of all orphanages

---

Comptoir von Hermann Beyer, 1876), as quoted in Sattler, *God's Glory, Neighbor's Good*, p. 55.

58. Richard Gawthorp argues that this emphasis placed the Halle educational vision in agreement with Enlightenment educational philosophy. See his "Pedagogy and Reform in Halle Pietism and the German Enlightenment," in *Interdisziplinäre Pietismusforschungen: Beiträge zum Ersten Internationalen Kongress für Pietismusforschung 2001*, vol. 2, ed. Udo Sträter, Hartmut Lehmann, Thomas Müller-Bahlke, and Johannes Wallmann (Tübingen: Max Niemeyer Verlag, 2005), pp. 529-35.

59. Shantz, *An Introduction to German Pietism*, p. 123.

60. James Van Horn Melton, "Pietism, Politics, and the Public Sphere in Germany," in *Religion and Politics in Enlightenment Europe*, ed. James E. Bradley and Dale K. Van Kley (Notre Dame: University of Notre Dame Press, 2001), p. 305.

61. See Shantz, *An Introduction to German Pietism*, p. 142.

62. Shantz, *An Introduction to German Pietism*, p. 117.

built between 1695 and 1802 in German lands were modeled after the Halle orphanage.[63]

Because of the generous support of various benefactors and connections at court in Berlin, most notably Karl Hildebrand Baron von Canstein (1667-1719), who became a key ally especially after the death of Spener in 1705, the Halle institutions grew and thrived. One especially important venture made possible by the generous support of von Canstein was the Bible Institute, whose principal mission was to make available Bibles and devotional literature at little or no cost. The work of the Bible Institute is impressive. One estimate puts the number of Bibles produced by Halle during the eighteenth century at three million.[64] It was especially through these publication ventures that Hallensian Pietism spread to Sweden, Russia and the Baltic region, and the Americas.[65]

Finally, the institutions founded by Francke at Halle also came to be identified with Protestant missionary endeavor. In response to a request for missionaries from the Danish king, Frederick IV, Bartholomäus Ziegenbalg (1682-1719) and Heinrich Plütschau (1677-1747), students at Halle University and associates of Francke, traveled to Tranquebar, India. They arrived in 1706, eighty-seven years before William Carey arrived in Bengal, India, under the auspices of the Baptist Missionary Society.[66] The work of Ziegenbalg was especially significant.[67] He set about learning the Tamil language as soon as he arrived. By 1707 he was preaching in Tamil and had founded separate schools for boys and girls, out of respect for the Tamil custom of segregating genders; he would later establish a seminary for training local Tamils for ministry. By 1711 he had translated the New Testament into Tamil, and would eventually publish a Tamil grammar in 1716.

---

63. Shantz, *An Introduction to German Pietism*, p. 140.

64. See Bernhard Dammermann, "Continental Versions from c. 1600 to the Present Day: German," in *The Cambridge History of the Bible: The West from the Reformation to the Present Day*, ed. S. L. Greenslade (Cambridge: Cambridge University Press, 1963), pp. 340-41.

65. See Sattler, *God's Glory, Neighbor's Good*, p. 77.

66. See Richard V. Pierard, "German Pietism as a Major Factor in the Beginnings of Modern Protestant Missions," in *The Pietist Impulse in Christianity*, ed. Collins Winn et al., pp. 285-90.

67. See Brijraj Singh, *The First Protestant Missionary to India: Bartholomaeus Ziegenbalg, 1683-1719* (Oxford: Oxford University Press, 2000).

Ziegenbalg's missionary practice and interest in the culture and religion of local Tamils were models both for culturally sensitive missionizing and for intercultural learning. This approach set him at odds with the Danish East India Company and its colonial ventures in the region[68] and made Francke uneasy, which is not surprising, given Francke's more conventional approach to missions and conversion.[69] Separating European identity from Christian identity, Ziegenbalg proclaimed, "If you wish to become Christian, we will not require you to imitate us Europeans in wearing clothes, eating, drinking, and other external things. You will have the freedom to do the things that your country requires. We do not want to change the external appearance of your body, but to look for the transformation of your heart and mind which alone means real conversion."[70] As scholars have also noted, the Halle missionaries were eager to recruit, develop, and include locals in their mission work.[71]

The Tranquebar mission was advertised broadly through the *Halle Report*, a periodical published by Halle that included the letters and accounts of mission work in East India. Halle's mission work also led to a strategic and ecumenical alliance with the Anglican Society for the Propagation of Christian Knowledge, which eventually led to a correspondence between Francke and the American Puritan Cotton Mather (1663-1728), a supporter of the Society for Promoting Christian Knowledge (SPCK).[72] The Halle-Danish mission inspired the creation of at least four additional missionary societies over the course of the eighteenth and nineteenth centuries.[73]

In addition to Francke's work organizing and managing the Halle

---

68. Singh, *The First Protestant Missionary to India*, pp. 146-63.

69. Shantz, *An Introduction to German Pietism*, p. 246.

70. Wilhelm Germann, *Ziegenbalg und Plütschau — Die Gründungsjahre der Trankebarschen Mission — Ein Beitrag zur Geschichte des Pietismus nach handschriftlichen Quellen und ältesten Drucken*, vol. 1 (Erlangen: Verlag von Andreas Deichert, 1868), pp. 290-92, as quoted in Daniel Jeyaraj, "The First Lutheran Missionary Bartholomäus Ziegenbalg: His Concepts of Culture and Mission from a Postcolonial Perspective," *Swedish Missiological Themes* 93, no. 3 (2005): 392.

71. See Shantz, *An Introduction to German Pietism*, pp. 248-50.

72. Richard F. Lovelace, *The American Pietism of Cotton Mather: Origins of American Evangelicalism* (Eugene, Ore.: Wipf & Stock Publishers, 1979), p. 33.

73. See Shantz, *An Introduction to German Pietism*, pp. 238-39.

foundations, he also participated in the life of the university. Under Francke's leadership the theological faculty sought to institutionalize the Pietist theological vision of Spener, to educate students in the living knowledge of God. Though less dramatic than the work that emanated out of the Halle *Stiftungen*, it was no less important. As Martin Brecht observes, "The success of Halle Pietism resulted in large part from the fact that he was able to win over and impress a whole generation of theologians at the new university."[74] The vision, as articulated by Francke, placed exegetical studies at the center, with dogmatic and other topics subordinated to study of the Bible.[75] In an attempt to clarify how Scripture was to be studied, Francke employed the distinction between the "kernel" and the "husk."[76] The latter was comprised of Bible study that was logical, philological, historical, and so on. To be sure, this was an important — even indispensable — element for theological study. However, it was only the "kernel" or inner truth of Scripture that was truly nourishing, transformative, and therefore salvific. It was the "literal sense intended by the Holy Spirit himself,"[77] which was arrived at through biblical exegesis, dogmatic analysis, and practical reading.

Critical in this was Francke's conviction that only *after* this sense had been assimilated into the heart of the reader could one speak of a real and true knowledge of the "kernel" of Scripture. Students, therefore, were to diligently apply themselves to being "interpreted" by the Scriptures through the practices of prayer, meditation, and struggle, or *oratio, meditatio,* and *tenatio*.[78] These practices were recommended because they placed the reader in a posture of openness to the true teacher of Scripture, the Holy Spirit. Theological study at Halle was not merely to be a scientific endeavor but had to include the cultivation of piety, because

74. Brecht, "August Hermann Francke und der Hallische Pietismus," p. 470.
75. Brecht, "August Hermann Francke und der Hallische Pietismus," p. 472.
76. See Matthias, "August Hermann Francke (1663-1727)," pp. 104-5.
77. August Hermann Francke, *Manuductio* (Halle: Zeitler, 1693), p. 66, as quoted in Matthias, "August Hermann Francke (1663-1727)," p. 105.
78. See August Hermann Francke, "Simple Instruction, or How One Should Read Holy Scripture for One's True Edification," *Lutheran Quarterly* 25, no. 4 (Winter 2011): 373-82; and Oswald Bayer, "Lutheran Pietism, or *Oratio, Meditatio, Tenatio* in August Hermann Francke," *Lutheran Quarterly* 25, no. 4 (Winter 2011): 383-97.

the subject of theology was the living God, with whom one was meant to enter into a relationship. And though Francke argued that the real core or kernel of Scripture was its witness to Jesus Christ, he also argued that only the reborn theologian could claim to have true knowledge of the Bible. In addition to placing a premium on exegetical studies, the Halle curriculum also included tutorials in homiletics, pastoral care, and catechetics.[79] Francke's innovations also led to the transformation of examinations for church appointments, which would eventually include, among other things, sermon preparation[80] and an account of the candidate's conversion.[81]

Of course, with the growth and development of Hallensian Pietism — both the Halle institutions and the innovations in the theological faculty at Halle — came controversy.[82] In fact, from the very beginning, with the publication of Spener's *Pia Desideria* in 1675, those identified with the Pietist movement were attacked, first by Lutheran Orthodox opponents and later by Enlightenment figures.[83] Opposition to Spener's reform program, to his doctrine of *Wiedergeburt* ("new birth") and other theological proposals, as well as to spiritualist and separatist tendencies within Pietist circles, is evident from 1679 onward. One of the most intensive periods of controversy occurred between 1695 and 1698 over the theological and spiritual significance and practice of confession in the Lutheran church.[84] Overlapping this period of controversy (1691-1698) was an intense exchange between Spener and five other Lutheran Orthodox theologians

79. Johannes Wischmeyer, "Continuity and Change: The Study of Protestant Theology in Germany between Reformation and the Humboldtian University Ideal," *Communio Viatorum* 47, no. 3 (2005): 248.

80. Wischmeyer, "Continuity and Change," p. 249.

81. Matthias, "August Hermann Francke (1663-1727)," p. 110.

82. For a discussion of the controversies surrounding Halle and Francke, see Brecht, "August Hermann Francke und der Hallische Pietismus," pp. 497-511. See also Timothy M. Salo, "Joachim Lange: Lutheran Pietist Theology and Halle Apologist," in *The Pietist Impulse in Christianity*, ed. Collins Winn et al., pp. 82-93.

83. See W. R. Ward, *Christianity under the Ancien Régime, 1648-1789* (Cambridge: Cambridge University Press, 1999), pp. 76-78, 100-103, 171-73. See also Eric Carlsson, "Pietism and Enlightenment Theology's Historical Turn: The Case of Johann Salmo Semler," in *The Pietist Impulse in Christianity*, ed. Collins Winn et al., pp. 97-106.

84. See Stein, *Philipp Jakob Spener*, pp. 140-43.

over his chiliastic eschatology. As a result, subsequent critiques of Pietism invariably included a critique of Pietist eschatology, especially forms of chiliasm.[85]

Conclusion

As we have seen, Spener and Francke were two of the key figures in the development of early Pietism in Germany. Through their writings, preaching, and tireless pastoral and organizational work — not the least of which includes the impressive institutions and various initiatives launched at Halle — they managed to give shape to a broad longing within Christian circles for a deeper commitment to a living Christianity. As our next chapter will show, their pietistic endeavors to renew the church and Christian society were accompanied by other, more radical approaches that sometimes led in the direction of separatism. We'll explore that story in our next chapter.

85. See Heike Krauter-Dierolf, *Die Eschatologie Philipp Jakob Speners: Der Streit mit der lutheranischen Orthodoxie um die "Hoffnung besserer Zeiten"* (Tübingen: Mohr Siebeck, 2005); Dietrich Blaufuss, "Zu Ph.J. Speners Chiliasmus und seinen Kritikern," *Pietismus und Neuzeit* 14 (1988): 85-108; and Stein, "Philipp Jakob Spener (1635-1705)," pp. 84-99.

CHAPTER FOUR

Reforming the Reformation

Classical Pietism's Beginnings, Part II

As we showed in our last chapter, Spener and Francke were key figures in formulating a program to reform and renew the church that worked primarily from within. Neither Spener nor Francke were interested in leaving the established church, but there can be little doubt that the association of more radical figures with the Pietist movement was also a motivating factor in many of the controversies surrounding the life and ministry of Spener, Francke, and their followers.

In this chapter, we will introduce some of the figures associated with the radical wing of the Pietist movement in German-speaking lands, as well as the remarkable personality Nikolaus Ludwig von Zinzendorf, as a way of filling out our picture of the early development of the Pietist movement. We will conclude with a discussion of the unique Pietist tradition that developed in the southwestern Duchy of Württemberg. Although in many ways dependent on impulses that came from Halle and the Moravian movement of Zinzendorf, Württemberg Pietism nevertheless represents a unique form of the larger Pietist tradition, one that continues to this day.

Radical Pietism

The relationship between what has come to be called radical Pietism and the Pietism of Spener and Francke — and, later, Zinzendorf — is fluid and complex, composed of permeable boundaries.[1] Radical Pietism appeared at the same time and developed alongside the more conventional Pietism of Spener and others. Fueled especially by the speculative elements in Jakob Böhme's thought, the Spiritualism of Caspar Schwenckfeld and others, the separatism of Jean de Labadie, and the eschatological musings of the English visionary Jane Leade (1624-1704),[2] the radicals tended to be more thoroughly chiliastic,[3] more decidedly separatist in their ecclesiology,[4] and more egalitarian in regard to the role of women in their communities and networks.[5] Radical Pietists like Gottfried Arnold (1666-1714) and Johanna Eleonora Petersen (1644-1724) enjoyed close personal contact with Spener and others. Spener and Francke were avid readers of certain strands of radical thought,[6] and when they did distance themselves from many radicals, their criticisms were qualified by a level of appreciation that the Orthodox would have found troubling.

This was particularly the case with Johanna Eleonora von Merlau (later Petersen). Born into a Hessian noble family in the city of Frankfurt during the later stages of the Thirty Years' War, Petersen was the most prolific female Pietist author during the early phases of the movement. After serving as a lady-in-waiting from 1657 to 1674 at the court (near Zwickau) of her godmother, Duchess Anna Margaretha, she returned to Frankfurt in 1675. She had become aware of the Pietist movement as early as 1672, when she met Spener. Through her correspondence with Spener, as well as her own religious inclinations and reading, von Merlau

1. For a fascinating study that shows the permeable nature of the boundaries between these different groups, see Douglas H. Shantz, *Between Sardis and Philadelphia: The Life and World of the Pietist Court Preacher Conrad Bröske* (Leiden: E. J. Brill, 2008).

2. See Donald F. Durnbaugh, "Jane Ward Leade (1624-1704) and the Philadelphians," in *The Pietist Theologians*, ed. Carter Lindberg (Oxford: Blackwell Publishing, 2005), pp. 128-46.

3. See Douglas H. Shantz, *An Introduction to German Pietism: Protestant Renewal at the Dawn of Modern Europe* (Baltimore: Johns Hopkins University Press, 2013), p. 158.

4. See Hans Schneider, "Understanding the Church: Issues of Pietist Ecclesiology," in *Pietism and Community in Europe and North America, 1650-1850*, ed. Jonathan Strom (Leiden: E. J. Brill, 2010), pp. 15-35.

5. See Shantz, *An Introduction to German Pietism*, pp. 179-203.

6. See W. R. Ward, *Early Evangelicalism: A Global Intellectual History, 1670-1789* (Cambridge: Cambridge University Press, 2006), pp. 35-39, 43-46.

became a committed follower of the new Pietist movement. When she arrived in Frankfurt, she immediately joined a conventicle meeting in the Saalhof — the former castle of the Hohenstaufen family — where she, Maria Juliana Baur von Eyseneck (1641-1684), and Johann Jakob Schütz would form the inner core of leadership. In 1680 she married Johann Wilhelm Petersen (1649-1727), a trained theologian and clergy-man. Spener, who was probably a key voice in suggesting the match, conducted the ceremony.[7]

By this point, the separatist impulse of the Saalhof group was already evident. In 1677, the group had already been visited by the Quaker William Penn (1644-1718), who was looking for potential settlers for Pennsylvania. Fearing future persecution, some in the Saalhof group, including Schütz, would establish the Frankfurt Land Company, acquiring some 15,000 acres of land in Pennsylvania, and eventually establishing Germantown, Pennsylvania.[8] Johanna Petersen also owned stock in the company, though she would never travel to North America.[9]

Petersen is most well-known because of her contributions to eschatology. Influenced by the thought of Jane Leade and the Philadelphians, an English apocalyptic sect, both Petersens became advocates of chiliasm and later of the doctrine of *apocatastasis ton panton,* or the "restoration of all things." Johanna Petersen's chiliasm, important for later forms of Pietism, especially the Württemberg variety discussed briefly below, consisted in a hope for a universal outpouring of the Spirit on the earth, which would effect a time of peace, a restoration of Israel (and the conversion of Jews), and a first resurrection of the reborn, who would rule on earth with Christ for a thousand years.[10] Far more controversial was their championing of the doctrine of the "restoration of all things." Johanna Petersen was convinced that eventually hell would be emptied and that all things would be

---

7. See Barbara Becker-Cantarino, "Volume Editor's Introduction," in Johanna Eleonora Petersen, *The Life of Lady Johanna Eleonora Petersen, Written by Herself,* edited and translated by Barbara Becker-Cantarino (Chicago: University of Chicago Press, 2005), pp. 12-13.

8. Shantz, *An Introduction to German Pietism,* p. 82.

9. Becker-Cantarino, "Volume Editor's Introduction," p. 10.

10. See Martin H. Jung, "Johanna Eleonora Petersen (1644-1724)," in *The Pietist Theologians,* ed. Lindberg, p. 150.

made new.[11] She published these ideas in 1698, though Spener had warned her against such an idea.[12] The Halle theologians also came out against the doctrine, which disappointed both of the Petersens, though Spener neither rejected nor championed it.[13]

Perhaps the most widely known of the radical Pietists who had connections with Spener was Gottfried Arnold. Arnold is most well-known for his *Unparteysche Kirchen- und Ketzer-historie, Vom Anfang des Neuen Testaments Bisz auf das Jahr Christi 1688* (1699-1700), or "A Nonpartisan History of the Church and Heresy, from the Beginnings to 1688." The work is notable for its use of primary sources, and for its working assumption of a "Constantinian Fall of the Church" — the assumption that the coming together of state and church symbolically represented in the person of Constantine was not necessarily a good thing.[14] This assumption led Arnold to consider the so-called heretics who populated church history in a different light.[15] Rather than the enemies of the gospel, he proposed, they were often its most ardent supporters, suffering at the hands of the authorities whose interests were more in maintaining power than in understanding the truth and living by it. Arnold critiqued the use of philosophy in the formation of Christian doctrine as the intellectual correlate of the use of the state in the enforcement of Christian faith and life. Both state power and an intellectualized faith corrupted and corroded true Christianity.[16] Needless to say, a history that featured the heretics as heroes — the book was also called "History of Heresy" — and the guardians of orthodoxy as villains was not going to win Arnold any friends in Lutheran Orthodox

11. Jung, "Johanna Eleonora Petersen (1644-1724)," pp. 154-55.

12. See Becker-Cantarino, "Volume Editor's Bibliography," p. 47.

13. Shantz, *An Introduction to German Pietism*, p. 164.

14. See Peter C. Erb, "Gottfried Arnold (1666-1714)," in *The Pietist Theologians*, ed. Lindberg, p. 179.

15. Arnold is widely recognized as marking a sea change in historiographical practice, not least because he highlighted how historiographical assumptions shape the writing of history. For a brief discussion of this, see Frank Roberts, "Gottfried Arnold on Historical Understanding: An Early Pietist Approach," *Fides et Historia* 14, no. 2 (Spring/Summer 1982): 50-59. See also Hans Schneider, *German Radical Pietism*, trans. Gerald T. MacDonald (Lanham, Md.: Scarecrow Press, 2007), pp. 32-35.

16. See F. Ernest Stoeffler, *German Pietism during the Eighteenth Century* (Leiden: E. J. Brill, 1973), pp. 178-81.

circles.[17] However, the impressive historical scholarship and rich source material provided in the book meant that it had to be taken seriously.[18]

Scholars are generally agreed that Arnold's radicalism was modified after he married in 1701.[19] His marriage to Anna Sprögel was followed by his decision to accept an appointment within the Lutheran church. By most accounts, Arnold's re-entry into the church didn't signal an end to his radicalism as much as an attempt to witness to his understanding of an authentic Christianity — which for Arnold included a variety of esoteric and apocalyptic elements[20] — within the structure of the church, for the sake of the church. As W. R. Ward notes, "Arnold's career . . . illustrates the way in which the activities of opposing wings of the Pietist movement were constantly interwoven,"[21] as his biography highlights the permeable boundaries that marked radical and ecclesial Pietism, and the dynamics of attempting to meld more radical ideas with traditional forms of Christian worship, theology, and piety.

Zinzendorf and the Moravian Movement

In some ways, our review of our last major figure, Nikolaus Ludwig von Zinzendorf (1700-1760), and the Moravian movement which he guided during the eighteenth century can also be understood as an attempt to bring together the radical and ecclesial forms of Pietism for the renewal of Christianity. By far the most fascinating and controversial of all the key figures in the Pietism of the eighteenth century, Zinzendorf possessed a remarkable spiritual attunement and religious genius combined with a penchant for organizing and an interest in practical devotion to the Savior.

17. See Erb, "Gottfried Arnold (1666-1714)," p. 179.

18. See Douglas H. Shantz, "'Back to the Sources': Gottfried Arnold (1666-1714), Johann Heinrich Reitz (1655-1720), and the Distinctive Program and Practice of Pietist Historical Writing," in *Commoners and Community: Essays in Honor of Werner O. Packull*, ed. C. Arnold Snyder (Kitchener, Ont.: Pandora Press, 2002), pp. 75-99.

19. For a discussion of this change, see Dale R. Stoffer, "The Life and Thought of Gottfried Arnold," *Brethren Life and Thought* 26 (Summer 1981): 140-45.

20. See Erb, "Gottfried Arnold (1666-1714)," pp. 181-86.

21. Ward, *Early Evangelicalism*, pp. 46-47.

At the same time, he had an "extraordinary capacity to combine a great ability to make a good first impression with an even greater inability to keep the loyalty of men of independent mind."[22] Thus, the opposition that Zinzendorf often encountered among his contemporaries had as much to do with his polarizing personality as with his innovative and radical ideas. Nevertheless, the Moravian movement, which experienced a revival under Zinzendorf's guidance in 1727 and to which he gave all of his considerable energies, has managed — though small in numbers — to have an enormous impact on Protestant Christianity.

Born in 1700 in Dresden to Austrian nobility, Zinzendorf was raised by his maternal grandmother, Henriette Catherina von Gersdorf (1648-1726), after the death of his father. Von Gersdorf was a remarkable woman, with facility in theological Latin, and was an early supporter of Spener, Francke, and the institutions at Halle. She was one of many among the nobility who gave generously to Francke's endeavors.[23] Zinzendorf was raised in the Pietism of Halle through his grandmother's influence, and was sent to study at the Halle *Paedagogium* in 1710. Zinzendorf's experience at Halle was difficult. A self-confident young man with a deep commitment to Jesus, Zinzendorf had never experienced the *Busskampf* (sorrow and trial) so cherished by Francke. Because of this, he was often accused of being unregenerate, and his self-assured demeanor was interpreted as arrogance and pride. To be sure, Zinzendorf also contributed to the latter assessment, as he would "exhort his fellow students toward greater religious dedication and zeal."[24]

In fact, one of the key differences between Moravian Pietism and Hallensian Pietism was Zinzendorf's disagreement with Francke over the experience of conversion and sanctification. Whereas Francke had developed a rather elaborate order of salvation, which was marked by *Busskampf*, Zinzendorf's Christocentrism led him to argue that the *Busskampf* had been experienced already in Christ:[25] "During the whole time he experi-

22. Ward, *Early Evangelicalism*, p. 99.

23. Baron von Canstein, responsible for founding and funding the Halle Bible Institute, was her brother-in-law. See Stoeffler, *German Pietism during the Eighteenth Century*, p. 132.

24. Stoeffler, *German Pietism during the Eighteenth Century*, p. 133.

25. See Craig D. Atwood, "The Mother of All Souls: Understanding Zinzendorf's Blood and Wounds Theology," *Journal of Moravian History* 1 (2006): 36.

enced everything that a human being can undergo in one's soul, all of our weaknesses, sickness, temptations, and practices. This was all pulled together when he sweated blood on the Mount of Olives, when he cried from the cross: 'My God! My God! Why have you forsaken me!'"[26] Zinzendorf reversed the Hallensian order of contemplating one's sin first, and then finding grace. Rather, grace first finds the individual, who then realizes the depth of his or her sin. In rather traditional Lutheran fashion, the intrusion of grace is described as faith: "We do not begin by becoming pious and holy; if we want to become partakers of the death and cross of Jesus, we become righteous through his merit, as sinners, without adding any work; if we are only able to trust him."[27] Faith, actively born in the heart by the Holy Spirit — the mother of the church[28] — was thus a gift of God, not one produced through human struggle.[29] Nevertheless, Zinzendorf believed that we must respond to God's unimaginable gift, as God would not coerce people into faith.[30]

Furthermore, Zinzendorf also understood the Christian life through a Christocentric lens. The atoning experience of Christ — one which encompassed the whole life of Jesus — configured Jesus as the principal medium in and through which humanity was both corporately and personally redeemed and made holy. In Zinzendorf's "blood and wounds theology," Jesus' life and death were not only the objective ground of Christian salvation, but also the subjective ground for the ongoing religion of the heart. Christians were called to enter, existentially or mystically,[31] into the ex-

---

26. Nikolaus Ludwig von Zinzendorf, *Christian Life and Witness: Count Zinzendorf's 1738 Berlin Speeches*, trans. Gary S. Kinkel (Eugene, Ore.: Pickwick Press, 2010), p. 99.

27. Zinzendorf, *Christian Life and Witness*, pp. 98-99.

28. For a discussion of Zinzendorf's provocative theology of the Holy Spirit, see Gary Steven Kinkel, *Our Dead Mother the Spirit: An Investigation of Count Zinzendorf's Theology and Praxis* (Lanham, Md.: University Press of America, 1990); and Craig D. Atwood, "The Mother of All Souls: Zinzendorf's Doctrine of the Holy Spirit," *Koinonia* 4, no. 2 (1992): 106-36.

29. See Nikolaus Ludwig von Zinzendorf, *Nine Public Lectures on Important Subjects in Religion*, translated and edited by George W. Forell (Eugene, Ore.: Wipf & Stock Publishers, 1998), pp. 69-71.

30. See Zinzendorf, *Nine Public Lectures on Important Subjects in Religion*, p. 64.

31. See Atwood, "The Mother of All Souls: Understanding Zinzendorf's Blood and Wounds Theology," p. 37.

perience of Jesus. "The Scripture says that our entire work of the Gospel is to portray Jesus, to paint Him before the eyes, to take the spirit's stylus and etch — yes, engrave — the image of Jesus in the fleshly tablets of the heart, so that it can never be removed again."[32] Through identification with the blood and wounds of Jesus in particular — a relationship often styled as mystical marriage[33] — the individual entered into the "way of Jesus" or the redemptive path which the Savior trod and which sanctifies and conforms the individual into the image of Christ. This resulted in a palpable, mystical identification between the believer and her Lord, the eternal Husband of the soul:[34]

> And when you have once caught sight of the beauty of his suffering, so that in all your life you will not be able to get rid of that sight, then he conducts you with his eyes wherever he will have you; then with his eyes he teaches you what good and evil is. Your knowledge of good and evil lies in his eyes; not in the tree from which Adam poisoned himself, from which Adam ate his curse, but rather in the eyes of the tortured Lamb, there lies your blessed, happy knowledge of good and evil. As far as this same image looks upon you, into the midst of your mortal bodies, so far shall you be changed, pervaded, captivated by the person of Jesus, so that your other brethren perceive you no longer as a man in your denomination, as a brother of the same persuasion only, but rather as a consort, as a playmate for the marriage bed of the blessed Creator and eternal Husband of the human soul.[35]

32. Zinzendorf, *Nine Public Lectures on Important Subjects in Religion*, p. 81.

33. See Arthur J. Freeman, *An Ecumenical Theology of the Heart: The Theology of Count Nicholas Ludwig von Zinzendorf* (Bethlehem, Pa.: The Moravian Church in America, 1998), pp. 192-96.

34. Regarding Zinzendorf's conception of "feeling," it is important to note two elements: (1) by the term "feeling," Zinzendorf meant something closer to a "perception" which may or may not have an emotional quality; (2) unlike Schleiermacher, Zinzendorf was careful to emphasize that this feeling or perception was to be based on faith, and not faith on the perception or feeling. See Peter Vogt, "Nicholas Ludwig von Zinzendorf (1700-1760)," in *The Pietist Theologians*, ed. Lindberg, pp. 213-17; and Arthur Freeman, "Count Nicholas Ludwig von Zinzendorf: An Ecumenical Pioneer," *Journal of Ecumenical Studies* 36, nos. 3-4 (Summer-Fall 1999): 296.

35. Zinzendorf, *Nine Public Lectures on Important Subjects in Religion*, p. 86.

In this experience, which Moravian devotional practice and worship were meant to facilitate throughout the life of the believer, the suffering of Christ was not only the source of forgiveness, but also the source and pattern for the new life of the reborn Christian. Both conversion and the Christian life were to be marked by joy and peace, though Zinzendorf did not believe that total freedom from sin was possible, a conviction which would also lead to a break between him and John Wesley.[36]

In 1716, Zinzendorf was sent to Wittenberg, the bastion of Orthodoxy, to study law. This experience, though difficult, also fueled his fertile imagination and desire for rapprochement between the Orthodox and Pietist factions within Lutheranism. His encounters with Catholics in France and with Reformed Christians in Holland during his "Grand Tour" (1719-1720) only deepened a growing ecumenical consciousness and conviction that he could work with anyone who had a genuine love of the Savior. In 1721, Zinzendorf took a post as court advisor in Dresden. The following year, he purchased the estate of Berthelsdorf, near his grandmother's estate at Gross Hennersdorf (near the modern-day German-Polish border), and married Erdmuthe Dorothea von Reuss.

That same year, Zinzendorf was made aware of the plight of the ancient Moravian church, whose roots lay in the Czech Hussite reformation of the fifteenth century. Since 1648, the existence of this pre-Reformation community had been under threat because their theological identity was not recognized under the Peace of Westphalia. Under the leadership of Christian David (1691-1751), the community migrated north and settled on Zinzendorf's estate. Because of his ecumenical aspirations, Zinzendorf also welcomed other religious minorities to the village of Herrnhut (meaning "under the Lord's watch"), which was established as a religious community on the estate.[37] Unfortunately, the religious diversity prized by Zinzendorf led to conflict, which became so severe that Zinzendorf left his post in Dresden in 1727 to devote himself wholly to the religious experiment of Herrnhut. Zinzendorf developed a constitution which he delivered to the community in the summer of that year. The community experienced a revival on August 13, 1727, after an especially powerful Eu-

---

36. See Freeman, *An Ecumenical Theology of the Heart*, pp. 188-90.
37. See Shantz, *An Introduction to German Pietism*, pp. 256-57.

charistic celebration, an event which is traditionally interpreted by most Moravians as a kind of second Pentecost.[38] At the time of the revival, there were some two hundred members of the community at Herrnhut; about two-thirds of them were Moravian.

Zinzendorf's conception of the church, and the constitution which he developed for the community at Herrnhut, were both ecumenical in nature. The community structure, and even Zinzendorf's vision for the Renewed Moravian Church, was to be a mixture of radical Philadelphian ideas shorn of their separatism, with the hope for renewal of traditional ecclesiological forms in the vein of Spener.[39] Arthur Freeman has pointed out that there were three different terms that Zinzendorf employed in ecclesiological reflections.[40] The term *Kirche* (literally "church") referred to the invisible, universal, spiritual church of God, which included both those who had gone before and those still alive. *Religion* was the term that he reserved to denote different denominations. Each of these denominations — in terms of both their ecclesiological structures and their unique doctrinal claims — were considered by Zinzendorf to be *Tropi Paidia* or different "ways of teaching" or manifestations of the Christian faith. Each of the different *Tropi* were considered necessary as schools within which people come to the one unifying center of faith, who is Christ. This approach to doctrinal pluralism was itself embodied in the constitution that Zinzendorf developed for the community at Herrnhut, where both the Lutheran Augsburg Confession and the Reformed Articles of the Synod of Berne were affirmed without either being declared as the final arbiter in matters of faith. To this was added "the ministerial orders of the ancient Moravian church,"[41] and together all three constituted the Renewed Moravian Church. In Zinzendorf's reflections on theological traditions

---

38. See John Greenfield, *Power from on High: The Story of the Great Moravian Revival of 1727* (Bethlehem, Pa.: The Moravian Church in America, 1928).

39. See Dietrich Meyer, "Zinzendorf und Herrnhut," in *Geschichte des Pietismus*, vol. 2: *Der Pietismus im achtzehnten Jahrhundert*, ed. Martin Brecht and Klaus Deppermann (Göttingen: Vandenhoeck & Ruprecht, 1995), p. 27.

40. What follows is heavily dependent on his "Gemeine: Count Nicholas von Zinzendorf's Understanding of the Church," *Brethren Life and Thought* 47, nos. 1-2 (Winter-Spring 2002): 5-12.

41. Freeman, "Gemeine," p. 6.

outside of the three brought together in the constitution of the Moravian Church, none were to be considered as the final "true church" on earth. Nevertheless, there was some indication that Zinzendorf often thought of the *Brüdergemeine* (the Moravian Church) as closer to the truth than the others, as it was considered a provisional, visible expression of the *Gemeine* (meaning "common" or "community").

Zinzendorf employed this third term more often than any other. It was meant to designate not only the local congregation, but also all reborn Christians who in and through community lived in an intimate relationship with Christ. Peter Vogt describes it this way:

> The term *Gemeine*, finally, signifies for Zinzendorf the spiritual brotherhood of all true believers across all confessional and denominational lines. This invisible body can become partially visible in a local *Gemeine* when true believers unite in fellowship. Zinzendorf is convinced that all who belong to Christ, even if they come from different churches, yearn for such fellowship.[42]

Though cast within a much broader, ecumenical horizon, this conception of the *Gemeine* was Zinzendorf's peculiar take on Spener's model of the "church within the church" — that is, *ecclesiola in ecclesia* or conventicles — whose primary purpose was renewal of the whole church. In Zinzendorf's view, the Moravian community was just such a *Gemeine*, and therefore he refused to see the community as a new or different church. Rather, Moravianism existed to renew the whole church, and should it succeed, it would pass away, having fulfilled its calling.

Zinzendorf's vision of the Moravian community as servant of the ecumenical church was put to the test in Pennsylvania in the early 1740s. Through the efforts of his colleague and eventual successor, August Gottlieb Spangenberg (1704-1792), Zinzendorf came to Pennsylvania with the hope of realizing a wider, even more inclusive *Gemeine* than the Moravian Church, one which would include all varieties of Protestants, including a variety of separatists. Because of its policy of religious tolerance, Pennsylvania offered ideal conditions for bringing together a variety of groups:

---

42. Vogt, "Nicholas Ludwig von Zinzendorf (1700-1760)," p. 216.

"Lutheran, Reformed, Presbyterians, Episcopalians, Quakers, Menno-nites, Dunkers, Sabbatarians, Inspired, and individual Separatists."[43] All of these met on New Year's Day in 1742 to discuss the proposed "Pennsyl-vania Congregation of God in the Spirit," which was to be an ecumenical *Gemeine* whose center was focused on the living Christ. Although a series of interdenominational synods were held — seven in all — Zinzendorf was unsuccessful in bringing his vision to concrete fruition. This was, at least in part, because his Moravian-influenced ecumenical vision, which dominated the proceedings, proved to be too overbearing for many of the other delegates.[44]

Zinzendorf was not able to realize his dream of a larger ecumenical *Gemeine;* nevertheless, the Moravian community was deeply committed to mission work. Though Zinzendorf was aware of the Danish-Halle mis-sion in Tranquebar, India, through the *Halle Report,*[45] it was a fortuitous visit to Denmark for the coronation of King Christian VI which ignited the Moravian missionary enterprise. There Zinzendorf and several of his companions met Anton Ulrich, a slave from the Caribbean island of St. Thomas who had been brought to Copenhagen, educated, and eventu-ally converted.[46] His description of the deplorable conditions in which slaves lived in the Danish West Indies moved Zinzendorf and his com-panions to launch a mission to the West Indies in 1732. This eventuated in the establishment of the first Afro-Caribbean church in the Americas, which was shepherded by men and women, most notably the free black woman Rebecca Protten (d. 1780), a significant early figure in the Mora-vian Church.[47]

43. John Joseph Stoudt, "Count Zinzendorf and the Pennsylvania Congregation of God in the Spirit," *Church History* 9, no. 4 (December 1940): 371.

44. See Harry Yeide Jr., *Studies in Classical Pietism: The Flowering of the Ecclesiola* (New York: Peter Lang, 1997), pp. 77-83.

45. See Daniel Jeyaraj, "Mission Reports from South India and Their Impact on the Western Mind: The Tranquebar Mission of the Eighteenth Century," in *Converting Co-lonialism: Visions and Realities in Mission History, 1706-1914,* ed. Dana L. Robert (Grand Rapids: Wm. B. Eerdmans, 2008), p. 33.

46. See Jon Sensbach, *Rebecca's Revival: Creating Black Christianity in the Atlantic World* (Cambridge, Mass.: Harvard University Press), p. 49.

47. For a discussion of Protten and the Moravian mission in St. Thomas, see Sens-bach, *Rebecca's Revival.*

The venture to the West Indies was soon followed by missions to Greenland (1733), Surinam (1735), South Africa (1737), Pennsylvania (1740), Labrador (1752), and Jamaica (1754).[48] The commitment to mission among Moravians during this period is evidenced in a 1736 government report which noted that there were only 47 people living in Herrnhut, while an additional 600 were out on the mission field.[49] Though the Moravian endeavor shared some commonalities with the Halle mission, there were some important distinctions. Halle missionaries were highly educated and stressed education in their mission practice. They tended to view conversion as a long-term process of education that was consummated in baptism. Herrnhuters tended to be skilled craftsmen or artisans. They eschewed focus on intensive religious education or "civilizing" in almost any form,[50] though with mixed results in regard to treating indigenous peoples and slaves justly.[51] One other important difference was the Moravian commitment to Zinzendorf's ecumenical vision. In distinction from the Halle missionaries, who were representatives of the Lutheran church, Moravian mission practice was not necessarily aimed at creating new converts to Moravianism. Rather, the aim was to bring people into relationship with Christ, even if that didn't mean baptizing people into the Moravian Church.[52]

The later 1740s was one of the most controversial and creative periods in the life of Zinzendorf and the Herrnhut community. Often called the "sifting time" (1743-1750), it was marked by an extreme emphasis on the "blood and wounds" devotion to Jesus, Zinzendorf's erotic poetry and hymnody, an excessive emotionalism, and serious financial problems

48. Vogt, "Nicholas Ludwig von Zinzendorf (1700-1760)," p. 219.

49. See Yeide Jr., *Studies in Classical Pietism*, p. 75.

50. See Richard V. Pierard, "German Pietism as a Major Factor in the Beginnings of Modern Protestant Missions," in *The Pietist Impulse in Christianity*, ed. Christian T. Collins Winn et al. (Eugene, Ore.: Pickwick Press, 2011), pp. 293-94.

51. See Jon Sensbach, "Pietism, Slavery, and the Emergence of Afro-Protestantism in the Atlantic World," *The Covenant Quarterly* 62, no. 4 (November 2004): 3-12; and Karl-Wilhelm Westmeier, "Zinzendorf at Esopus: The Apocalyptical Missiology of Count Nicholas Ludwig von Zinzendorf — A Debut to America," *Missiology: An International Review* 22, no. 4 (October 1994): 419-36.

52. See Yeide Jr., *Studies in Classical Pietism*, pp. 75-77. This was an especially important emphasis for Moravian missionaries in largely Christian lands.

leading to almost total collapse.[53] As F. Ernest Stoeffler notes, the period "threatened to cut Moravians off from most other Christians."[54] And resistance came not only from Orthodox and Enlightenment figures, but also from other Pietists, especially those identified with Halle. By 1750, Zinzendorf had sought to curb the more excessive elements, and after his death in 1760, almost every practice, writing, or liturgical development from this period came under serious scrutiny by successors at Herrnhut, who suppressed the more radical aspects of Zinzendorf's theology, hymnody, and poetry.[55] Only recently, since the Second World War, has Zinzendorf been re-embraced in the wider circles of Moravianism, and his contribution to Christian theology and devotion has begun to garner the attention it deserves in even wider circles.[56] Although Zinzendorf was by far the most controversial of all the figures we have discussed, he was the only one able to translate his Pietist vision of the church into a sustainable model which endures in the contemporary Moravian Church.

Württemberg Pietism

Although this branch of Pietism deserves a lengthy discussion of its own, we will conclude with some brief comments on the leading figures of the Pietism that emerged in southwestern Germany. Although significantly influenced by the Pietism of Spener, Halle, and Zinzendorf, Württemberg Pietism is marked by its own kind of originality. Owing to devastation from the Thirty Years' War as well as a series of repressive rulers — one of whom was a Catholic ruling a largely Protestant region — the Lutheran Church in Württemberg in the seventeenth and eighteenth centuries was susceptible to an apocalyptic mood, was reform-minded, and was more

53. See Peter Vogt, "'Honor to the Side': The Adoration of the Side Wound of Jesus in Eighteenth-Century Moravian Piety," *Journal of Moravian History* 7 (2009): 83-106; and W. R. Ward, *Christianity under the Ancien Régime, 1648-1789* (Cambridge, U.K.: Cambridge University Press, 1999), p. 122.

54. Stoeffler, *German Pietism during the Eighteenth Century*, p. 151.

55. See Meyer, "Zinzendorf und Herrnhut," pp. 57-64.

56. See, for example, *Neue Aspekt der Zinzendorf-Forshung*, ed. Martin Brecht and Paul Peucker (Göttingen: Vandenhoeck & Ruprecht, 2006).

friendly to the impulses of Pietism.[57] Most scholars agree that because of these dynamics, Lutheranism in Württemberg became almost synonymous with Pietism.[58] Therefore, Pietism in Württemberg was also a grassroots movement, boasting a number of significant lay theologians. At the same time, key luminaries like Johann Albrecht Bengel and Friedrich Christoph Oetinger also placed an enduring stamp on Swabian[59] Pietism.

Johann Albrecht Bengel

Perhaps the greatest of the "Württemberg fathers," Johann Albrecht Bengel (1687-1752) studied theology in Tübingen, after having been afforded an outstanding education in Stuttgart,[60] where he was exposed to the impulses of Pietism and reform-minded Orthodoxy. It was probably through the influence of Johann Wolfgang Jäger (1647-1720) — an Orthodox theologian — that Bengel developed his ecclesial orientation, moving away from more radical forms of Pietism.[61] While in Tübingen, his deep and abiding interest in New Testament textual studies was born. As a number of scholars have noted, Bengel was alarmed by the numerous textual variants he encountered in the Greek New Testament. In 1713 he became preceptor at the gymnasium (i.e., secondary school) in Denkendorf, where he taught Latin, Greek, and Hebrew, as well as a range of other subjects. This was the context in which Bengel pursued his interest in the manuscript history of the Greek New Testament, or what has come to be called textual criticism.

In 1734 he published his *Novum Testamentum Graecum*, which offered a careful reconstruction of the original Greek text, including a critical apparatus that offered a classification system for distinguishing between variant readings in the New Testament.[62] His more expansive (and ultimately

---

57. See Stoeffler, *German Pietism during the Eighteenth Century*, pp. 88-91.

58. See Martin Brecht, "Der württembergische Pietismus," in *Geschichte des Pietismus*, vol. 2: *Der Pietismus im achtzehnten Jahrhundert*, ed. Brecht and Deppermann, p. 225.

59. "Swabia" is the more ancient name for the Württemberg region.

60. See Shantz, *An Introduction to German Pietism*, p. 230.

61. See Brecht, "Der württembergische Pietismus," p. 251.

62. See Lyle O. Bristol, "New Testament Textual Criticism in the Eighteenth Century," *Journal of Biblical Literature* 69, no. 2 (June 1950): 108-9.

more influential) *Gnomon Novi Testamenti* of 1742 included a commentary, a Latin translation of the New Testament, and a more refined version of his earlier critical apparatus.[63] The commentary included "concise explanations, or pointers, on matters of philology, exegesis, literary structure, figures of speech, and practical edification to assist pastors with their sermon preparation."[64] Bengel also spelled out more clearly the underlying principles that guided his variant classification system. Included among these is an axiom that stands to this day among textual critics: "The more difficult reading is to be preferred over the easier one."[65]

Bengel's interest in the Bible, however, lay not only in textual criticism but also in interpretation — above all, the interpretation of the Apocalypse of John. Bengel's interpretation of the Apocalypse was decidedly chiliastic, and he went so far as to predict that the last chapter in history would begin on June 18, 1836. Within this last chapter, a number of dramatic events would occur: the conversion of the Jewish people; the fall of the Antichrist (which Bengel identified with the Roman Catholic Church); the thousand-year reign of the saints with Christ on earth (cf. Rev. 20); and the final judgment. Tucked within this chronology, Bengel placed Spener's "hope for better times for the church," and gave to the Pietism of the region a strong biblical basis for the eschatological orientation that predated Bengel.[66] Of course, his prediction about June 18, 1836, was wrong, which resulted in a general disillusionment for many of his followers when the date came and went.[67] Scholars are divided over whether his particular form of eschatology produced an activist or quietist spirituality, though most agree that his insistence on discerning the "signs of the times" was a significant contribution to later forms of Württemberg Pietism and eventually to the larger Christian tradition.[68]

63. Bengel's *Gnomon* was the basis for Wesley's 1754 *Explanatory Notes on the New Testament*. See Shantz, *An Introduction to German Pietism*, p. 235.

64. Shantz, *An Introduction to German Pietism*, p. 234.

65. See Stoeffler, *German Pietism during the Eighteenth Century*, p. 100.

66. See Martin Brecht, "Chiliasmus in Württemberg im 17. Jahrhundert," *Pietismus und Neuzeit* 14 (1988): 25-49.

67. See Brecht, "Der württembergische Pietismus," p. 256.

68. For an activist interpretation, see C. John Weborg, "The Eschatological Ethics of Johann Albrecht Bengel," *The Covenant Quarterly* 36 (May 1978): 31-43. For a quietist interpretation, see Frank Macchia, *Spirituality and Social Liberation: The Message of*

Friedrich Christoph Oetinger

Although Bengel's predictions proved wrong, his interest in apocalyptic chronology and his development of a "salvation history" *(Heilsgeschichte)* form of biblical theology were very important for the development of the Württemberg tradition. So also were Bengel's students, the most important of whom was Friedrich Christoph Oetinger (1702-1782). Because of a remarkable capacity for creativity and free thinking, and because of his deep interest in theosophy and alchemy, Oetinger should be considered a student of Bengel in a qualified sense. He was undoubtedly influenced by Bengel's Biblicism and by his interest in apocalyptic eschatology. And in the vein of Bengel's chronological endeavors, Oetinger was also convinced that through access to God's revelation, one could gain knowledge of the workings of the cosmos. However, unlike Bengel, Oetinger allowed for a second source of revelation alongside Scripture: the book of nature. He also showed himself much more open to the influence of Böhme and other theosophists and visionaries.

In 1722, Oetinger came to study in Tübingen and eventually met Bengel, who was serving as preceptor at Denkendorf, located about thirty miles northeast of Tübingen.[69] Before arriving in Tübingen, Oetinger had developed an interest in the philosophy of Gottfried Wilhelm Leibniz and Christian Wolff. Over time he found himself unable to reconcile the philosophical worldview of Leibniz with the Bible, to the detriment of the latter. This crisis was finally resolved when Oetinger was introduced to the writings of Böhme by a local miller in Tübingen. What Oetinger found in Böhme was the insistence that God was living and active, *actus purissimus* ("pure act"),[70] a conception that Oetinger felt helped to explain how the physical and the spiritual dimensions of the universe fit together.

---

the Blumhardts in the Light of Wuerttemberg Pietism (Metuchen, N.J.: Scarecrow Press, 1993), pp. 9-11.

69. See Martin Weyer-Menkhoff, "Friedrich Christoph Oetinger (1702-1782)," in *The Pietist Theologians*, ed. Lindberg, p. 241.

70. See Friedrich Christoph Oetinger, "Genealogy of the Thoughts of the Well-Grounded Theologian," in *European Pietism Reviewed*, edited and translated by Frederick Herzog (San Jose, Calif.: Pickwick Publications, 2003), p. 125.

Oetinger's attraction to the alchemical and theosophical traditions is emblematic of the general sense of crisis that the Enlightenment had produced for many. Through Böhme, Paracelsus, Cabbala, and other sources, Oetinger sought to fashion a physico-spiritual theosophy which would explain both the physical and the spiritual workings of the world, and heal the rupture which Enlightenment rationalism had created.[71] This attempt to heal the rift between spirit and matter made itself felt in many of Oetinger's writings, where he showed a lifelong concern with astronomy, mathematics, medicine, geology, botany, zoology, and the burgeoning scientific interest in magnetism and electricity,[72] alongside and integrated with a deep concern for biblical commentary, the Christian life, and, above all, Christology. Oetinger was clearly concerned to describe a holistic and comprehensive theological vision of reality in which materiality and the body played an integral part, and where the Incarnation occupied the central position. His Christocentrism is captured well in his famous phrase "all of God's ways end in the flesh," which was meant to denote that corporeality or embodiment was not a side issue for God, but was rather the ultimate purpose and goal, a truth revealed in Jesus Christ.[73] This notion, and the metaphysic that Oetinger developed to explain it, would have a profound impact on later German idealism, especially the philosophy of Hegel.

Oetinger's interests in the theosophical and alchemical traditions, originating with Böhme and Paracelsus, should also be seen as occurring within the framework of his eschatology. As Friedhelm Groth has pointed out, Oetinger sought to "out-Bengel Bengel."[74] Oetinger was convinced — in line with Bengel's apocalyptic predictions — that he was living on the eve of the millennium and that, as a consequence, more and more

71. See Robert T. Llewellyn, "Friedrich Christoph Oetinger and the Paracelsan Tradition: A Disciple of Boehme in the Age of Romanticism," in *From Wolfram and Petrarch to Goethe and Grass: Studies in Literature in Honor of Leonard Foster*, ed. D. H. Greene, Leslie P. Johnson, and Dieter Wuttke (Baden-Baden: Verlag Valentin Koerner, 1982), pp. 539-48.

72. See Ernst Benz, *The Theology of Electricity*, ed. Dennis Stillings (Allison Park, Pa.: Pickwick Publications, 1989), pp. 27-104.

73. See Weyer-Menkhoff, "Friedrich Christoph Oetinger (1702-1782)," p. 251.

74. See Friedhelm Groth, "Chiliasmus und Apokatastasishoffnung in der Reich-Gottes-Verkündigung der beiden Blumhardts," *Pietismus und Neuzeit* 9 (1983): 60.

revelations would be forthcoming, giving indications to the faithful of what the "Golden Times" would really be like. The visionary and theosophical traditions were valid as potential sources of revelation because they offered a glimpse into the inner workings of history and the cosmos on the eve of its final liberation and restoration. Following in the wake of Bengel, Oetinger was also a proponent of the *apocatastasis ton panton*, or the "restoration of all things," in which God, the One in whom all things cohere and live, would eventually empty hell and reconcile all things to himself.[75] The combination of a holistic worldview and an emphasis on eschatology led to a reconceptualization of "piety" and "new birth." More clearly connected to the life-giving powers of the resurrection of Jesus,[76] Oetinger's conception of piety moved away from moralism toward a vital participation in the life of God. The reborn Christian, through the transformation of "new birth," begins to participate, in a limited way, in the final transformation of all things, with love of neighbor as a key component of Oetinger's ethical vision.[77]

The Württemberg tradition stands as a unique expression of Pietism. Pietism in Swabia was able to make extensive inroads into the local church in the region, becoming almost synonymous with Lutheranism. This gave it a very grassroots and communal orientation, which, through the work of figures like Bengel, Oetinger, and others, also bore the marks of a deep commitment to the Scriptures and an abiding interest in all things eschatological. Along with Zinzendorf — who had a controversial relationship with Bengel and Oetinger[78] — and the Moravian movement, the Württemberg tradition continues to exert an enormous amount of influence on subsequent generations, especially through German idealism and later developments in German theology in the nineteenth and twentieth centuries.

---

75. Groth, "Chiliasmus und Apokatastasishoffnung in der Reich-Gottes-Verkündigung der beiden Blumhardts," pp. 60-61.

76. As Pierre Deghaye puts it, "The resurrection of Jesus is the key to our rebirth" ("Das Wort als Himmel und Hölle," in *Glauben und Erkennen: Die Heilige Philosophie von Friedrich Christoph Oetinger: Studien zu seinem 300. Geburstag*, ed. Guntram Spindler [Metzingen: Ernst Franz Verlag, 2002], p. 159).

77. See Stoeffler, *German Pietism in the Eighteenth Century*, pp. 116-17.

78. See Ward, *Early Evangelicalism*, pp. 117-18.

Conclusion

From its inception, Pietism was an internally diverse phenomenon that included both ecclesial and separatist wings. These last two chapters have showcased that variety not only by focusing on Spener and Francke, but also by offering sketches of radical Pietism, the remarkable figure of Nikolaus Ludwig von Zinzendorf and the Moravian movement, as well as the unique form of Pietism that developed in the region of Württemberg. Even with this diversity, however, we would argue that there were certain shared emphases or concerns which formed a core of Pietist identity. This core emphasized a concern for a more vital Christian faith, which included a deeper expression of love of God and service to neighbor. We will elucidate these emphases in our next chapter.

CHAPTER FIVE

A Portrait of Pietism

Its Authentic Hallmarks

One of the first caveats a student of Pietism encounters — and so it will be repeated here — is that defining Pietism is at best a challenging and at worst an impossible task. The purpose of this chapter is not to define Pietism but to describe it by identifying and expounding its main common features. That's also challenging. Any such attempt will inevitably involve judgment calls based on who are perceived to be the leading prototypes of the movement and what are considered the main themes of the movement and its ethos overall. As has been shown, nearly all scholars of Pietism distinguish between its two broad wings or branches — "churchly" (or "mainstream") and "radical" Pietism. So there's diversity within it. But how much diversity? Scholars are not united about which advocates of "heart Christianity" should be included in an account of Pietism. Should Zinzendorf be treated as a Pietist? A growing consensus now says yes. But not all scholars agree. *If* Zinzendorf is included among the crucial prototypes of Pietism, the founding movers and shakers of the movement and representatives of its ethos, then *feeling* will be given greater emphasis in describing the Pietist ethos than otherwise. That's just one example of the problem faced in any attempt to describe Pietism. There is no uniform scholarly consensus on who counts as a Pietist or on a definitive list of characteristics or hallmarks of Pietism as an ethos.

In previous chapters we have focused on describing Pietism by delineating its history and especially its leaders and representative figures. In this chapter our description will proceed by focusing on the early movement's hallmarks, common features, characteristics, and family resemblances. In this, we follow Donald Durnbaugh's suggestion that "Pietism can best be understood by looking at its characteristics."[1] Here, as in most cases, the common characteristics will be drawn from the early personal prototypes of the Pietist movement, with an occasional glance at later developments. Those include, by all accounts, Spener and Francke[2], and we will also include Zinzendorf. Others we will consider include Gottfried Arnold, Gerhard Tersteegen, Johann Albrecht Bengel, Friedrich Christoph Oetinger, the Blumhardts, and occasionally even Johann Arndt (as Pietist precursor). What did these and all others normally included in the story of Pietism share in common that was *not* common in other Protestants? Here we will consider ten hallmarks — as themes distinctive of (but not necessarily unique to) Pietism among Protestant Christians.

Scholars' Lists of Pietist Hallmarks

Most lists of Pietism's chief, distinctive characteristics are shorter than what we offer here. Durnbaugh classifies Pietism as "experiential, emotional, individual, biblically-centered, and ethically minded."[3] For Ted Campbell, "Pietism stressed personal religious experience, especially repentance . . . and sanctification."[4] W. R. Ward sees "the crux" of Pietism

1. Durnbaugh, quoted in Stephen J. Stein, "Some Thoughts on Pietism in American Religious History," in *Pietism in Germany and North America, 1680-1820*, ed. Jonathan Strom, Hartmut Lehmann, and James Van Horn Melton (Burlington, Vt.: Ashgate, 2009), p. 27.

2. Pietist scholar Peter James Yoder is surely right that any account of historical, classical Pietism must treat Spener and Francke as the movement's main, defining prototypes. Spener, he cogently argues, was the "very soul of the movement" at its beginning (with Arndt as a major influence on him). Francke became the movement's "principal representative" after Spener. According to Yoder, depending on philosopher George Lakoff, "prototypes merely speak of a cognitive centrality and allow for fluid, fuzzy boundaries." See "'Rendered Odious' as Pietists: Anton Wilhelm Böhme's Conception of Pietism and the Possibilities of Prototype Theory," in *The Pietist Impulse in Christianity*, ed. Christian T. Collins Winn et al. (Eugene, Ore.: Pickwick Press, 2011), pp. 17-26.

3. Durnbaugh, quoted in Stein, "Some Thoughts on Pietism in American Religious History," p. 27.

4. Ted A. Campbell, *The Religion of the Heart: A Study of European Religious Life in*

as "the inner spring of spiritual vitality, the New Birth, a doctrine which became the Pietist party badge. . . . The essence of the matter was how best to realize the priesthood of all believers."[5] Dale Brown emphasizes that Pietism was and is primarily a type of Christianity that considers "religion an affair of the heart."[6] For him, as for many other scholars, "the heart of Pietist theology is its focus on regeneration" — the new birth, being "born again."[7] He also lists concern for the reformation of the church through focus on practical Christianity, emphasis on the Bible for devotional reading and a guide to lifestyles, reformation of life, "orthopraxis" over "orthodoxy," and hope for the world as Pietism's main features.[8] Mary Fulbrook lists the distinctive hallmarks of Pietism's ethos as fundamental Biblicism, preaching to arouse experience of conversion, emphasis on regeneration and conversion, Christian life as struggle, and millenarianism and eschatological hope.[9]

These lists should suffice to demonstrate that scholarly accounts of Pietism's shared ethos, its distinctive motifs, both vary and overlap considerably. The closer scholars stick to Spener and Francke as defining founders and prototypes of Pietism, the more similar are their accounts of the ethos. The further they go afield into Pietism's frontiers, toward and even across its boundaries, attempting to include, for example, radical Pietists, the more their accounts vary. We agree with Pietist scholars F. Ernest Stoeffler and Jonathan Strom that Pietism is a category with a strong center, and therefore a relatively stable identity, but with permeable boundaries.[10]

---

the Seventeenth and Eighteenth Centuries (Columbia, S.C.: University of South Carolina Press, 1991), p. 71.

5. W. R. Ward, *The Protestant Evangelical Awakening* (Cambridge, U.K.: Cambridge University Press, 1992), p. 57.

6. Dale Brown, *Understanding Pietism* (Grand Rapids: Wm. B. Eerdmans, 1978), p. 109.

7. Brown, *Understanding Pietism*, p. 28.

8. Brown, *Understanding Pietism*, pp. 27-28.

9. Mary Fulbrook, *Piety and Politics: Religion and the Rise of Absolutism in England, Württemberg, and Prussia* (Cambridge, U.K.: Cambridge University Press, 1983), pp. 32-35.

10. F. Ernest Stoeffler, *The Rise of Evangelical Pietism* (Leiden: E. J. Brill, 1971), p. 12; and Jonathan Strom, *Pietism and Community in Europe and North America, 1650-1850* (Leiden: E. J. Brill, 2010), pp. 1-2.

That is, its boundaries cannot be easily or absolutely identified, which permits somewhat diverse interpretations of its character. We agree especially with Stoeffler that Pietism should be judged by its *center* and not by its *circumference*.[11] For example, *some* radical Pietists abandoned church altogether and became anti-church "seekers" of a mystical spirituality. Some of those and other radical Pietists dabbled in alchemy, esoteric mysticism, and theosophical speculations.[12] We do not deny these Pietists space in a scholarly account of the movement, but we consider them marginal to the movement and their distinctive, radical contributions less than helpful for describing the general Pietist ethos.

Here we will describe ten key hallmarks, characteristics, common, unifying affinities of Pietism. We make no claim that these are *unique* to Pietism *except* in terms of the *emphasis* they receive among Pietists. For Pietists they are all crucial to a healthy, holistic, authentic Christianity. And, from Spener on, Pietists have believed that these characteristics are always in danger of being lost and forgotten — especially by so-called mainline religion. They were all developed at least in part in response to the perceived "crisis of piety" in late-seventeenth and early-eighteenth-century European state church (Lutheran and Reformed) religion, which was, by most accounts, formalistic and lifeless. Church historian Justo González rightly describes that religion as "increasingly stale and objectified, as if the significance of theology were to be found primarily in a series of truths that could be formally stated in propositions to be transmitted from one generation to another."[13] Pietism arose against this "dead orthodoxy" of state Protestantism. These ten common motifs, then, were all somewhat reactionary. But Pietists of all generations have considered them worthy of renewed emphasis because Christianity is always in danger of falling back into dead orthodoxy and always stands in need of renewal.

The ten key hallmarks of Pietism treated here are these: (1) embrace

---

11. Stoeffler, *The Rise of Evangelical Pietism*, p. 12.

12. See, for example, Hans Schneider, *German Radical Pietism*, trans. Gerald T. MacDonald (Lanham, Md.: Scarecrow Press, 2007); and Douglas H. Shantz, "The Origin of Pietist Notions of New Birth and the New Man: Alchemy and Alchemists," in *The Pietist Impulse in Christianity*, ed. Collins Winn et al., pp. 29-41.

13. Justo González, *A History of Christian Thought*, vol. III, rev. ed. (Nashville: Abingdon Press, 1987), p. 300.

and acceptance of orthodox Protestant Christian doctrine, broadly defined; (2) experiential, transformative Christianity; (3) conversion, the regeneration of the "inner person"; (4) conversional piety — a strong devotional life and a personal relationship with God through Jesus Christ crucified and risen; (5) visible Christianity — holy living and transformed character; (6) love of the Bible understood as a medium of an immediate relationship with God; (7) Christian life lived in community; (8) world transformation toward the kingdom of God; (9) ecumenical, irenic Christianity; and (10) the common priesthood of true believers. Together these ten hallmarks provide a profile, as it were, of Pietism in terms of its common, distinctive beliefs. Of course, not all ten will appear in every Pietist individual, church, or expression, but together they constitute a kind of portrait or list of family resemblances of Pietism.

Pietism and Orthodox Doctrine

First, let it be understood that, contrary to many myths and misconceptions, historic, authentic Pietism embraced and accepted *orthodox Protestant Christian doctrine, broadly defined.* In other words, in its reaction to dead orthodoxy and Protestant Scholasticism, it did not throw the baby of correct doctrine out with the bathwater of lifeless formalism. Of course, it's possible to find individual Pietists who abandoned orthodox Christianity, but they are the exceptions. If Pietism is defined by its center and its roots and not by its margins and offshoots, then Pietism is a form of orthodox Protestantism. True, Pietism reacted *against* "Protestant Orthodoxy" — a term typically used for highly systematic, dogmatic theology that tended to define true Christianity in cognitive terms — as belief in rigid doctrinal systems (usually *either* Lutheran *or* Reformed). Orthodox Protestantism is simply belief in the great doctrines of ancient and Reformation Christian faith: the incarnation of God in Jesus Christ (Christ's true deity and humanity), the Trinity, salvation by grace alone, justification by grace through faith alone without works, the Bible as God's inspired and authoritative Word, and so on. The main Pietist leaders never abandoned these core doctrines. Critics of Pietism are fond of pointing out that Friedrich Schleiermacher, the father of modern, liberal theology, did deviate significantly from orthodox Protestant doctrines, but they must remember that he was also Reformed. Should Reformed theology be blamed for his deviations from orthodox Christianity? Conservative Reformed theologians would be quick to say no. Neither should Pietism be blamed for his departures from orthodoxy.

Stoeffler expresses the general scholarly consensus about Pietism and Reformation doctrine: "The frequent charge of extremism or fanaticism against the early Pietists . . . needs to be considered. The fact is that they abhorred any departure from Reformation doctrine quite as much as their opponents."[14] Stoeffler puts his finger on the key difference between Pietism and Protestant Orthodoxy: "While to them [the Orthodox theologians] the essence of Christianity consisted primarily in assent to a series of theological propositions, to him [the Pietist theologian] it consisted in a personal relationship to God expressed in a life lived according to his revealed will."[15] The doctrinal differences between the early Pietists and their faithful heirs, on the one hand, and the theologians of Protestant Orthodoxy, on the other, was one of emphasis — except in the details. For example, most of the Pietists did not believe in the "dictation theory" of biblical inspiration; at least some theologians of Protestant Orthodoxy did. However, all Pietists believed in the Holy Spirit's unique inspiration of Scripture's authors and in the Bible's supreme authority in matters of doctrine. Theodore Tappert concludes that "Pietism . . . did not materially alter the doctrinal content inherited from the Scholastics or Orthodoxists of the seventeenth century."[16]

Few opponents of early, original Pietism have accused Spener or Francke or any other Pietist prototypes of denying the deity of Christ, Christ's miracles and resurrection, or the Trinity. Most of the debate has centered on whether they, and their faithful heirs, believed in the great Reformation doctrines of salvation — especially justification by grace through faith alone. Again, the problem is one of *emphasis*, not substitution. The early Pietists and their faithful progeny affirmed the doctrine of justification, but they

14. Stoeffler, *The Rise of Evangelical Pietism*, p. 12.

15. Stoeffler, *The Rise of Evangelical Pietism*, pp. 242-43.

16. Theodore G. Tappert, "The Influence of Pietism in Colonial American Lutheranism," in *Continental Pietism and Early American Christianity*, ed. F. Ernest Stoeffler (Grand Rapids: Wm. B. Eerdmans, 1976), p. 22.

also emphasized doctrines of salvation they felt were lost during the time when, so they believed, *sola fides* (faith alone) was being emphasized one-sidedly to the exclusion of regeneration and sanctification. That is, they believed that Protestant Orthodoxy and the practice of the state churches emphasized salvation as an external change, a change of legal status before God, a *forensic* (declaratory) change to the exclusion of *inward transformation* and the need for *personal decision* to repent and trust in God through Jesus Christ. In *Pia Desideria*, Spener wrote, "Although our Evangelical Lutheran Church is a true church and is pure in its teachings, it is in such condition, unfortunately, that we behold its outward form with sorrowful eyes."[17] By its "outward form" he meant, among other things, its teaching about salvation, which *tended* toward a purely "objective faith" to the neglect of "subjective faith."[18] By "objective faith" he meant cognitive assent to doctrines; by "subjective faith" he meant inward trust in God that transforms the whole person (the subject of the next two hallmarks).

K. James Stein rightly affirms that the early Pietists displayed "stout adherence to Lutheran confessionalism."[19] That is, they embraced the great doctrines of the Protestant Reformation such as "imputed righteousness" in justification.[20] They even embraced Luther's idea of *simul justus et peccator* — that the Christian is always both righteous (through imputation) and sinful at the same time.[21] However, they did not want to leave salvation there — as simply forgiveness of sins and imputation of Christ's righteousness forever in tension with ongoing sinfulness; they wanted to *add* to the orthodox Reformation doctrine of salvation *inward transformation* of the whole person — without any idea of perfection. To some critics, this addition somehow detracted from salvation by grace alone through faith alone, but there's no reason why it should. And it didn't in the cases of the leading Pietist theologians.[22]

---

17. Philip Jacob Spener, *Pia Desideria*, trans. Theodore G. Tappert (Philadelphia: Fortress Press, 1964), p. 67.

18. Theodore G. Tappert, "Introduction," in *Pia Desideria*, p. 26.

19. K. James Stein, *Philipp Jakob Spener: Pietist Patriarch* (Chicago: Covenant Press, 1986), p. 151.

20. Stein, *Philipp Jakob Spener*, pp. 191-92.

21. Stein, *Philipp Jakob Spener*, p. 194.

22. By "addition" we do not mean that Pietism's emphasis on inward, transforming

But what about later Pietists? Did they all hold firmly to orthodox Protestant doctrine? It's always risky to universalize about any religious movement. The word "all" is problematic. Isolated, extreme cases often pop up to falsify sweeping claims. Nevertheless, nearly all scholars of Pietism agree that, with notable exceptions such as Schleiermacher (whom we will discuss in a later chapter), the vast majority of Pietist prototypes have affirmed basic orthodoxy, including justification by grace through faith alone. Speaking about American Pietists, Paul Kuenning notes that they upheld "forensic" (declaratory) justification (imputed righteousness) while at the same time emphasizing sanctification:

> The genius of classical Pietism lay not in any rejection of justification by grace alone but in the revitalization and expansion of Martin Luther's original insights into the meaning of sanctification.[23]

Kuenning further notes,

> Pietism was never content to allow the justification of the believer through faith in Christ to exist in isolation. To be justified meant to receive the goodness of God and simultaneously to be consumed with the compulsion to do good for others. It meant to be filled with the desire to witness and to serve.[24]

Pietism's Living Christianity

Pietism's second hallmark or characteristic feature is *experiential, transformative Christianity*. This is where Pietism went beyond Protestant Orthodoxy's emphasis on sacramental spirituality, doctrinal correctness,

---

experience of God's grace in conversion and regeneration — new birth — and in sanctification was a "mere addition" that did not alter the whole doctrine of salvation. It did. Our point is simply that it did not and does not imply *denial* of the classical Reformation doctrine of justification by grace through faith alone.

23. Paul P. Kuenning, *The Rise and Fall of American Lutheran Pietism* (Macon, Ga.: Mercer University Press, 1988), p. 20.

24. Kuenning, *The Rise and Fall of American Lutheran Pietism*, p. 71.

and extrinsic salvation. All Pietists highlighted salvation as experience of inward transformation by the Holy Spirit through faith as personal appropriation of God's grace. Eighteenth-century Pietist Philip Otterbein (1726-1813) expressed this distinctive Pietist view vividly: "Christ and his death do us no good unless Christ enters within us, destroying the kingdom of Satan within us, penetrating and renewing our spirit, soul, and body with His light and life."[25] Because Pietists stressed inward experience as a necessary part of salvation, some critics accused them of abandoning salvation by grace alone and relying on experience as a meritorious work of righteousness. Like other original Pietists, Otterbein went out of his way to say that every aspect of salvation, including inward transformation, is by grace alone: "It is . . . certain that we can deserve eternal blessedness neither fully nor in part. It is certain that everything is by free grace and that we become blessed by grace."[26]

For all Pietists, this inward, transforming experience of God in the soul or heart was necessary for authentic Christian life and constituted a "direct encounter with the divine" that was not dependent on the mediation of the traditional "appointed means of grace"[27] except Scripture or the preached Word of God. Pietists did not reject sacraments, but the inward, subjective, transforming experience of God was believed to depend only on the Holy Spirit through the gospel: "Though Pietism does insist upon direct communion with God through the Holy Spirit, such is not a communion to be brought about without the means of the Word."[28] Thus, although Pietism's experience of God was not thought of as absolutely unmediated, because it depended on the Word, it was thought of as immediate — as God working directly in the heart. Spener speaks of this interior, immediate experience of God in *Pia Desideria:*

> You hear the Word of God. This is good. But it is not enough that your ear hears it. Do you let it penetrate inwardly into your heart and allow

---

25. Otterbein, quoted in J. Steven O'Malley, *Early German-American Evangelicalism* (Lanham, Md.: Scarecrow Press, 1995), p. 29.

26. O'Malley, *Early German-American Evangelicalism*, p. 75.

27. Campbell, *The Religion of the Heart*, p. 90.

28. Brown, *Understanding Pietism*, p. 71.

the heavenly food to be digested there, so that you get the benefit of its vitality and power, or does it go in one ear and out the other?[29]

For all Pietists, this was the difference between merely nominal Christianity, the religion of mere "professors of the faith," and true Christianity. The former trusted in belief and ritual for salvation; the latter knew God experientially and transformatively in a personal and immediate way. "Both from without and from within his very being," the Pietist "felt keenly the need for the appropriation of divine grace on a personal and experiential level."[30] Francke likened this experience of God being available to every Christian to a foretaste of the life to come in heaven.[31] For him it constituted a spiritual transfiguration of Christ inwardly and could be "better" than the disciples' own experience of Christ during his life on earth. Especially for Francke, Zinzendorf, and later Pietists (more than for Spener), this inward experience of God would always result in *feelings* together with a "complete existential re-orientation" of life.[32]

Zinzendorf probably dwelled on the feelings accompanying inward experience of God more than any other early Pietist. He called the experience an "immediate contact with God"[33] and argued, "The only valid road to personally meaningful religious reality is . . . 'feeling.' The meaning of religious affirmations is to be found basically in the way in which they meet the religious needs of the believer."[34] He did *not*, however, make religious feelings the objective basis for religious authority or the final criterion of religious truth.[35] For him, as for all true Pietists, that would be the Word of God, the gospel attested in Scripture. Stoeffler sums up Zinzendorf's approach to these matters, and by extension that of all Pietists, this way: "For Zinzendorf . . . meaningful religious faith was trust in God as

---

29. Spener, *Pia Desideria*, p. 66.

30. Stein, *Philipp Jakob Spener*, pp. 156-57.

31. August Hermann Francke, "The Foretaste of Eternal Life," in *The Pietists*, ed. Emilie Griffin and Peter C. Erb (San Francisco: HarperSanFrancisco, 2006), pp. 42-66.

32. F. Ernest Stoeffler, *German Pietism during the Eighteenth Century* (Leiden: E. J. Brill, 1973), pp. 14-15, 18.

33. Stoeffler, *German Pietism during the Eighteenth Century*, p. 143.

34. Stoeffler, *German Pietism during the Eighteenth Century*, p. 144.

35. Stoeffler, *German Pietism during the Eighteenth Century*, p. 145.

revealed in Christ, based upon the testimony of Scripture, authenticated in religious experience, and productive of an affective identification with Christ which is clearly felt."[36]

For Pietists such as Francke, Zinzendorf, and others, however, religious experience and feelings were never ends in themselves. The feelings are evidences of religious experience, not the goal. A religious experience has the purpose of uniting an individual with Christ and empowering him or her to live a changed life. As Francke noted, "True faith is a divine work in us, which transforms us and bestows upon us the new birth from God, which kills the old Adam, and fashions us into a man [sic] who is entirely different in heart, soul, mind, and in all his powers."[37] A "progressive amendment of life," then, was the purpose of inward experience of God.[38]

Conversion

Pietism's third hallmark is *conversion, regeneration of the "inner person."* This is the *event* of inward, transforming experience of God, where it begins. James Tanis rightly notes that "Pietism's cornerstone was the doctrine of rebirth."[39] Dale Brown calls it the *locus classicus* of Pietist theology and explains it this way: "Regeneration results in the overcoming and eradication of sin and the participation in the divine nature, which is the formation of oneself in the likeness of Jesus. Through this birth Jesus Christ acquires form in each believer."[40] However, for most Pietists this does not mean "sinless perfection." Classical Pietists denied perfection in this life but held out hope, even expectation, of progressive growth in holiness, by which they meant Christ-likeness.

Spener and Francke especially introduced and emphasized the concept of the "inner man,"[41] which became a hallmark of Pietism. They derived

36. Stoeffler, *German Pietism during the Eighteenth Century*, p. 145.
37. Stoeffler, *German Pietism during the Eighteenth Century*, p. 145.
38. Stoeffler, *German Pietism during the Eighteenth Century*, p. 8.
39. James Tanis, "Reformed Pietism in Colonial America," in *Continental Pietism and Early American Christianity*, ed. Stoeffler, p. 72.
40. Brown, *Understanding Pietism*, p. 99.
41. Throughout, when we place "inner man" in quotation marks, we do so because

it from Johann Arndt, Pietism's precursor and the author of *True Christianity*. Arndt wrote about the transforming experience of God resulting in a "new inner man."[42] According to Arndt — and Spener and Francke followed him in this — this new or renewed inner person, the core of one's personality, the "heart," is brought about and into conformity with Jesus Christ through repentance and heartfelt trust in the Savior through the Word of God: "This is true repentance when the heart internally through sorrow and regret is broken down, destroyed, laid low, and by faith and forgiveness of sins is made holy, consoled, purified, changed, and made better so that an external improvement in life follows."[43] Also, speaking of true faith, Arndt said, "By this deep trust and heartfelt assent, man gives his heart completely and utterly to God, rests in God alone, gives himself over to God, clings to God alone, unites himself with God. . . ."[44]

Spener picked up Arndt's emphasis on new birth and the inner person in *Pia Desideria*, declaring, "Our whole Christian religion consists in the inner man or the new man [sic], whose soul is faith and whose expressions are the fruits of life, and all sermons should be aimed at this."[45] Also, according to Spener, "true orthodoxy" is aimed at the inner person. Doctrine disconnected from it is useless. He challenged churchgoers who thought they were Christians by making this declaration:

> It is not enough that we hear the Word with our outward ear, but we must let it penetrate to our heart, so that we may hear the Holy Spirit speak there, that is, with vibrant emotion and comfort feel the sealing of the Spirit and the power of the Word. Nor is it enough to be baptized, but the inner man, where we have put on Christ in Baptism, must also keep Christ on and bear witness to him in our outward life.[46]

---

that is how the phrase appears in published English translations of *Pia Desideria* and other Pietist books. For the sake of inclusiveness, we use *inner person* when not quoting the phrase.

42. Johann Arndt, *True Christianity*, in *Pietism*, ed. G. Thomas Halbrooks (Nashville: Broadman Press, 1981), p. 169.

43. Arndt, *True Christianity*, p. 165.

44. Arndt, *True Christianity*, p. 166.

45. Spener, *Pia Desideria*, p. 116.

46. Spener, *Pia Desideria*, p. 117.

In other words, Spener and other Pietists were asking why one would just be forgiven and declared righteous. Why not be transformed, changed inwardly, created new in the image of Christ Jesus? That's the goal of salvation — forgiveness *and* new birth. And with new birth comes a new feeling of experiencing God and desiring to do the will of God.

Francke experienced a dramatic conversion that he later labeled *Busskampf* — a "struggle of repentance." He described it vividly and called it "the thunder of the power of God" that gives new birth and a "new beginning."[47] Without stating that every Christian must have exactly the same dramatic conversion or even be able to date one, Francke did insist that every Christian must experience repentance and conversion resulting in regeneration and amendment of life. This became a hallmark of true Pietism. Zinzendorf expressed it most vividly and with emotion:

> When the Holy Spirit comes into the heart, he melts the heart; then the eyes fill with tears, then body and soul rejoice. As the occasion requires, the heart is grieved at its misery and rejoices at the grace, at the peace, at the blessedness which it feels, not knowing how it came about.[48]

The Moravian leader asked people who wondered if they were truly saved, "Do you feel a condition which you have not had before?"[49] All Pietists believe that *some* measure of feeling of Christ in the heart accompanies salvation. That is usually understood to be first a feeling of sorrow for sin and then a feeling of joy for forgiveness and a new beginning.

What did early Pietists think a person must *do* to experience this conversion, this regeneration of the inner person? Although differing from Francke in some ways, Zinzendorf nevertheless expressed the general consensus: only hear and believe with the heart:

> If we only are passive and gladly passive to let good be done to us, then there is no difficulty in obtaining salvation. What then at last is the con-

47. Francke, "The Foretaste of Eternal Life," p. 59, p. 44.

48. Nicholas Ludwig von Zinzendorf, *Nine Public Lectures on Important Subjects,* translated and edited by George W. Forell (Iowa City: University of Iowa Press, 1973), p. 53.

49. Zinzendorf, *Nine Public Lectures on Important Subjects,* p. 53.

dition? None other than believing in Him; not looking upon the Savior as an imposter and upon His teaching as a fable; honoring His suffering and death as a divine truth.[50]

Early Pietists set this doctrine of conversion and rebirth within the context of the "paradox of grace." Gary Sattler expresses it this way: "Seen theocentrically, all that happens [in salvation] is of God. Experienced anthropocentrically, there is human effort required and expended in the cleansing of one's heart."[51] The "human effort," however, is not works or merit but mere acceptance of God's work. Theologically, this is what is called "synergism." All the early Pietists affirmed the freedom of the human will *as a result of the promptings of grace* ("prevenient grace") to either accept or reject God's saving work in the heart.[52]

Conversional Piety

The fourth Pietist hallmark is *conversional piety — a strong devotional life and a personal relationship with God through Jesus Christ crucified and risen.* Of course, this hallmark is not unique to Pietism. The Puritans, for example, emphasized this as well.[53] The distinctive Pietist expression of

50. Zinzendorf, *Nine Public Lectures on Important Subjects*, p. 70.

51. Gary R. Sattler, *Nobler than the Angels, Lower than a Worm: The Pietist View of the Individual in the Writings of Heinrich Müller and August Hermann Francke* (Lanham, Md.: University of America Press, 1989), p. 49.

52. All one has to do to see this is read major scholarly works on early Pietism. Nearly all take note of the implicit — if not explicit — synergism in its doctrine of salvation. Lutheran scholar Paul Kuenning, for example, traces Spener's and other early Pietists' concepts of divine initiative and free acceptance of grace back to Philip Melanchthon, Luther's right-hand man in the Reformation and successor as leader of the Wittenberg party of Lutheranism after Luther's death. (See Kuenning, *The Rise and Fall of American Lutheran Pietism*, p. 23.) I (Roger) find the pattern of soteriology in early Pietism similar, if not identical to, that of Jacob Arminius and the early Remonstrants.

53. See, for example, *The Devoted Life: An Invitation to the Puritan Classics*, ed. Kelly Kapic and Randall Gleason (Downers Grove, Ill.: InterVarsity Press, 2004). Many scholars have compared the two movements and concluded that they had much in common. However, there are notable differences as well. One is that the vast majority of Puritans were Calvinists, whereas the vast majority of early Pietists were not. As noted

this concept appears in the phrase "intimacy with the Savior" — a favorite phrase of Zinzendorf's to describe the true Christian life.[54]

According to Stoeffler, "A feeling of intimacy with the Savior remained the most important aspect of [Zinzendorf's] piety."[55] Fleshing this out more, Stoeffler notes, "What he insisted on was that the heart of Christian piety must not be considered a set of regulations but a joyful, affective, unutterably satisfying, personal relationship with 'the Savior.'"[56] For Zinzendorf, as for other early Pietists, this began with conversion and continued on throughout the converted Christian's entire life. They denied perfection, allowing that the relationship between the believer and Christ would have its ups and downs, but they all described it as joyful. Stoeffler describes early Moravian piety vividly, and much, if not all, of his description could apply equally to all Pietism as a whole:

> Early Moravian piety . . . was . . . essentially a joyful, emotional, perhaps basically romantic, attachment of the individual Christian to the "Savior," whose will regarding all the prosaic duties of everyday existence was thought to be apprehended most fully within a fellowship of likeminded people. The most immediate result was that religion to these people became a most profoundly satisfying reality at the very center of their personal existence. A further result was that they had an extremely vivid sense of religious fellowship which helped them to transcend radically life's ambiguities and difficulties.[57]

Many critics have accused Pietism of legalism, of moralistic preaching and living according to extremely rigid rules of behavior. In fact, Zinzendorf explicitly denied that such was necessary for a person truly converted and in love with the Savior: "Now there is no need to preach one point of

---

in the exposition of the third hallmark above, the Pietists were synergists with regard to salvation — believing that human cooperation with God's grace was necessary, while nearly all Puritans condemned synergism in salvation as heresy.

54. Zinzendorf, quoted in Stoeffler, *German Pietism during the Eighteenth Century*, pp. 152, 153.

55. Stoeffler, *German Pietism during the Eighteenth Century*, p. 152.

56. Stoeffler, *German Pietism during the Eighteenth Century*, p. 153.

57. Stoeffler, *German Pietism during the Eighteenth Century*, p. 159.

morality after the other at [such a person], not even of the most refined and subtle. . . . For every loving look from the Savior indicates our morality to us throughout our whole life."[58] What Zinzendorf meant, as is clear from the context and the entire sermon, is that a truly converted person whose life is permeated by this relationship with Christ will naturally want to live a life pleasing to God and will strive to do it without outward compulsion.

So, what are the *means* and *marks* of such a life of conversional piety? For Francke, the *means* were self-examination, daily repentance, prayer, hearing of the Word, and sacraments,[59] while the *marks* were trials, cross-bearing, obedience to God's law, trust in God, and joy.[60] While much of this hallmark of Pietism is at least vaguely familiar to most modern American (and other) Protestant Christians, especially those who consider themselves evangelicals, it was outside the norm for state church Protestantism in the post–Reformation era. Stoeffler, like other historians, notes that territorial, state Protestantism was then mired in "shallow and superficial Christianity."[61] The majority of people, including pastors and church leaders, thought a Christian to be any baptized person who maintained a formal connection with the church.[62] Devotional life was crucial to the Pietists, and they considered it necessary for authentic Christianity, much to the chagrin and even horror of many state church leaders.

Visible Christianity

The fifth common feature characteristic of Pietism is *visible Christianity — holy living and transformed character*. Again, this is a hallmark shared with other Christian movements, but Pietism offers its own distinctive twist. To be sure, some Pietists allowed their Pietism to become distorted into a legalistic, moralistic emphasis on behavioral "dos" and "don'ts." The

58. Zinzendorf, *Nine Public Lectures on Important Subjects*, p. 84.
59. Stoeffler, *German Pietism during the Eighteenth Century*, p. 21.
60. Stoeffler, *German Pietism during the Eighteenth Century*, p. 19.
61. Stoeffler, *The Rise of Evangelical Pietism*, p. 18.
62. Stoeffler, *The Rise of Evangelical Pietism*, pp. 17-18.

original Pietist vision of visible Christianity, holy living, is summed up in "love of neighbor." Francke, for example, talked about the "inner person" (already discussed above) and the "outer person" and argued that the transformation wrought in conversion-regeneration, affecting the inner person, would inevitably result in a transformation in the outer person. "Because the Christian has the mind of Christ," Francke said, "he or she lives gladly in community and cannot avoid serving neighbor in unselfish love."[63] Neither Spener nor Francke insisted on escapism from the world or harsh asceticism.[64] Movie portrayals of Pietism such as *Babette's Feast* present a distorted view. It's true that the early Pietists criticized alcohol consumption and dancing, for example, but their aim was not asceticism. The prohibition of alcohol had to do with avoiding drunkenness, all too common in that society, and the prohibition of dancing was aimed at the common practice of lewd dancing. The emphasis was on positive behaviors, not prohibitions.[65]

Love of the Bible

The sixth hallmark of Pietism is *love of the Bible understood as a medium of an immediate relationship with God.* One of Spener's suggestions for reform and renewal of the churches was a new emphasis on Bible reading; his conventicles primarily studied the Bible. Beyond any doubt or debate, the Bible played a major role in Pietist efforts to revivify Christianity. Brown rightly says that "Pietism definitely represented a back-to-the-Bible movement."[66] Spener, Francke, and Zinzendorf all affirmed the Protestant doctrine of *sola scriptura;* they did not elevate experience to a level alongside or above Scripture. They all affirmed Scripture's unique inspiration and authority, but they rejected a mechanical view of inspiration and held that it was the authors of Scripture who were inspired, not the words.[67] Re-

63. Francke, quoted in Sattler, *Nobler than the Angels, Lower than a Worm*, p. 117.
64. Sattler, *Nobler than the Angels, Lower than a Worm*, p. 170.
65. Gary R. Sattler, *God's Glory, Neighbor's Good: A Brief Introduction to the Life and Writings of August Hermann Francke* (Chicago: Covenant Press, 1982), p. 74.
66. See Brown, *Understanding Pietism*, p. 65.
67. Stein, *Philipp Jakob Spener*, p. 152.

jecting the Protestant scholastic doctrine of exhaustive biblical inerrancy, they "limited inerrancy to what the Bible said about human salvation."[68] They emphasized the role of the Holy Spirit in inspiring and illuminating the written Word to readers.[69] Without the Holy Spirit, they argued, it is impossible to understand the Bible truly. Without the Spirit, it is just a dead letter; with the Spirit, it is a life-giving medium of God's transforming power and grace.

For most if not all of the early Pietists, the main point of Scripture is to be found not in its literal, historical sense but in its ability to give life. One scholar has described Francke's approach to the interpretation of Scripture as a "hermeneutics under the sign of rebirth."[70] For Francke, Zinzendorf, and most other early Pietists, Scripture was to be read primarily for its *sensus mysticus,* because the divine intention behind the words of the human author — which the human author did not necessarily always know — was to give life. Thus, Francke and others differentiated between "living knowledge" and "theoretical knowledge" of God.[71] The bare, historical meaning, the factual reference, is the "husk," while the inner, life-giving, spiritual meaning is the "kernel" of Scripture.[72] That is not to say that Pietists advocated a fanciful allegorical interpretation that tore the spiritual meaning away from the historical meaning. It is only to say that the main purpose of Scripture, according to Pietism, is not to *inform* but to *transform:*

> Pietists believed the Bible had been communicated to man in order to edify, console, encourage, warn, reprimand, and help the church and its members as well as to lead men and women to God by bringing about repentance and change. For Pietists the Bible became a devotional resource rather than a source of doctrine, a guide to life rather than just the source of belief.[73]

68. Stein, *Philipp Jakob Spener,* p. 151.
69. Stein, *Philipp Jakob Spener,* pp. 152-53.
70. Markus Matthias, "August Hermann Francke (1663-1727)," in *The Pietist Theologians,* ed. Carter Lindberg (Malden, Mass.: Blackwell, 2005), pp. 104-5.
71. Matthias, "August Hermann Francke (1663-1727)," p. 106.
72. Matthias, "August Hermann Francke (1663-1727)," p. 105.
73. Brown, *Understanding Pietism,* p. 68.

Pietists loved the Bible not because it contains propositional truths about God to feed the mind, but because it is the principal medium for the Christian's relationship with God, helping to guide and develop a deep and genuine intimacy between the Christian and God. Pietists loved the Bible because they believed they had discovered that its essential, spiritual truth can be understood by any Spirit-led and enlightened person. "The theory was . . . that the Spirit of God is able to commend the truth of the Bible to men's minds and hearts without the tortured interpretations of the professionals [i.e., biblical scholars]."[74] Pietists believed that *they* had discovered the "open Bible," in contrast to the "closed Bible" of the Protestant Orthodox and scholastic scholars and church leaders, who taught that *they* were the only ones who could interpret it rightly.

Life Together

The seventh common motif of Pietism is *Christian life lived in community.* One of the most common false views of Pietism is that it promotes spiritual individualism. It's true that there was the separatist and sometimes individualistic impulse that was especially evident in more radical forms; nevertheless, Pietists valued highly both the church and the Christian community outside the church. Spener's conventicles, or *collegia pietatis*, were also referred to as *ecclesiola in ecclesia* — small groups associated with the church but meeting outside its formal structures and boundaries for fellowship, prayer, and Bible study. Johannes Wallmann goes so far as to claim, "The concept of community *(ecclesiola in ecclesia)* [is] essential to Pietism."[75]

Franklin Littell also rejects the idea of individualism as natural to Pietism. He admits that today "we often encounter this teaching [that is, Pietism] in an individualistic form, removed from the setting of the church and hostile to the organized life of the Christian community."[76] While the

74. Stoeffler, *The Rise of Evangelical Pietism*, p. 21.

75. Johannes Wallmann, "Johann Arndt (1555-1621)," in *The Pietist Theologians*, ed. Lindberg, pp. 35-36.

76. Franklin H. Littell, "Radical Pietism in American History," in *Continental Pietism and Early American Christianity*, ed. Stoeffler, p. 164.

early Pietists emphasized "a deeply personal, vitally significant experience of the living God . . . even those preachers and teachers most critical of the religious establishments were devoted to a vision of the true church as the inspired community of God's people."[77] Even those Pietists who, often under persecution by the state churches, broke away to found separate sects or house churches practiced "a full communal life."[78]

Harry Yeide Jr. has labored hard to correct the mistaken interpretation of Pietism as individualistic, describing the movement as "anything but individualistic, introverted, and emotional."[79] In fact, he goes so far as to identify the phenomenon of *ecclesiola in ecclesia* as *the* distinctive feature of Pietism.[80] He defines Pietism as "an ecclesiola movement in which a great premium is placed on divinely initiated experiential religion as the foundation for renewal actions."[81]

World Transformation

The eighth hallmark and distinguishing emphasis of Pietism is *world transformation toward the kingdom of God (through social action and missions)*. People who label Pietism otherworldly and withdrawn from social endeavors ("quietism") have clearly not studied Pietism. Unfortunately, the unjustified image of Pietism as a religion that is "so heavenly minded that it is no earthly good" persists. But nothing could be further from the truth about historical Pietism.

Modern Pietism scholarship highlights Spener's, Francke's, and later Pietism's optimistic views of the potential for the kingdom of God to be approximated, if not achieved, on earth before Christ returned. In *Pia Desideria*, Spener spoke warmly about "hope for better times for the church" and for society through renewal of the churches. Mary Fulbrook rightly claims,

77. Littell, "Radical Pietism in American History," p. 164.
78. Littell, "Radical Pietism in American History," p. 166.
79. Harry Yeide Jr., *Studies in Classical Pietism: The Flowering of the Ecclesiola* (New York: Peter Lang, 1997), p. xi.
80. Yeide Jr., *Studies in Classical Pietism*, p. 30.
81. Yeide Jr., *Studies in Classical Pietism*, p. 144.

Unlike the increasingly pessimistic and quietistic Luther, Pietists believed in the possibility of the active transformation of this world, the achievement of the kingdom of God on earth; and they believed . . . that it was their duty towards God, for the greater glory of God, to attempt to change conditions in the here and now.[82]

In *Pia Desideria*, Spener laid out a specific program for social improvement. According to Stein, "Spener has been considered a pioneer in public relief and in care for the poor."[83] Also, "Spener taught that the Christian life is devoted to world-formation, that is, to contribution to the well-being of society."[84] For example, Spener believed and argued that it is the duty of the government to provide work for all able-bodied people.[85]

In a similar vein, Sattler notes, "Despite their zealous intolerance of 'worldly desires' and 'course sins,' it was the Pietists who fed, clothed, and educated poorer neighbors."[86] Francke, for example, built the "Franckean Institutes" or "Hallensian Institutes" at Halle and made that city a center not only of spiritual renewal of church and society but also of social transformation. For him, "the earth itself would ultimately be transformed" through Christian endeavors on behalf of society.[87] "Francke's concern for the glory of God and the good of humankind extended as far as the range of his mind."[88]

In his study of Württemberg Pietism, Frank Macchia discusses several Pietist leaders who became social reformers, some even taking government positions in order to heal the social order. Theologian Jan Milic Lochman, in the introduction to Macchia's book, notes,

Wuerttemberg Pietism of the 19th century offered European, above all German-speaking, theology the fruitful possibility of a connection be-

---

82. Fulbrook, *Piety and Politics*, p. 25.
83. Stein, *Philipp Jakob Spener*, p. 241.
84. Stein, *Philipp Jakob Spener*, p. 238.
85. Stein, *Philipp Jakob Spener*, p. 240.
86. Sattler, *God's Glory, Neighbor's Good*, p. 49.
87. Sattler, *God's Glory, Neighbor's Good*, p. 70.
88. Sattler, *God's Glory, Neighbor's Good*, p. 74.

tween a deeply personal piety that is faithful to the scriptures and an alert attention to the burning social questions of industrialized society.[89]

Macchia focuses mainly on two modern Pietists of Württemberg, father-and-son Lutheran pastors Johann Christoph Blumhardt and Christoph Friedrich Blumhardt. Christoph especially was a social activist, but he was building on his father's legacy — and earlier pietistic impulses toward social transformation. According to Macchia, "Christoph's primary loyalty was always to the kingdom of God and its manifestation in the liberation of the poor and oppressed."[90] However, well before the Blumhardts appeared, Württemberg Pietism was deeply involved in social transformation "for God's glory and neighbor's good."

Michelle A. Clifton-Soderstrom echoes similar sentiments regarding Spener:

> Wherever he ministered, Spener demonstrated his knowledge of and advocacy for the "least of these" — widows, orphans, peasants, unemployed, refugees, migrants, beggars, and invalids. He encouraged his parishes to work as Christians in partnership with the government to provide things like aid, jobs, relief, homes, and medical care.[91]

Clifton-Soderstrom exegetes Francke's sermon "The Duty to the Poor" (1697) to show that he not only founded institutions for the poor and disadvantaged but also preached that "everything Christians do . . . is to be motivated by sincere love for the poor."[92] Francke's church in Halle "became God's instrument of justice in the streets of Glaucha" (a poor suburb of Halle).[93]

Kuenning notes a similar dynamic. In his analysis of Lutheran Pietism in America, specifically the Franckean Evangelical (Lutheran) Synod and

89. Jan Milic Lochman, "Introduction," in Frank D. Macchia, *Spirituality and Social Liberation* (Metuchen, N.J.: Scarecrow Press, 1993), p. xv.

90. Macchia, *Spirituality and Social Liberation*, p. 128.

91. Michelle A. Clifton-Soderstrom, *Angels, Worms, and Bogeys: The Christian Ethic of Pietism* (Eugene, Ore.: Cascade Books, 2010), p. 45.

92. Clifton-Soderstrom, *Angels, Worms, and Bogeys*, p. 80.

93. Clifton-Soderstrom, *Angels, Worms, and Bogeys*, p. 81.

its father-and-son leaders J. G. Schmucker (1771-1854) and Samuel Simon Schmucker (1799-1873), Kuenning describes a synod that was explicitly Pietist and revivalist *and* deeply involved in social causes, including anti-war efforts, pro-temperance efforts, and the abolition of slavery. The Synod ordained the first African-American Lutheran pastor in America (Daniel Payne). Kuenning concludes,

> Samuel Schmucker as an individual leader and the Franckean Synod as a corporate body were the most vigorous exponents of abolitionism in the Lutheran church. It appears that this concern issued directly from the theological traditions that they had mutually imbibed from the classical Lutheran Pietism of the Spener-Francke school in Germany.[94]

Kuenning speaks about Pietism more broadly when he says, "Conversion to the Lord resulted in service to one's neighbor. To be converted was to commit oneself concretely to the building of God's Kingdom on earth."[95]

To be sure, not all Pietists have been socially active in terms of world transformation. Some have withdrawn from any attempt to Christianize the social order. Some, especially in the twentieth century under the influence of fundamentalism, have even disavowed and demonized the so-called Social Gospel. However, we believe that, at its best, Pietism always includes an impulse toward social transformation "for God's glory and neighbor's good."

Ecumenical Christianity

The ninth common feature of Pietism is *ecumenical, irenic Christianity*. Although Spener, Francke, and Zinzendorf were all Lutherans, they also all

---

94. Kuenning, *The Rise and Fall of American Lutheran Pietism*, p. 221.

95. Kuenning, *The Rise and Fall of American Lutheran Pietism*, p. 236. In case someone is tempted to think the social activism of the Franckean Synod in the U.S. is unique and not illustrative of modern Pietism, scholar Mark Safstrom offers a parallel illustration of Pietist social activism in Sweden around the same time in "The 'Waldenström Party' in Swedish Politics, 1868-1917: Interpreting the Political Activism of the Swedish Awakening" in *The Pietist Impulse in Christianity*, ed. Collins Winn et al., pp. 175-85. According to Safstrom, Pietists were in the forefront of bringing democracy and socialism to Sweden.

sought to transcend narrow sectarianism, moving toward a more ecumenical Christianity through emphasis on the invisible church, the universal body of Christ that includes all true believers, seeking especially to overcome dogmatism and harsh polemics in Christian theology and church life.

Donald Durnbaugh rightly highlights one characteristic of Pietism that cannot be denied: "the spacious, trans-territorial and transconfessional character of Pietism which tended toward a religion of the heart rather than of the mind."[96] Durnbaugh argues, "One constituent element of Pietism is its eclectic or . . . ecumenical stance which sought adherents and like-minded spirits across ecclesial, territorial, class, and economic boundaries . . . the self-understanding that true Christians can be found in many confessions."[97] Zinzendorf, for example, gladly accepted as fellow Christians those from Catholic and Reformed traditions at a time when many Orthodox Lutherans (or those embedded in Lutheran Orthodoxy) rejected them as unbelievers. The Moravian leader even planned a universal church that he would call "The Congregation of God in the Spirit" that would transcend denominational boundaries. According to Hans Schneider, "By de-emphasizing the confessional differences and stressing the godly lifestyle as a sign of true Christians, Pietism paved the way for Protestant unions in the nineteenth century."[98]

A traditional Pietist saying about doctrines is this: "In essentials unity, in non-essentials liberty, in all things charity [love]." The exact source of the saying is debated, but Pietists picked it up and used it to express their irenic and tolerant approach to doctrinal differences. Spener and Francke, as well as later Pietists, sought to rediscover "apostolic simplicity" to dampen the fires of theological controversy. "Spener, Francke, and their colleagues desired to walk the middle ground between dogmatic inflexibility and dogmatic indifference."[99] This irenic, tolerant, and flexible

96. Donald F. Durnbaugh, "Communication Networks as One Aspect of Pietist Definition," in *Pietism in Germany and North America, 1680-1820*, ed. Strom et al., p. 49.

97. Durnbaugh, "Communication Networks as One Aspect of Pietist Definition," pp. 33-34.

98. Hans Schneider, "Understanding the Church: Issues of Pietist Ecclesiology," in *Pietism and Community in Europe and North America, 1650-1850*, ed. Strom, p. 34.

99. Brown, *Understanding Pietism*, p. 43.

approach to secondary matters of doctrine, which tended to fuel the fires of Protestant divisions and arguments, angered Pietism's Protestant Orthodox critics. The latter accused them of doctrinal indifference, which was simply untrue — at least concerning the great dogmas of ancient Christianity and the Protestant Reformation.

Much to the chagrin of his critics and opponents, Spener not only criticized useless speculation and harsh polemics in theology; he also urged the "practice of heartfelt love toward all unbelievers and heretics."[100] As for doctrinal disputation within the church, Spener did not reject disputation altogether, but he argued that "disputing is not enough either to maintain the truth among ourselves or to impart it to the erring. The holy love of God is necessary."[101] Spener believed that "much that is alien, useless, and reminiscent of the world's wisdom has here and there been introduced gradually into theology."[102] According to him (and this was clearly aimed at his opponents among the Protestant Orthodox), "Indeed we may say that the highly enlightened apostle [Paul], if he came among us today, would probably understand only a little of what our slippery geniuses sometimes say in holy places." His solution to all this was to return to "apostolic simplicity,"[103] shedding our "sacks full of useless questions" in theology, and treating one another with love even when we disagree about doctrines.[104]

The Common Priesthood of True Believers

The tenth and final hallmark of Pietism is *the common priesthood of true believers*. Of course, Luther and other Reformers emphasized the priesthood of every believer. The Anabaptists probably took that more seriously than any other Protestant group. But by the time of Spener and Francke, that Protestant principle had been largely forgotten or watered down in a new clericalism — at least in the state churches. A major thrust of Spener's ministry was to elevate the laity to a new spiritual position — not to

100. Spener, *Pia Desideria*, p. 99.
101. Spener, *Pia Desideria*, p. 102.
102. Spener, *Pia Desideria*, p. 51.
103. Spener, *Pia Desideria*, p. 57.
104. Spener, *Pia Desideria*, p. 51.

replace ordained ministry as a teaching office, but to equip non-ordained Christians to study the Bible, pray, and engage in devotional practices without having to have clergy present. This infuriated many of his critics in the official churches.

Jonathan Strom rightly stresses this hallmark of Pietism: "The common or spiritual priesthood was a major component of early Pietist reform proposals."[105] According to Strom, "It was Philipp Jacob Spener in the 1675 *Pia Desideria* who gave the common priesthood the greatest prominence in the seventeenth century, and his interpretation of it became a centerpiece of his attempts to revitalize Christianity."[106] Spener published a tract entitled "The Spiritual Priesthood" in 1677 in which he advocated keeping the authority of ordained ministry in the churches while at the same time promoting lay reading and studying of the Word of God.[107] That may not sound revolutionary in the early twenty-first century, but in the late seventeenth century it caused great controversy. At that time laypeople were only supposed to read and study and discuss the Bible with the help and oversight of ordained clergymen. Some territories and even nations outlawed lay gatherings for Bible study and discussion in an attempt to crush Pietism. Spener and later Pietist leaders steadfastly defended the right and ability of converted laypeople to read, study, and discuss the Bible. They were advocates of what later was called an "open Bible" policy.

For Spener and other early Pietist leaders, the *collegia pietatis* were the forums for exercising the common priesthood. "Direct encounter with Scripture becomes [there] a central task for all Christians."[108] Nothing infuriated Spener's enemies more than his argument that laypeople had the right and duty to judge whether their ministers were rightly interpreting Scripture.[109] And, much to his critics' dismay, Spener was not averse to

105. Jonathan Strom, "The Common Priesthood and the Pietist Challenge for Ministry and Laity," in *The Pietist Impulse in Christianity,* ed. Collins Winn et al., p. 42.

106. Strom, "The Common Priesthood and the Pietist Challenge for Ministry and Laity," p. 47.

107. Strom, "The Common Priesthood and the Pietist Challenge for Ministry and Laity," p. 49.

108. Strom, "The Common Priesthood and the Pietist Challenge for Ministry and Laity," p. 49.

109. Strom, "The Common Priesthood and the Pietist Challenge for Ministry and Laity," p. 49.

allowing women to participate equally with men — even though this happened primarily in groups associated with Spener, rather than in Spener's own conventicle.[110] Brown concludes that "early Pietism worked to eliminate the great chasm which separated clergy and laity."[111]

Various Pietist groups throughout history have taken the common priesthood of believers to different levels and interpreted it differently, but all have sought to minimize the difference between clergy and laity, usually relegating it to a matter of education and training. According to classical Pietism — Spener through the Blumhardts and beyond — a minister is a spiritual guide and mentor, an equipper and encourager, and a believing layperson is a priest capable of going directly to God in prayer and of interpreting Scripture in matters crucial to salvation.

Conclusion

What we have attempted to do here is simply paint a portrait of classical Pietism that highlights its characteristic, distinctive features — many of them matters of *emphasis* rather than *absolute difference*. In other words, other Christian movements share many of these features or hallmarks, but Pietism puts them together in a distinctive way and emphasizes them in a manner most others do not. Sometimes that distinctive emphasis lies in their connection with each other — something missing in other Christian movements. By no means do we claim that Pietism stands alone or above or apart from other spiritual movements within Protestantism; it shares much with the classical Reformation (of which it saw itself as the completion), the radical Reformation (e.g., Anabaptists), and Christian mysticism. Nevertheless, we believe that Pietism has its own distinctive ethos, stemming from Arndt, Spener, Francke, Zinzendorf, and their faithful heirs, and that its contribution to what is called "evangelicalism" in the late twentieth and early twenty-first centuries has too often been overlooked.

---

110. Strom, "The Common Priesthood and the Pietist Challenge for Ministry and Laity," p. 49.

111. Brown, *Understanding Pietism*, p. 57.

CHAPTER SIX

Where Pietism Flourished on New Soil

Great Britain and North America

A major thesis of this book is that Pietism, as described here, the movement launched in Germany by Philipp Jakob Spener and carried forward by August Hermann Francke, Nikolaus Ludwig von Zinzendorf, and others, and its ethos, is a largely neglected root of contemporary evangelicalism worthy of being rediscovered and embraced by evangelicals. Scholars of Pietism often point out a bias in the literature about American religious history in favor of New England Puritanism that has tended to obscure other equally important impulses, including especially Pietism.[1] In many public school history classes and even in courses on American religion in Christian colleges and universities founded by Pietists, Puritanism gets more attention than Pietism. And yet, according to many contemporary historians, Pietism is just as significant an influence in colonial American religious life as Puritanism, and its ethos has lasted longer and filtered into that life in broader and deeper ways. In fact, F. Ernest Stoeffler argues, "There can no longer be any doubt that the evangelicalism which became the dominant pattern for the individual and corporate religious self-understanding of American Protestants is heavily indebted to the Pietist heritage."[2]

1. See, for example, F. Ernest Stoeffler, "Introduction," in *Continental Pietism and Early American Christianity,* ed. F. Ernest Stoeffler (Grand Rapids: Wm. B. Eerdmans, 1976), p. 10.

2. Stoeffler, "Epilogue," in *Continental Pietism and Early American Christianity,* ed. Stoeffler, p. 267.

Of course, that includes Great Britain, because much of American Pietism was imported from there or from Germany via Great Britain. The evangelical awakenings in Great Britain associated with John and Charles Wesley, and the early Methodist movement, were greatly impacted by Pietism, as we will explain in this chapter. Indeed, it's doubtful that there would have been a Methodist movement without Pietism. Stoeffler rightly points out that "early Methodism owed a considerable debt to the older movement of Continental Pietism."[3] For many Pietists emigrating to America, Great Britain was a stopping-off point, which also made it a launching pad for Pietism into the American colonies. Although European Pietists of many kinds settled temporarily in England on their way to America, there can be no doubt that America is the fertile soil in which Pietism took root and flourished and became, at least in some way, the common folk religion of the people.

James Tanis, among others, emphasizes the influence of Pietism on American religious life and American society generally. What he says is in agreement with the majority of the scholarship:

[Pietism] established a new pattern of evangelism and a new form of revivalism; it had opened unforeseen and uncontrived avenues of ecumenism; and it had created America's own odd mixture of personal piety, moralism, and national faith. Each characteristic was one of a series of safeguards for a biblically oriented faith.[4]

Pietism, even among Lutheran immigrants to the American colonies, opened the door to the Great Awakening — a series of revivals led by George Whitefield and Jonathan Edwards, among others, which shook the colonies throughout the 1740s and left an indelible stamp on American culture. The Great Awakening, in turn, gave great momentum to the Pietism that was already firmly planted among the colonists, especially in the middle colonies.

3. Stoeffler, "Pietism, the Wesleys, and Methodist Beginnings in America," in *Continental Pietism and Early American Christianity*, ed. Stoeffler, p. 201.

4. James Tanis, "Reformed Pietism in Colonial America," in *Continental Pietism and Early American Christianity*, ed. Stoeffler, p. 72.

Pietism's Influence on American Culture

What, then, were Pietism's main contributions to British and American religious life? The majority of this chapter will unfold the history of how these influential elements of Pietism were planted in English-speaking lands in the seventeenth through the nineteenth centuries. First, however, it will be helpful to spell them out.

Stoeffler argues that Pietism continues to be felt in American religious life, especially among that portion of it broadly labeled "evangelical," in seven main ways. These will easily be recognized as aspects of the Pietist ethos described earlier in this book. According to Stoeffler, these elements have filtered from Pietism into general American evangelical Protestantism.

The first is an emphasis on *evangelism* — saving souls and giving them religious nurture in order to keep them in the "saved" state.[5] By and large, Stoeffler says,

> American churches have been more interested in the "saving of souls" than in problems of theology, or ecclesiology. The traditional emphasis has been to help the would-be believer into a new state of being, and then to provide for him the kind of religious nurture which is designed to keep him in that state.[6]

This religious emphasis cannot be taken for granted. It is more pronounced in American Christianity as compared to other forms of Christianity (even if it has been transplanted to many other places in the world), and it is primarily drawn from Pietism. Stoeffler recognizes that something of this emphasis was part of the Puritan tradition, but, he insists, "it was Pietism which during the eighteenth century transformed the Puritan tradition in America into the kind of new-life centered evangelicalism which meets us in American religious history."[7]

Stoeffler's second Pietist emphasis that has shaped American evan-

5. Stoeffler, "Epilogue," p. 268.
6. Stoeffler, "Epilogue," p. 268.
7. Stoeffler, "Epilogue," p. 268.

gelicalism is *experiential religion:* "This . . . has been a prominent part of Pietism's traditional message, expounded in a myriad number of sermons, hymns, and other devotional guides."[8] The point is that Pietism and much of American evangelical Christianity regard the essence of being religious as having a spiritual experience that helps the individual transcend life's problems and "look to the future in the confidence that . . . this evil world is also his Father's world."[9]

A third element of both Pietism and American evangelical Protestantism is, in Stoeffler's words, "*a strong biblical emphasis* . . . [that] needs no demonstration."[10] According to him, "America's early frontier situation became fertile soil for the Bible-centered theology of . . . Pietists."[11] And to this day, he avers, this simple biblicism is in much of American religious life "as sure-footed and untouched by hermeneutical uncertainties as when it came from the hands of its eighteenth-century advocates."[12] To be sure, the Puritans also stressed biblical authority, but Stoeffler and other scholars of Pietism point out that Pietism reinforced a special love for the Bible, which made biblicism "a dominant characteristic of a very large section of Protestantism in America."[13]

Fourth, Pietism introduced into the stream of European and American Protestantism an *ethical impulse focused on social need,* as Stoeffler notes: "It was Pietism . . . which first began to call attention to the needs of orphans, of prisoners, of the aged, of the sick, of slaves, and of all manner of suffering humanity."[14] In this regard, Stoeffler sees Wesleyan evangelicalism in England and Pietism as belonging inseparably together: "It was this sensitivity to human need which Pietism helped transmit to the American churches and which has remained a widely acknowledged element of American Christianity."[15]

A fifth emphasis of Pietism that shaped evangelicalism is *Protestant*

---

8. Stoeffler, "Epilogue," p. 268.
9. Stoeffler, "Epilogue," p. 268.
10. Stoeffler, "Epilogue," p. 268; italics ours.
11. Stoeffler, "Epilogue," p. 269.
12. Stoeffler, "Epilogue," p. 269.
13. Stoeffler, "Epilogue," p. 269.
14. Stoeffler, "Epilogue," p. 269.
15. Stoeffler, "Epilogue," p. 269.

hymnody. Zinzendorf was a prolific hymn-writer who influenced Charles Wesley, who, in turn, wrote hundreds of evangelical hymns that indelibly stamped British and American Christianity. Hymns and hymn-singing in churches and revivals became a major feature of British and American Christianity because of Pietism. Worship that was intended to provoke deep spiritual feelings and life-transforming decisions came into American Christianity, especially evangelicalism, through Pietism. And, Stoeffler argues, "It is a moot question . . . whether it was the pulpit, the church school, or the typical hymnal with its manifestly Pietist leanings which communicated most effectively the traditional insights and values of American Protestantism."[16]

Sixth, Stoeffler offers the *pronounced role of the laity* as a major practice contributed by Pietism to English-speaking — especially American — Protestant Christianity. True, Martin Luther highlighted the priesthood of the believer as a mark of reformed and restored Christianity, but, Stoeffler rightly says, "it is a matter of record that the sixteenth-century doctrine of the priesthood of all believers was dramatically implemented on the pragmatic level within Pietism."[17]

Seventh, and finally, another major feature of Pietism that influenced English-speaking and especially American Protestantism is an *ecumenical vision* of Christianity. Zinzendorf was among the first Pietist leaders to come to America, and there he attempted to birth a trans-denominational Christian movement called the "Fellowship of God in the Spirit" (or "Congregation of God in the Spirit") — an ecumenical movement that would embrace Lutherans, Reformed, Moravians, Brethren, and even Quakers. In Great Britain, Wesley directed this motto to Christians of other traditions: "If your heart is as my heart, give me your hand."[18] Stoeffler concludes that "whatever social and cultural factors may have moved American Protestantism in an ecumenical direction, Pietism's contribution . . . must be taken far more seriously than it has been."[19]

Stoeffler rightly points out that there is "the other side of the ledger" on which Pietism has "contributed its share to some of those features of

16. Stoeffler, "Epilogue," p. 269.
17. Stoeffler, "Epilogue," p. 270.
18. Stoeffler, "Epilogue," p. 270.
19. Stoeffler, "Epilogue," p. 270.

American Protestantism which are widely regarded as less admirable."[20] These are all well-known and have been made the hallmarks of Pietism by critics: escapist theology, otherworldliness, anti-intellectualism, and so on. However, as we are attempting to show in this book, these are not characteristic of the original vision that animated figures like Spener, Francke, Zinzendorf, and others, but represent, rather, a distortion.

The (Mis)Understanding of Pietism's Important Role

The rest of this chapter will be devoted to spelling out in some detail Pietist-like figures and movements in Great Britain and early America — persons and groups that stemmed in some way from the original Spener-Francke-Zinzendorf Pietist movement in Germany and embodied its ethos. First, however, it will be helpful to pause again, just for a moment, to remind readers why this is important, why this "reclaiming" project matters.

Virtually all of the major histories of British and American evangelical Christianity, including ones written by self-identified evangelicals, ignore Pietism. Evangelical historian Donald Dayton raised many evangelicals' consciousness of this imbalance, and even bias, in evangelical historiography in a ground-breaking article in *Christian Scholar's Review* entitled "The Search for Historical Evangelicalism."[21] There he identified two paradigms of evangelical history — one emphasizing its Puritan and Presbyterian roots, as in Protestant Orthodoxy and scholasticism, and the other emphasizing its Pietist and Pentecostal roots, as in the Wesleyan–Holiness movement. I (Roger) have come to refer to these two paradigms as the "Puritan–Presbyterian paradigm" and the "Pietist–Pentecostal paradigm." One example of evangelical historians' tendency to favor the first, even to the point of virtually ignoring the second, is the popular book *The Evangelical Heritage* by Bernard Ramm (1973). There, as in so many other books of evangelical history, Pietism is hardly mentioned. The focus is

---

20. Stoeffler, "Epilogue," p. 270.

21. Donald Dayton, "The Search for Historical Evangelicalism," *Christian Scholar's Review* 23, no. 1 (September 1993): 12-33.

nearly exclusively on evangelicalism's roots in the Reformation and later Protestant Orthodoxy (including Puritanism).

Evangelical theologian Stanley Grenz, whom we will discuss further in our final chapter, sought to correct this one-sided emphasis on orthodoxy as the essence of evangelical faith in his 1993 book *Revisioning Evangelical Theology.* When he argued there that the true essence of evangelical Christianity is a certain kind of spirituality — which he termed "convertive piety" — a firestorm of controversy erupted among evangelicals. Nevertheless, Grenz was harking back to Pietism as evangelicalism's most authentic soil.

Modern, contemporary evangelicalism in Great Britain and especially America is an unstable compound of Protestant Orthodoxy that regards Puritanism and its later manifestations, such as mid-to-late-nineteenth-century Princeton Orthodoxy (Charles Hodge, B. B. Warfield, et al.), as the standard, and Pietism (here including Wesleyan Holiness and Pentecostalism) that regards renewalism (emphasis on church renewal, evangelism, and the transforming experience of God) as the standard. Both sides of the compound recognize validity in the other, but their emphases and certainly their accounts of evangelical history and theology differ.

I (Roger) once spoke on this subject to the presidents of the thirteen member colleges of the Christian College Consortium at their annual meeting. All are evangelical Christian liberal arts colleges that attempt to hold *both* orthodoxy *and* convertive (or conversional) piety together. After my presentation, the presidents seemed to forget that I was in the room and began to argue with each other about whether *correct doctrine* or *transforming experience* was the key to identifying what they all meant when they called their institutions "evangelical." It was effectively a laboratory experience of the problem of evangelical identity and its main tension. Not a single president wanted to deny either aspect, but they all disagreed vehemently about which aspect is controlling of the evangelical identity.

One thing became clear to me (Roger) as I listened and later interacted with these evangelical Christian college presidents, and also as I had many conversations about evangelical identity with numerous evangelical scholars and leaders during the years I served as editor of *Christian Scholar's Review.* It was (and is) the case that even those evangelicals who lean more toward the Pietist-Pentecostal paradigm in terms of *practice* know little to nothing about Pietism as a historical movement and spiritual ethos or its role in shaping American Christianity from the start. Their knowledge of American evangelical roots is almost always limited to Puritanism, in part because that's been the focus of the majority of the scholarship.

Our task in this chapter will be to explore and explain this missing link in American evangelical history in particular (with some nods toward British evangelical history). The main question to be answered is this: How did the Spener-Francke-Zinzendorf (et al.) type of Pietism get transferred to Great Britain and especially America? Who were the prototypes of early American Pietism? What institutions and denominations did they found and spawn? It's an exercise in rediscovering an almost forgotten root — not just branch — of the evangelical family tree.

Pietism's Presence in England

On one matter historians of Pietism in America are largely agreed: it tended to settle and flourish mainly in the middle and southern colonies rather than in Puritan-dominated New England. Pennsylvania was especially a hotbed of Pietist activity, but so was New Jersey. Pietism made its way into New York and southward into North Carolina early on. From the middle colonies it moved westward into what was then the "frontier" of English-speaking North America: the Appalachian regions and beyond. Although it had its influences in Puritan New England (e.g., on Puritan leader Cotton Mather), that region never became a "hotbed" of Pietism. The same could be said of the Deep South — South Carolina, Florida, and the westward regions. The American Deep South was heavily influenced religiously by later revivalism, which can be seen as an offshoot of Pietism, but early colonial Pietism was concentrated mainly in the middle colonies.

The story of Pietism's transmission to North America, however, ought rightly to begin in Great Britain, and especially England, where many persecuted continental Pietists fled and settled. As we saw earlier, German Pietism, especially those forms centered in Halle (Francke's) and Herrnhut (Zinzendorf's), launched missions to other lands early in the life of their communities. Both sent emissaries into Scandinavia and established strong Pietist communities there, many of which came under persecution by the state churches. This led their followers to emigrate to Great Britain and America — especially in the nineteenth century. Early Pietist missionaries reached India and Central America, while others went to Great Britain and North America. Historian Richard Pierard laments that due to popular regard for William Carey, the "father of the modern missions movement," who was a British Congregationalist and then a Baptist, "on the popular level, particularly in the United States, the Pietist antecedents of Protestant missions remain largely unknown."[22] He rightly corrects this popular ignorance:

> Those in the English-speaking world must not forget that the foundation for their enormous missionary outreach in the nineteenth century was laid in eighteenth-century Pietism. It is not unrealistic to say that the early English missionary endeavor was even a product of it.[23]

Pietist influence in Great Britain began with emissaries sent by Francke from Halle to England. Most prominent among them was Anton Wilhelm Böhme (known in England as Anthony William Boehm), who arrived from Halle in 1701 and immediately began establishing close relations between Halle Pietism, especially its missionary endeavors, and newly founded British groups such as the Society for Promoting Christian Knowledge (SPCK) and the Society for Propagating the Gospel (SPG). Böhme also translated some of Francke's works into English and spread the news of German Pietism as a "new reformation" throughout England.[24] Together with another Halle emissary to England named Friedrich Michael Ziegenhagen, Böhme helped Pietist refugees from Germany travel to the American colonies through Great Britain, which became a major stopping-point on their way. The goal of Böhme and Ziegenhagen was not just to help emigrants to their new land; it was also to train them to help struggling Pietist Lutheran congregations in the colonies.

22. Richard Pierard, "German Pietism as a Major Factor in the Beginnings of Modern Protestant Missions," in *The Pietist Impulse in Christianity,* ed. Christian T. Collins Winn et al. (Eugene, Ore.: Pickwick Press, 2011), p. 285.
23. Pierard, "German Pietism as a Major Factor in the Beginnings of Modern Protestant Missions," p. 295.
24. Pierard, "German Pietism as a Major Factor in the Beginnings of Modern Protestant Missions," p. 289.

Another connection between original Pietism and Great Britain was the Moravians, who were also actively involved in missionary work. (In fact, there was considerable competition and even tension between the emissaries of Halle and those of Zinzendorf's Herrnhut during the eighteenth century.) Just as Francke sent Böhme and Ziegenhagen to England, so Zinzendorf commissioned Moravians to establish a foothold there. From England, many Moravians continued on to America, where their form of Pietism became a fixture of the religious landscape, something that did not happen in Great Britain, at least not to the same extent. According to Pierard, Moravians established thriving churches in England and Holland which became launching pads and financial support groups for Moravian missions to the West Indies and other places under British and Dutch control or influence.[25]

Two of the most important Moravian emissaries to Great Britain were August Gottlieb Spangenberg, the man who would eventually succeed Zinzendorf as leader of the Moravian movement, and Peter Böhler, who established Moravian churches (called "meetings" because at that time only the Church of England's churches could be called churches) and who eventually became bishop of all the Moravians in England and America. Both Spangenberg and Böhler spent most of their adult lives traveling from Herrnhut to England to America, raising money for Moravian missions, and founding Moravian meetings and churches. Both also greatly influenced John and Charles Wesley. Indeed, according to Stoeffler and other historians,[26] Wesleyan Methodism could not have come into being in the form that it did without Pietism, which was mediated to it primarily by Spangenberg and Böhler.

Pietism in America: Room to Flourish

As mentioned before, Pietism did not "catch on" in England as it did in America. Many reasons for this have been suggested. For example, Pi-

25. Pierard, "German Pietism as a Major Factor in the Beginnings of Modern Protestant Missions," p. 292.

26. See Scott Thomas Kisker, *Foundation for Revival: Anthony Horneck, the Religious Societies, and the Construction of an Anglican Pietism* (Lanham, Md.: Scarecrow Press, 2008).

etism flourished and became firmly established in those American colonies that lacked an established state church — Pennsylvania, New Jersey, and North Carolina. Later, of course, the United States rejected political establishment of religion, giving free rein to Pietism, which often resisted the confining authority of state churches. In England, official Anglicanism did not exactly persecute Pietist conventicles, but it did not provide a hospitable religious environment for radical, separatist, dissenting religious groups, even though many still existed there. The same could be said of Germany and the Scandinavian kingdoms, even though for a time Denmark's royal family favored Pietism. Only America offered the freedom for Pietists to break free of the bonds of traditional, liturgical, sacramental Protestant Orthodoxy and experiment with new forms of Christian life. In short, Pietism was a more dynamic force that found the old wineskins of Protestantism confining. Pietism flourished where those structures were not enforced by law.

Pietism began among Lutherans in Germany and grew among them in Scandinavia. Therefore it is understandable that German and Scandinavian immigrants to the American colonies were often seen as a fertile and receptive mission field by Pietist leaders in Halle and Herrnhut (and their emissaries in England, where many German and Scandinavian emigrants to America stopped and spent some time).

Swedish Lutheran immigrants began arriving in the "new world" as early as 1638, when they founded a colony on the Delaware River christened "New Sweden." By 1639 they were sufficiently numerous to petition the state church of Sweden for ministers. Dutch Lutherans mingled with Dutch Reformed in the Hudson River Valley colonies and appealed for their own Lutheran pastor in 1649. German Lutherans settled in the Philadelphia area ("Germantown") in 1683 and quickly outnumbered Swedes and Dutch. Along with the Lutherans came what were known as "sect people" — Mennonites, Quakers, and Dunkers (Old German Baptists or German Brethren). Of course, in the middle colonies that lacked established churches, the term "sect" quickly lost its negative European meaning.

German settlers, lacking Lutheran pastors, often worshiped with Anglican or Dutch Reformed congregations even as they continued to lobby Europe for ministers of their own denomination. Some Lutheran ministers came from the state churches in Europe, but, as Theodore Tappert reports,

> By far the most productive response to appeals . . . came from leaders of the institutions founded a generation earlier in Halle, Saxony, by August Hermann Francke. As a matter of fact, the spirit and practices of Halle informed most of the others who helped the distressed and forsaken Lutherans in North America.[27]

The first Lutheran synod (denomination), founded in the New World in 1748, was controlled by Halle Pietist clergymen and excluded non-Pietists.[28]

The image that most contemporary Americans have of Lutheranism is of formal, if not liturgical, worship and rather somber religious celebrations. That was not the case with early American Pietist Lutheranism. While they "did not materially alter the doctrinal content inherited from the Scholastics and Orthodoxists [of Europe]," they did "shift the emphasis from the head to the heart, from the Christ-for-us to the Christ-in-us."[29] The Pietist Lutheran pastors of colonial America regularly visited both their members and others, seeking "to produce a consciousness of sin, repentance, and faith, culminating in a holy life."[30] Their worship was revivalistic, with emotional demonstrations. The preaching "was often accompanied by tears of sorrow or joy" such that, according to one contemporary record, "many hearers wept, and the floor was moistened as by a shower."[31] The emphasis of preaching and pastoral care was on "spiritual awakening" rather than doctrine or morality.[32] Early American Lutheranism, stamped as it was by Halle Pietism, represented "revivalism within the liturgical framework of a structured institutional church."[33]

---

27. Theodore G. Tappert, "The Influence of Pietism in Colonial American Lutheranism," in *Continental Pietism and Early American Christianity*, ed. Stoeffler, p. 15.

28. Tappert, "The Influence of Pietism in Colonial American Lutheranism," p. 17.

29. Tappert, "The Influence of Pietism in Colonial American Lutheranism," p. 22.

30. Tappert, "The Influence of Pietism in Colonial American Lutheranism," p. 30.

31. Tappert, "The Influence of Pietism in Colonial American Lutheranism," p. 30.

32. Tappert, "The Influence of Pietism in Colonial American Lutheranism," p. 32.

33. W. R. Ward, *The Protestant Evangelical Awakening* (Cambridge, U.K.: Cambridge University Press, 1992), p. 260.

The leading light of early American Lutheran Pietism was, by all accounts, Francke's handpicked emissary Henry Melchior Muhlenberg, often called the patriarch of American Lutheranism.[34] Muhlenberg was a university-trained theologian and ordained Lutheran pastor who attached himself to Francke's Halle Institutions. He left for America in 1741 with the assignment to lead German Lutherans in Pennsylvania, New Jersey, and New York, where they were most concentrated. He was also assigned to oppose the ministry of the Moravians, who were moving into the same areas among the same people. At that time there was great tension developing between the Pietism of Halle and that of Herrnhut — especially in the New World, where they saw each other as competitors.

Muhlenberg was a true "churchly Pietist," committed to the Augsburg Confession and confessional Lutheranism generally, but he was also profoundly Pietist in ethos. He had no use for renegades and separatists, including many "radical Pietists," but he did celebrate and promote the experience of *Busskampf*.[35] Muhlenberg preached fervently against unconverted ministers, dead orthodoxy, and reliance on sacraments for salvation. He fell into conflict with the preachers of Lutheran Orthodoxy in New Jersey and with Zinzendorf's followers in Pennsylvania. While he was himself open to cooperation with non-Lutherans, and supported the Great Awakening ministries of the Dutch Reformed preacher Theodore Frelinghuysen and the famous Anglican preacher George Whitefield, he passionately sought to keep Lutherans within the Lutheran fold and out of, for example, Zinzendorf's ecumenical "Congregation of God in the Spirit."

By all accounts, Muhlenberg was the most influential Lutheran leader in early American history, passionately articulating Francke's version of Pietism in the colonial context. After Muhlenberg died, American Lutheranism began to fall into division between those who wanted to preserve his Pietist ethos, requiring something like conversion for full membership and recognition as true Christians, and those who fell back into Lutheran

---

34. The Francke who handpicked and sent Muhlenberg was not August Hermann but his son and successor at Halle, Gotthilf August.

35. Hermann Wellenreuther, "Heinrich Melchior Mühlenberg and the Pietisms in Colonial America," in *Pietism in Germany and North America, 1680-1820*, ed. Jonathan Strom, Hartmut Lehmann, and James Van Horn Melton (Burlington, Vt.: Ashgate, 2009), p. 129.

Orthodoxy, with its emphasis on sacraments and doctrinal rigidity. The latter became known as the "Old Lutherans" while the others were known simply as Pietists or — and this was intended as an insult — "enthusiasts." The Pietist impulse within pre–Civil War American Lutheranism was strongest in New York.[36] Historians of Lutheran Pietism regard Muhlenberg's main successors as the revivalist, social reformer, and confessional Lutheran J. G. Schmucker and his son, Samuel Simon Schmucker, founder of Gettysburg Lutheran Seminary in Pennsylvania.

The Schmuckers and their followers "looked favorably upon the revivalism that characterized so much of Protestantism in the United States [e.g., the Second Great Awakening] because it was largely compatible with their own traditions."[37] They required testimony of personal conversion for confirmation and full church membership[38] and used "new measures" introduced into revivalism by Second Great Awakening preachers such as Charles Finney. J. G. Schmucker organized one of the first Lutheran synods in America known as The General Synod, which had its strongest presence in New York and Ohio. It was stalwartly abolitionist as well as revivalist — two things that led to its eventual demise. Samuel Schmucker, who was converted at a revival in Kentucky, helped to form the Franckean Synod, which was strongest in upstate New York but also included churches scattered throughout the Midwest. Schmucker and the Franckean Synod were noted for being anti-war, anti-slavery, pro-temperance, pro-Sabbath observance, pro-women's rights, and pro-equality. The synod was the first mainline American denomination to ordain a black man.

Paul Kuenning argues that for the Schmuckers, "conversion to the Lord resulted in service to one's neighbor. To be converted was to commit oneself concretely to the building of God's kingdom on earth."[39] According to him, this social concern and commitment stemmed from "the classical Lutheran Pietism of the Spener-Francke school in Germany."[40]

---

36. The material here, about pre-Civil War Pietist Lutheranism, comes mainly from the excellent book *The Rise and Fall of American Lutheran Pietism* by Paul P. Kuenning (Macon, Ga.: Mercer University Press, 1988).

37. Kuenning, *The Rise and Fall of American Lutheran Pietism*, p. 77.

38. Kuenning, *The Rise and Fall of American Lutheran Pietism*, pp. 77-79.

39. Kuenning, *The Rise and Fall of American Lutheran Pietism*, p. 236.

40. Kuenning, *The Rise and Fall of American Lutheran Pietism*, p. 221.

Kuenning also argues that a recovery of American Lutheranism's Pietist roots and of the reform-minded revivalism of the Schmuckers could help renew both contemporary Lutheranism and evangelicalism.[41]

Not only were early American Lutherans influenced by Pietism, but so were Reformed Protestants in colonial America. Although there had been Pietist impulses among Reformed (Dutch, German, Swiss, and Presbyterian) Protestants in Europe in the seventeenth and eighteenth centuries, Pietism seems really to have taken hold among them in America. The Reformed counterpart to the Lutheran Muhlenberg was the Dutch revival preacher Theodore Frelinghuysen of New Jersey. Also instrumental in bringing Pietism into American Reformed Protestantism was his mentee, Gilbert Tennant.[42] European Reformed Protestantism tended to be more confessionally oriented, and many European Reformed leaders strongly opposed Pietism as dangerous if not outright heretical. One reason for this is that Pietist Reformed preaching and teaching leaned distinctly *away* from traditional Calvinism, as defined by the Synod of Dort, with its strong emphasis on God's sovereignty in salvation (predestination). James Tanis notes that "for the most part, Pietists emphasized man's rejection of God in refusing Christ, rather than God's rejection of man according to foreordained decrees."[43] Also, "for the Reformed Pietists, both on the Continent and in the Colonies, the central Reformed doctrines of election and certainty of faith were cast in a new form."[44] Frelinghuysen and other Pietist Reformed preachers believed that " 'in the day of judgment God will not deal with men according to election and reprobation but according to their obedience and devoutness.' "[45] Thus, "Frelinghuysen's 'summons to repentance' was clearly a break with Reformed theology according to [the Synod of] Dort, in spite of his intentions."[46]

Frelinghuysen and Tennant both cooperated freely and enthusiasti-

---

41. Kuenning, *The Rise and Fall of American Lutheran Pietism*, p. 230.

42. The information here comes primarily from the excellent chapter by James Tanis, "Reformed Pietism in Colonial America," in *Continental Pietism and Early American Christianity*, ed. Stoeffler, pp. 34-73.

43. Tanis, "Reformed Pietism in Colonial America," p. 71.

44. Tanis, "Reformed Pietism in Colonial America," p. 55.

45. Tanis, "Reformed Pietism in Colonial America," p. 56.

46. Tanis, "Reformed Pietism in Colonial America," p. 56.

cally with the Great Awakening revivals that swept the American colonies under the preaching of Whitefield. Their preaching, like Whitefield's, was emotional, appealing for decisions of repentance and faith, and condemned reliance on baptism and church membership for salvation. Their central doctrine was the experience of rebirth, conversion with regeneration, but they also promoted care for the poor and education of the young. They strongly condemned unconverted clergy and founded "Log Colleges" for the education of converted preachers in order to supply candidates for Reformed church pulpits. These directly rivaled official Reformed and Presbyterian ministerial training institutions such as The College of New Jersey (later Princeton).

As in the case of Muhlenberg and the Schmuckers among Lutherans, the revivalism of Reformed Pietists such as Frelinghuysen and Tennant gave rise to division among Reformed colonists. More traditional Reformed ministers rejected their new measures and especially the centrality of conversion. The people involved in this rejection came to be known as "Old Side," while the Pietist-Revivalists came to be called "New Side." New Side Reformed and Presbyterian Protestants went on to be instrumental in the Second Great Awakening of the early nineteenth century.

Moravians in America

Perhaps one of the strangest and most difficult to comprehend developments of Pietism in colonial America, which had long-lasting ramifications for several groups calling themselves "Brethren," was the mission and ministry of the Moravians to America. Zinzendorf probably considered the New World fertile ground for his hoped-for unified Pietist "Congregation of God in the Spirit" — a unity of true Christians that would lead to a kingdom of God on earth. First he sent Spangenberg, together with several small bands of Moravians, to Georgia in 1735 in order to form a kind of wilderness community with outreach efforts to Native Americans and immigrants from Great Britain and Europe. It was there that John Wesley became impressed with Moravian spirituality. However, the mission failed, and the Moravians moved north to Pennsylvania, spreading out from there into New Jersey and finally, especially, North Carolina.

Spangenberg established two permanent Moravian settlements in Pennsylvania, one in what came to be called Bethlehem and the other in Nazareth. From there, Spangenberg sent bands of Herrnhutters out to other places, with the highest concentration finally forming around Salem (now Winston-Salem), North Carolina. By 1748 there were thirty Moravian "localities," communities modeled after Herrnhut in Germany. Each locality, including the original ones at Bethlehem and Nazareth, had two classes of adherents — "communicant members" and "society members" — an outer and an inner membership similar to that of Herrnhut.[47] The society members lived semi-communally on land owned by the church, and worked in small industries run by the community. Communicant members lived as near as possible on their own land, working their own farms and enterprises, but otherwise participated fully in the life of the church.

The Moravians brought uniquely Herrnhut practices to America, such as fervent singing, emotional prayer meetings, small groups ("choirs") for devotion and spiritual formation, New Year's Eve "watch night" services, Easter "sunrise" services, and respect — if not veneration — for Zinzendorf, who arrived among them in 1741. During his time in Pennsylvania, Zinzendorf led four main efforts. First, he helped Spangenberg organize Bethlehem as a "peculiar place" — a center of spiritual renewal in the New World for all people.[48] Second, he visited not only Moravian meetings and homes but also and especially non-Moravian Lutheran churches and homes. Muhlenberg and other Lutheran leaders became concerned that he was attempting to proselytize their congregants into his fold, which he probably was. At these meetings, Zinzendorf asked people about their relationship with God, preached his peculiar brand of Jesus-mysticism, and condemned unconverted church leaders and ministers. Third, Zinzendorf organized the "Pennsylvania Synods" of Moravians, including as many non-Moravian Lutherans as possible, and also began setting up his "Congregation of God in the Spirit." Finally, he attempted to evangelize Native American communities, an effort that met with little success. Eventually

---

47. John R. Weinlick, "Moravianism in the American Colonies," in *Continental Pietism and Early American Christianity*, ed. Stoeffler, pp. 151-52.

48. Weinlick, "Moravianism in the American Colonies," p. 145.

he left the American Moravian movement in Spangenberg's capable hands, but the American Moravian Church did not gain complete independence from Herrnhut until the mid-nineteenth century.

According to John Weinlick, "Colonial Moravians may be seen as a tiny minority which, as is so often the case with minorities, made a contribution to American life far beyond what might have been expected."[49] The Moravian Church still exists well into the twenty-first century, although it is not numerically large and is concentrated still in North Carolina and Pennsylvania. However, its influence in American religious history is far greater than its size would suggest, partly because of all the other denominations it has spawned or directly influenced.

Before turning finally to the single most significant organizational influence of Pietism in British and American religion, Methodism and its offshoots, some account must be given of the various "Brethren" churches spawned by Pietism — not to be confused with the Moravian Brethren. The story of the Brethren churches is so complicated and convoluted that it requires an entire volume even to begin to do justice to it. Here only a few aspects of that story can be told. Let it be known to the reader, however, that most of the American denominations known as "Brethren" are rooted in Pietism.[50]

The European beginnings of the Brethren movement(s) are murky; there is no single founding person or event. According to the earliest Brethren records, the movement arose out of radical Pietist dissatisfaction with state churches in Southwestern Germany and a religious revival which swept through that area at the beginning of the eighteenth century. Sometime during the summer of 1708, a group of these revived Protestants, having experienced an evangelical awakening that led them out of the state churches and into Anabaptist-like practices of believer's baptism and foot-washing, met to form a new church network. One of the earliest descriptions of the group comes from a Quaker who interviewed Brethren

49. Weinlick, "Moravianism in the American Colonies," p. 162.
50. Donald F. Durnbaugh has been the foremost American historian of the Brethren movement and its offshoots in America. Speaking of this movement, which some historians consider primarily Anabaptist, Durnbaugh proclaims, "Brethren rootage in Pietism is irrefutable." See "The Brethren in Early American Church Life," in *Continental Pietism and Early American Christianity*, ed. Stoeffler, p. 227.

about their beginnings. Although they could not identify a particular event or person as the catalyst,[51] they described a revival in Germany much like the Great Awakening. Donald Durnbaugh, speaking of these Brethren beginnings, writes,

> The realization of personal sinfulness, the criticism of unregenerate ministers, the unwillingness to commune with a mixed multitude [in church life — converted and unconverted worshiping together equally as members], the rejection of formalized prayers and liturgies, the meetings outside the church structures for small prayer fellowships — these are hallmarks of the revival spirit.[52]

Eventually this Pietist group with Anabaptist features became known throughout Europe (and later in America) as "Dunkers," because they baptized only believers by immersing them three times — in the name of the Father, then in the name of the Son, and then in the name of the Spirit. They were also known especially in English-speaking countries as "German Baptist Brethren." For the most part, they were pacifists, refusing to participate in war and regarding peace-making as a major part of the gospel message. They were also radically congregational with no denominational hierarchy. It has always been easy to confuse them with Anabaptists and, indeed, the two have mingled much.

To make a long and complicated story ridiculously brief and overly simplistic, these German Brethren came to America due to persecution in Germany, settling first in Pennsylvania in 1719, then spreading out into the middle colonies. Some of them founded utopian religious communities, such as the famous Ephrata, in Pennsylvania; such communities were also founded in Missouri and Oregon. The main group, however, settled into typically American church life, mingling with Mennonites, Methodists, and even Pietist Lutherans. One notable difference between this group and their theological cousins, the Mennonites, was that "the Brethren were

---

51. Durnbaugh and some other Brethren scholars identify the leader of the original Brethren as Alexander Mack, "a miller stemming from a well-situated burgher family near Heidelberg, Germany." See *The Believers' Church: The History and Character of Radical Protestantism* (London: Macmillan, 1968), p. 120.

52. Durnbaugh, *The Believers' Church*, p. 231.

much more zealous and lively than the quiet Mennonites."[53] They tended
to be revivalistic and activist in terms of social reform efforts, made mainly
by means of communal experiments meant to demonstrate the spirit of
the kingdom of God to the larger world around them.

Philip William Otterbein emerged as a Brethren spokesman and
leader, though not all Brethren followed him. Born in Germany and a
minister of Reformed churches in America, Otterbein eventually joined a
Brethren church and helped organize Brethren congregations into a new
denomination that came to be called the United Brethren in Christ — a denomination that divided several times in several ways over the next couple
of centuries. Its remnants and relics remain, including one by the original
name, and Otterbein is regarded as an important theological influence by
most of these groups. He intentionally bridged the gap between Reformed
Protestants (who originally ordained him) and Methodists (who he also
joined and served as an elder). According to Otterbein, "Christ and his
death do us no good unless Christ enters within us, destroying the kingdom of Satan within us, penetrating and renewing our spirit, soul, and
body with His light and life."[54]

Out of the original Dunkers or German Baptist Brethren movement
emerged many uniquely American Pietist denominations, colleges, and
missionary agencies. Some of them remain fervently evangelical into the
twenty-first century, whereas others have tended more toward mainline
Protestantism. The largest is the mainline Church of the Brethren, a member of the National Council of Churches. Somewhat smaller and more
conservative are the Brethren Church (Ashland), the Brethren in Christ
Church, the Church of the United Brethren in Christ, and the Fellowship
of Grace Brethren Churches. Some Brethren groups merged with other
denominations to form ecumenical unions such as the United Churches
of Christ and even the United Methodist Church (formed by a union of
the Evangelical United Brethren and the Methodist Episcopal Church).
Because these Brethren, stemming from the German Baptist Brethren,
are broken up into numerous small groups, the movement as a whole

---

53. Durnbaugh, *The Believers' Church,* p. 237.

54. Otterbein, quoted in J. Stephen O'Malley, *Early German-American Evangelicalism* (Lanham, Md.: Scarecrow Press, 1995), p. 29.

gets undeserved inattention in accounts of American religious history. Their influence, however, has been far greater than their numbers — especially by means of the colleges they have founded such as Messiah College (Grantham, Pennsylvania) and Grace College (Winona Lake, Indiana).

Pietism and Methodism

As mentioned previously, Pietism had a major influence on the Wesleys and early Methodism. Stoeffler notes that some "religious societies" in England influenced the Wesley family; some of them were similar to Pietism but lacked the experience of peace and joy common in true Pietism.[55] One has to distinguish between "piety" as deep devotion and "Pietism" as a life-transforming experience that includes feelings of peace and joy. It was the latter that John Wesley felt during and after his famous Aldersgate Street (London) experience on May 24, 1738, when his heart was "strangely warmed": he knew for the first time that his sins were forgiven, and he felt a new dimension of relationship with God through Jesus Christ.

That experience happened to the founder of Methodism at a Moravian meeting, which he reluctantly attended with his Pietist/Moravian friend Peter Böhler. There are many stories of Wesley's contacts with Pietists (mostly Moravians), and a number of these stories appear in Wesley's own journals, so there can be no doubt about Pietism's influence on him and early Methodism. After his heart-warming experience at the Moravian meeting in London, Wesley traveled to Herrnhut in Germany and spent time with Zinzendorf. They had lengthy conversations about many subjects, including theology. Eventually they agreed to disagree about some doctrines, including Wesley's idea of "Christian perfection." Wesley went home thinking that Zinzendorf was more than a little odd, and he regarded the Moravians' treatment of him as far too reverential. Still, many of Zinzendorf's ideas and especially his profound love of Jesus shaped the piety and theology of both John and Charles Wesley.

55. Stoeffler, "Pietism, the Wesleys, and Methodist Beginnings in America," pp. 186-88.

Stoeffler examines another influence on John Wesley's thought — Johann Albrecht Bengel. Bengel's writings, including *Gnomon Novi Testamenti*, were Wesley's "constant companion while he wrote the bulk of his *Notes* [on the New Testament]."[56] According to Stoeffler, "In the writings of both men one finds an uncommon devotion to a way of life which is centered in love for God and man."[57]

Stoeffler expresses the scholarly consensus when he writes that "early Methodism owed a considerable debt to the older movement of Continental Pietism"[58] and that "it was his contact with the Moravians . . . which gradually turned Wesley the seeker into Wesley the possessor of that experiential 'knowledge' of God which Pietists universally considered basic to the religious life."[59] Early Wesleyan Methodism, then, became a major conduit of Pietism to Great Britain and America as Methodism spread to the colonies and then became the major form of Protestantism in the United States during the nineteenth century. This early Methodism displayed virtually all of the common hallmarks of the Pietist ethos described in Chapter Five.

Radical Pietism in America

Very little mention has been made here of the many radical Pietist social experiments in colonial America. One of the earliest and most notable ones was the famous Ephrata community in Pennsylvania, founded by Pietist leader Conrad Beissel. But perhaps the best-known one (at least to twenty-first-century Americans) is the Amana Colonies of Iowa. Tourists still flock to what's left of them near Iowa City, and, of course, Amana appliances fill the kitchens and laundry rooms of American homes. Many people wrongly identify Amanas with Anabaptists such as the Amish, though there's no historical connection between them. The Amanas were (and are) Pietist followers of German spiritual leaders Eberhard Gruber and Johann Rock, founders of the Community of True Inspiration, the

---

56. Stoeffler, "Pietism, the Wesleys, and Methodist Beginnings in America," p. 199.
57. Stoeffler, "Pietism, the Wesleys, and Methodist Beginnings in America," p. 200.
58. Stoeffler, "Pietism, the Wesleys, and Methodist Beginnings in America," p. 201.
59. Stoeffler, "Pietism, the Wesleys, and Methodist Beginnings in America," p. 191.

official name of the Amana church. Like many radical Pietists, they emigrated to America in the early nineteenth century, eventually settling in Iowa. There they founded seven villages where they attempted to restore the communal life of the early Christian church in Jerusalem.

Pietist intentional Christian communities like Ephrata and the Amanas flourished across America during colonial times and into the nineteenth century. Many died out or changed so dramatically that they are no longer representative of what they were. Some exist now only as historic "pioneer" villages for tourists. Still, similar Christian intentional communities based on a Pietist ethos occasionally come into existence. A more recent one is Bethany Fellowship in suburban Minneapolis, Minnesota, that flourished especially in the 1950s and 1960s and founded several industries, including a well-known publishing house.

During the nineteenth century, many immigrants to America from Scandinavia were Pietists who left under persecution when fines and even the threat of jail sentences were imposed on Christians who met in conventicles for prayer and Bible study outside the confines of the state churches. Several American denominations that exist into the twenty-first century were founded by these Scandinavian Pietists, including most notably the Baptist General Conference (originally the Swedish Baptist Conference and now Converge Worldwide), the Evangelical Free Church (a union of the Swedish Evangelical Free Mission and the Norwegian-Danish Evangelical Free Church Association), and the Evangelical Covenant Church of America (originally the Swedish Evangelical Mission Covenant of America). These three strongly evangelical denominations and their institutions (Bethel University, Trinity University and Divinity School, and North Park University) have been influential in the formation of evangelicalism in the twentieth century and remain influential among evangelicals into the twenty-first century. Many of their adherents have forgotten their Pietist (to say nothing of their Scandinavian) roots, but they and many other American denominations arose out of Pietism and continue to embody a Pietist ethos, whether or not they call it that.

Conclusion

Pietism, both as a movement and as an ethos, made an early and enduring imprint on North American Christianity. In fact, some scholars of American religion see Pietism, along with Puritanism, as the two most influential types of Christianity in America. High school and college courses still emphasize Puritanism, however, and tend to neglect Pietism. The evidence compiled in this chapter justifies the call to rediscover Pietism as a formative "flavor" of American religion and to reclaim it as a main ingredient in the evangelical recipe.

CHAPTER SEVEN

Pietism for a New Era

The Re-invention of Pietism in the Nineteenth Century

The story of Pietism in nineteenth-century Europe is one of re-invention. The older Pietism of Spener, Francke, and Zinzendorf faded, as historical movements are wont to do, but this did not spell the end of Pietism — simply its recombination in new and surprising expressions which can be read as attempts to deal with new challenges. These new expressions of the older Pietist impulse were often at odds with each other. The goal of this chapter is not to offer an exhaustive portrait, but to highlight some of the key developments and to indicate some of the most important trajectories that the Pietist impulse took in the nineteenth century.

In what follows, we offer a brief consideration of the breakdown of the older Pietism at the end of the eighteenth century, followed by a discussion of some attempts to grapple with the Enlightenment by figures influenced by Pietism. We finish with a consideration of the most significant trajectories of the Pietist ethos in the nineteenth century: the Awakening movement and impulses associated with the Blumhardts.

Modernity and the Breakdown of the Older Pietism

As the eighteenth century came to a close, the older Pietism, particularly in northern Germany, was undergoing transformation due to both developments from within the movement and challenges from without. The internal development has much to do with the vacuum of leadership that developed after the passing of the earliest key figures. Two of the most important movements discussed earlier — Hallensian and Moravian Pietism — both suffered after the deaths of Francke (d. 1727) and Zinzendorf (d. 1760). The leadership of the Halle Institutions fell to Francke's son, Gotthilf August Francke (1696-1769), who, not possessed of the charismatic personality and strong will of his father, was unable to hold together the various strands within the Hallensian family.[1] Although the Halle vision had managed some success in the courts of Europe — notably in Prussia and Denmark — by the mid-eighteenth century, its influence had waned considerably.[2]

The Moravian movement fared somewhat better after Zinzendorf's death, though under the leadership of August Gottlieb Spangenberg (1704-1792), the dynamism of the theological and ecclesiological experimentation of Zinzendorf was tempered, and the Moravian movement became more conservative both theologically and ecclesially, as it embraced the Augsburg Confession in an attempt to avoid being labeled a sect.[3] Nevertheless, the spiritual energy and innovations unleashed by the earlier Pietists had made their impact on the larger society, and the important Pietist phenomenon of the "conventicle meeting" continued to exert a profound influence in certain circles.[4]

The transformations within the Pietist movement were also prompted in part by the remarkable transformations within Western society nor-

1. See Benjamin Marschke, "Halle Pietism and Politics in Prussia and Beyond," in *A Companion to German Pietism (1600-1800)*, ed. Douglas H. Shantz (Leiden: E. J. Brill, forthcoming).

2. For a discussion of Halle Pietism's fortunes at the Prussian court, see Benjamin Marschke, "Halle Pietism and Politics in Prussia and Beyond"; and Marschke, "Halle Pietism and the Prussian State: Infiltration, Dissent, and Subversion," in *Pietism in Germany and North America, 1680-1820*, ed. Jonathan Strom, Hartmut Lehmann, and James Van Horn Melton (Burlington, Vt.: Ashgate, 2009), pp. 217-28. For a discussion of the Danish context, see Christopher B. Barnett, *Kierkegaard, Pietism, and Holiness* (Burlington, Vt.: Ashgate, 2001), pp. 37-47. See also Nicholas Hope, *German and Scandinavian Protestantism, 1700-1918* (Oxford: Clarendon Press, 1995), pp. 154-65.

3. See Dietrich Meyer, "Zinzendorf und Herrnhut," in *Geschichte des Pietismus*, vol. 2: *Der Pietismus im achtzehnten Jahrhundert*, ed. Martin Brecht and Klaus Deppermann (Göttingen: Vandenhoeck & Ruprecht, 1995), pp. 60-63.

4. See Horst Weigelt, "Der Pietismus im Übergang vom 18. zum 19. Jahrhundert," in *Geschichte des Pietismus*, vol. 2, ed. Brecht and Deppermann, pp. 744-45.

mally gathered together under the heading "modernity." Although complex and reaching back into the seventeenth century, modernity is generally associated with the intellectual ferment produced by the Enlightenment and the subsequent process of "secularization," or gradual removal of religious (i.e., Christian) mores and ideas from public discourse and reasoning. Though scholars argue about the nature and extent of secularization, and though the process of secularization looked different in different contexts,[5] there can be little doubt that Western culture, especially in Europe, changed remarkably in regard to the public role of religion, and in regard to the intellectual and theological content of the Christian faith. The hegemony of theological and religious explanations of natural phenomena quickly receded as new discoveries in the natural sciences occurred rapidly. At the same time, the social sciences (sociology, economics, and so on) and potent political philosophies — especially communism after 1848 — also offered comprehensive explanations of human behavior and society without recourse to God. Of great importance for the beginning of the period were the French Revolution (1789) and the Napoleonic Wars (1803-1815), both of which shook the foundations of the *Ancien Régime.*

The movements of Rationalism, Romanticism, and Idealism each contributed to the intellectual and religious fervor in Germany and beyond. The effect of Enlightenment thought on the status of Hallensian Pietism is amply illustrated by the return of rationalist philosopher Christian Wolff to the university faculty in 1740. Through the opposition of August Hermann Francke, Wolff had been unceremoniously asked to leave the University of Halle in 1723 by Friedrich Wilhelm I because his "lectures 'contradicted revealed religion.'"[6] However, Friedrich's successor, Friedrich II (called Friedrich the Great), was far more congenial to Enlightenment ideas, and immediately upon his accession to the throne of Prussia in 1740, he invited Wolff to resume his teaching career at the University of Halle. The return of Wolff was hailed as a major victory for the Enlighten-

5. For the most recent and extensive treatment of "secularization," see Charles Taylor, *A Secular Age* (Cambridge, Mass.: Belknap Press of Harvard University Press, 2007).

6. Thomas Albert Howard, *Protestant Theology and the Making of the Modern German University* (Oxford: Oxford University Press, 2006), p. 96.

ment in Germany, and marked the end of Pietist hegemony at Halle, such that the university "became a leading centre of what was often labeled 'rationalism' *(Rationalismus)* or 'neology' *(Neologie)* in the late eighteenth century."[7]

The intellectual challenge that modern thought presented to Christianity was substantial. In Germany in particular, the philosophical revolution initiated by Immanuel Kant (1724-1804) reduced theological knowledge to the status of moral postulates. In Kant's system, "God" could not be known as a loving and self-giving relational person because God existed beyond the categories of human reason. God was relegated to the "noumenal" realm — the realm of spirit or the metaphysical realm, inaccessible to human reason — while human reason was geared to deal only with the "phenomenal" realm — or the realm of sense experience.

This, of course, did not mean that God did not exist; it simply meant that God couldn't be known through the categories of theoretical or "pure" reason, an assertion which ruled out the possibility that divine revelation — if such a thing existed — was possessed of rational content. Kant conceded, however, that the idea of "God" could be affirmed in the realm of ethics, as "God" represented the animating force which compelled human beings to choose to do the good.[8] Kant argued that "God" represented the idea that those who do good will receive their just reward, whether in this life or the next.[9] According to Kant, the content and end of religion was moral. However, even here, revealed religion was to be subject to the religion of reason.[10]

7. Howard, *Protestant Theology and the Making of the Modern German University,* p. 98.

8. See Gary Dorrien, *Kantian Reason and Hegelian Spirit: The Idealistic Logic of Modern Theology* (Oxford: Wiley-Blackwell, 2012), pp. 49-50.

9. See Hendrikus Berkhof, *Two Hundred Years of Theology: Report of a Personal Journey* (Grand Rapids: Wm. B. Eerdmans, 1989), pp. 1-15.

10. See Immanuel Kant, *Religion within the Boundaries of Mere Reason,* in Immanuel Kant, *Religion and Rational Theology,* translated and edited by Allen Wood and George Di Giovanni (Cambridge: Cambridge University Press, 1996), pp. 138-46.

Friedrich Schleiermacher: A "Herrnhutter of a Higher Order"?

Although offering a concession that there might be a God after all and that this God might have some formal role in public and private morality, Kant's philosophy, if embraced, made traditional theology almost impossible and its status in the intellectual culture of Europe deeply problematic.[11] Among theologians, Friedrich Schleiermacher (1768-1834) made the most serious attempt to deal with the implications of Kant's philosophy for theology. Schleiermacher offered an alternative theological orientation built on the category of the "feeling of absolute dependence," which is not to be confused with simple "feelings" or "emotions."[12] Rather, accepting Kant's strictures on human knowledge, Schleiermacher conceded that human reason has access only to the phenomenal realm. However, he argued that the pre-cognitive intuition that every living thing and the cosmos as a whole are absolutely dependent for their existence on a greater power (i.e., God)[13] is itself a feeling that occurs within the phenomenal realm and, as such, can be known. Schleiermacher argued that through careful analysis of the various states of Christian consciousness, one can deduce many of the postulates of traditional Christian theology, though shorn of their traditional metaphysical garb.[14]

Like many of the great German luminaries from the late eighteenth and early nineteenth century, Schleiermacher's relationship vis-à-vis Pietism is complicated. Raised in the conservative Moravianism of the late eighteenth century,[15] Schleiermacher experienced a crisis of faith while

---

11. For instance, J. G. Fichte (1762-1814), one of Kant's most important successors, argued that theology should not have its own faculty in the university. See Dorrien, *Kantian Reason and Hegelian Spirit*, p. 97; and Howard, *Protestant Theology and the Making of the Modern German University*, pp. 130-211.

12. For an accessible discussion of this concept, see Terrence N. Tice, *Schleiermacher* (Nashville: Abingdon Press, 2006), pp. 18-31.

13. See Friedrich Schleiermacher, *On Religion: Speeches to Its Cultured Despisers*, trans. John Oman (New York: Harper & Brothers, 1958), p. 36.

14. This was the intention behind Schleiermacher's dogmatic text *The Christian Faith*. See Friedrich Schleiermacher, *The Christian Faith*, 2 vols., ed. H. R. Mackintosh and J. S. Stewart (New York: Harper & Row, 1963), pp. 76-93.

15. See Dorette Seibert, "Auf dem Weg zum 'Herrnhuter höherer Ordnung'? Schleiermacher und Herrnhut," *Evangelische Theologie* 56, no. 5 (1996): 400-406.

attending the Moravian seminary at Barby, near Wittenberg. The crisis was brought on by his exposure to Enlightenment writers like Goethe and Kant; Schleiermacher helped to smuggle their works into the closed environment at Barby.[16] By 1786, a year after his matriculation at Barby, Schleiermacher revealed to his father, a strict Moravian, the doubts he was harboring about the traditional doctrines of Christ's divinity.[17] Schleiermacher's existential crisis, and a conflict with the seminary authorities, led him to leave the school in 1787 to study at the University of Halle, then a bastion of Enlightenment thought. He would eventually inaugurate a new era in the history of theology with the publication of his *On Religion: Speeches to Its Cultured Despisers* (1799). With the publication of this volume, Schleiermacher's name would forever be associated with German liberal theology.

Schleiermacher's direct connection with late-eighteenth-century Moravianism, the central role that he gave to piety and *Gefühl* ("feeling"), his deep-seated Christocentrism, the emphasis that he placed on the importance of community in his theology — all these things placed him on the boundary of a consideration of the re-invention of Pietism in the nineteenth century. In *Speeches*, Schleiermacher described true religion as the "sense and taste for the infinite,"[18] which he also named "piety." His appeal to this term, especially given the derision with which it was perceived by his audience — the so-called cultured despisers — was rooted in his own pietistic upbringing,[19] and his assertion that true religion consisted in a genuine, heartfelt experience also clearly echoed Pietist sentiments.[20] Schleiermacher's Jesus-centered conception of redemption also shared some formal parallels with Moravian, Jesus-centered piety:

> He [Christ] is the unity and center of our common life, and we are each only limbs of his body, animated by him, and so effective through him

16. See Martin Redeker, *Schleiermacher: Life and Thought* (Philadelphia: Fortress Press, 1973), p. 12.

17. See Redeker, *Schleiermacher*, pp. 13-14.

18. Schleiermacher, *On Religion*, p. 39.

19. See Tenzan Eaghll, "From Pietism to Romanticism: The Early Life and Work of Friedrich Schleiermacher," in *The Pietist Impulse in Christianity*, ed. Christian T. Collins Winn et al. (Eugene, Ore.: Pickwick Publications, 2011), p. 110.

20. See Schleiermacher, *On Religion*, p. 91.

and for him. Our goal and aspiration consist solely in furthering that work which God sent him into the world to accomplish, and everything else must relate to that purpose.[21]

It would be hard to deny that such a sentiment could be embraced by someone like Zinzendorf. Likewise, as other scholars have argued, both the stress laid on the communal nature of faith and the structural shape of those communities owe something to Pietism.[22]

Nevertheless, despite the formal parallels, the great "Herrnhutter of a higher order," as Schleiermacher called himself,[23] was largely, though not totally, rejected by the heirs of Pietism in the nineteenth century. There were, of course, good grounds for this. As James Nelson puts it, "For Moravian piety the experience of God par excellence was feeling *(Gefühl)*, not of 'utter dependence' or of the 'World Spirit,' but of being with Jesus of Nazareth, who was also 'very God' as he walked on this earth."[24] Schleiermacher described Jesus as the great exemplar of "God-consciousness" (Schleiermacher's term for the awakened and cultivated "feeling of absolute dependence" within a given individual); Jesus' influence as Redeemer had filtered into the historical process and made its way across the ages to the present. This was a far cry from the Pietist assumption that it was the living, risen Jesus who was encountered in the event of faith. Baron von Kottwitz (1757-1843), a leading figure in the German Awakening (about which we will speak shortly), summed up the general judgment of Schleiermacher among members of the Awakening movement when he opined that Schleiermacher's Christ was "shrouded in mist."[25]

21. Friedrich Schleiermacher, "Christ the Liberator," in Friedrich Schleiermacher, *Servant of the Word: Selected Sermons of Friedrich Schleiermacher,* trans. Dawn De Vries (Philadelphia: Fortress Press, 1987), p. 55.

22. See Eaghll, "From Pietism to Romanticism," pp. 114-18; and Redeker, *Schleiermacher,* pp. 50-54.

23. See Richard Crouter, "Introduction," in Friedrich Schleiermacher, *On Religion: Speeches to Its Cultured Despisers,* translated and edited by Richard Crouter (Cambridge: Cambridge University Press, 1996), p. xiii.

24. James D. Nelson, "Piety and Invention: A Study of the Dynamic Roots to Intellectual Creativity in Schleiermacher," in *The Impact of the Church upon Its Culture,* ed. Jerald C. Brauer (Chicago: University of Chicago Press, 1968), p. 315.

25. Gustav Adolph Benrath, "Die Erweckung innerhalb der deutschen Landes-

Søren Kierkegaard and the Critique of Danish Christendom

Another heir of earlier Pietism — especially of the Moravian form — who sought to wrestle with the critical legacy of the Enlightenment was Søren Kierkegaard (1813-1855). Born in Copenhagen, Kierkegaard was the seventh child of Michael Pedersen Kierkegaard (1756-1838),[26] who had been exposed to Moravian Pietism at least since 1773 and was a prominent member of the Moravian Society in Copenhagen. Hallensian Pietism had come to Denmark in the early eighteenth century, with the Danish court offering an especially fertile ground for the Halle missionary movement. Moravianism's presence in Denmark began in the late 1720s; the 1731 visit of Zinzendorf to Copenhagen to attend the coronation of Christian VI marked an important turning point. The *Brødersocetet* of which Michael Pedersen was later a member was founded in Copenhagen in 1739.[27]

Søren, a brilliant child, grew up in a context indelibly shaped by his father's pietistic leanings.[28] In addition to attending Moravian Society meetings on Sunday afternoons, the family had a library containing numerous volumes of *Erbauungsliteratur*, or "devotional literature," which was a key literary genre in Pietism.[29] There is ample evidence that Kierkegaard read and was familiar with this literature. His journals show special affection for Johann Arndt, but also reveal knowledge of Spener, Francke, and Gerhard Tersteegen, as well as the Danish Pietist hymnodist Hans Adolph Brorson.[30]

Scholars debate the precise effect of this literature and the attendant

---

kirchen 1815-1888. Ein Überblick," in *Geschichte des Pietismus*, vol. 3: *Der Pietismus im neunzehnten und zwanzigsten Jahrhundert*, ed. Ulrich Gäbler (Göttingen: Vandenhoeck & Ruprecht, 2000), p. 162.

26. Joachim Garff, *Søren Kierkegaard: A Biography* (Princeton: Princeton University Press, 2004), p. 8.

27. Barnett, *Kierkegaard, Pietism, and Holiness*, p. 43.

28. Kyle Roberts, "The Living Word and the Word of God: The Pietist Impulse in Kierkegaard and Gruntvig," in *The Pietist Impulse in Christianity*, ed. Collins Winn et al., p. 124.

29. Barnett, *Kierkegaard, Pietism, and Holiness*, p. 55.

30. See Barnett, *Kierkegaard, Pietism, and Holiness*, pp. 63-107.

themes of Pietism in Kierkegaard's thought.[31] Kierkegaard's own assessment of Pietism highlights the complexity:

> Yes, indeed, pietism (properly understood, not simply in the sense of abstaining from dancing and such externals, no, in the sense of witnessing for the truth and suffering for it, together with the understanding that suffering in this world belongs to being a Christian, and that a shrewd and secular conformity with this world is unchristian) — yes, indeed, pietism is the one and only consequence of Christianity.[32]

In light of the long qualifier, the element in Pietism that Kierkegaard was drawn to was clearly the search for an "authentic Christianity." The themes in Kierkegaard's thought that either resonate with or are to some extent dependent upon Pietism are those concerned with genuine Christian existence. As Joseph Ballan describes it, "In response to what he perceives as the cheapening of grace and the corruption of Christianity, Kierkegaard follows Arndt in stressing the centrality of discipleship and the imitation of Christ in the lives of individual Christians."[33] Themes such as the "imitation of Christ," "subjectivity," "truth as appropriation," the centrality of Scripture as a means for spiritual transformation, the radical attack on Christendom — all these owe something to Pietism's relentless search for a living Christianity. Likewise, the genre of "upbuilding discourses" or edifying literature whose purpose was to encourage the individual in the search for an authentic Christian life, of which Kierkegaard wrote quite a bit, also bears the mark of Pietism.

At the same time, however, Kierkegaard was also critical of the legal-

---

31. For instance, see the following: Marie Mikulová Thulstrup, "Pietism," in *Kierkegaard and Great Traditions*, ed. Niels Thulstrup and M. Mikulová Thulstrup (Copenhagen: C. A. Reitzels Boghandel, 1981), pp. 173-222; Joseph Ballan, "Johann Arndt: The Pietist Impulse in Kierkegaard and Seventeenth-Century Lutheran Devotional Literature," and "August Hermann Francke: Kierkegaard on the Kernel and Husk of Pietist Theology," in *Kierkegaard and the Renaissance and Modern Traditions*, vol. 2: *Theology*, ed. J. Stewart (Burlington, Vt.: Ashgate, 2009), pp. 149-56, 21-30; and Barnett, *Kierkegaard, Pietism, and Holiness*.

32. Søren Kierkegaard, *Journals and Papers*, vol. 3 (Bloomington: Indiana University Press, 1976), p. 3318.

33. Ballan, "Johann Arndt," p. 28.

istic and pusillanimous aspects of Pietism which he particularly discerned in Halle Pietism as it had developed into the early nineteenth century. "For Kierkegaard, Halle Pietism is, above all, a sociopolitical phenomenon, subject to his developing critique of the history of established Christianity as the history of Christianity's decline or annulment."[34] The author of the "Attack upon Christendom" saw the Hallensian project, especially as it melded with the Lutheran State Church in Denmark, as an expression of almost total hypocrisy. Rather than working to transform individuals into passionate imitators of Christ, Halle Pietism developed into a social-political project which promoted "a Christianity centered on expedient civic works and 'proper' ethical conduct."[35] In Kierkegaard's estimation, it missed the point of imitation by replacing the intense and passionate life of Christian discipleship with a set of rules:

> Among the reasons against dancing Francke gives there is one which is so lofty or high that one almost has to laugh — he says that dancing conflicts with "the imitation of Christ." No doubt a dancing partner really does not look like an "imitator of Christ," but here, as we say of the voice, Francke's voice breaks into a falsetto; it is too high.[36]

Kierkegaard's critique of the routinization and embourgeoisement of Pietism — that is, its transformation into establishment Christianity, the very thing it initially revolted against — was, as we will see, shared by many of the heirs of Pietism in the nineteenth century. As such, this was a critique that was internal to Pietism itself.[37]

The German Awakening Movement

Of far greater importance than either Schleiermacher or Kierkegaard for understanding the re-invention of Pietism in the nineteenth century was the so-called German Awakening movement *(Erweckungsbewegung)*. Al-

---

34. Ballan, "August Hermann Francke," p. 151.
35. Barnett, *Kierkegaard, Pietism, and Holiness*, p. 138.
36. Kierkegaard, *Journals and Papers*, vol. 3, p. 3322.
37. Barnett, *Kierkegaard, Pietism, and Holiness*, p. 90.

though there is much debate about whether or not the "Awakened" actually saw themselves as involved in a single "movement,"[38] scholars use the term to identify a set of common commitments among figures located in northern Germany (Wuppertal and especially Prussia) and southwestern Germany (Württemberg and Basel).[39] These neo-Pietists, as they have also been called, were committed to resisting what they perceived as a rising tide of rationalism and anti clericalism flowing from the French Enlightenment through works of mercy in the form of organized voluntary societies bent on expressing "faith active in love."[40] Doctrinally and politically conservative, these neo-Pietists were industrious in establishing voluntary societies committed to foreign mission work, publishing, and especially poor relief.

Connected to other movements in Europe, such as the Dutch *Réveil*, which later produced Abraham Kuyper (1837-1920),[41] and the Swedish revival sparked by the preaching of the Scottish Methodist George Scott (b. 1804) and the work of Carl Olof Rosenius (1816-1868),[42] it is nevertheless difficult to establish precisely when the Awakening movement began in German-speaking lands. The year 1815 has become a useful historical marker, as it often appeared in the writings and preaching of the Awakened.[43] This was the year of Napoleon's defeat and the restoration of the Prussian monarchy. In general, the Awakened in northern Germany, like Schleiermacher, were deeply committed Prussian patriots. Their desire for the liberation of Prussia from French domination was shared in small

---

38. See Hartmut Lehmann, "*Erweckungsbewegung* as Religious Experience or Historiographical Construct: The Case of Ludwig Hofacker," in Hartmut Lehmann, *Religiöse Erweckung in gottferner Zeit: Studien zur Pietismusforschung* (Göttingen: Wallstein Verlag, 2010), pp. 120-31; and David Crowner and Gerald Christianson, "General Introduction," in *The Spirituality of the German Awakening*, ed. David Crowner and Gerald Christianson (Mahwah, N.J.: Paulist Press, 2003), p. 6.

39. See Crowner and Christianson, "General Introduction," pp. 16-20.

40. See Crowner and Christianson, "General Introduction," p. 7.

41. See Ulrich Gäbler, "Evangelikalismus und Réveil," in *Geschichte des Pietismus*, vol. 3, ed. Gäbler, pp. 64-74.

42. See Karl A. Olsson, *By One Spirit: A History of the Evangelical Covenant Church in America* (Chicago: Covenant Press, 1984), pp. 42-58.

43. See Benrath, "Die Erweckung innerhalb der deutschen Landeskirchen 1815-1888," p. 155.

group meetings (whose roots went back to the older Pietism) throughout Berlin and other cities and villages in Prussia. The restoration of the
Prussian monarchy was widely hailed as an event of eschatological significance, while another key date was the 1840 accession of the pious king
Frederick Wilhelm IV (1795-1861), himself a friend and promoter of Awakening causes until he succumbed to mental illness in 1857.[44]

Awakened preachers exhibited a dialectical relationship to the Enlightenment. Although they emphatically rejected the rationalism of the
Enlightenment, neo-Pietists did embrace elements of German Idealism,
especially the emphasis on "personhood, the inner life, and life in the eternal world."[45] And neo-Pietists shared a number of other broad assumptions with the Enlightenment as well:

> In their skepticism of traditional church structures, as well as in their or-
> ganization of new initiatives, they shared a spirit of rational inquiry that
> does not simply accept the status quo. Like the leaders of the Enlighten-
> ment, the Awakened desired liberation from strictures of the past and
> were optimistic about what could be achieved. Both camps espoused
> more individual autonomy, more personal responsibility, and a greater
> sense of individual worth. The ecumenical spirit of the Awakening was
> also related, if only indirectly, to the scientific method's dispassionate
> and unified view of the world, and the Awakening's emphasis on the
> practice of faith and on the importance of experience corresponds to
> the Enlightenment's delight in empirical proof.[46]

Their relationship to the older Pietism was equally complex. The perception among the Awakened was that by the end of the eighteenth century,
the older Pietism had become too withdrawn, expressing itself only in
the form of small cell-group meetings.[47] What was required in the cur-

---

44. See John E. Groh, *Nineteenth-Century German Protestantism: The Church as
Social Model* (Washington, D.C.: University Press of America, 1982), p. 101. Nicholas
Hope notes that by 1830, "an awakened, Evangelical mood was visible in most German
lands. . . ." See Hope, *German and Scandinavian Protestantism, 1700-1918*, p. 367.

45. Groh, *Nineteenth-Century German Protestantism*, p. 109.

46. Crowner and Christianson, "General Introduction," pp. 13-14.

47. See Groh, *Nineteenth-Century German Protestantism*, p. 105.

rent situation was a renewed commitment to engaging society, with a new attention to history and nature.[48] Interest in traditional soteriology (i.e., sin, salvation, and the experience of new birth) was placed alongside growing interest in theological anthropology (i.e., the pious "inner self" and a fully embodied Christian existence). A concern for the authority and reliability of Scripture was combined with eschatologically derived theories of "salvation history" which enabled the Awakened to read "the signs of the times." And, of course, the importance of community and social-ethical action was infused with certain strands of nationalism.[49] The Awakened were committed to a vision of living Christianity which resonated deeply with the earlier thought of Arndt, Spener, and Zinzendorf, but they were also committed to revitalizing — re-Christianizing, as they saw it — their culture, which required that they engage the public realm in a new way.

Friedrich August G. Tholuck

August Tholuck (1799-1877) was by far the most important theological figure of the *Erweckungsbewegung*. Born in Breslau in 1799, Tholuck was a brilliant linguist, having reasonably mastered some nineteen languages by the age of thirteen. Although his parents initially dissuaded him from pursuing an educational path, he enrolled at the University of Berlin in 1817, intent on becoming an Orientalist.[50] It was in Berlin that Tholuck came into contact with the Awakening movement through the circle associated with Baron von Kottwitz. Von Kottwitz, a Silesian nobleman who was highly regarded for his piety, was something of a social entrepreneur and philanthropist, having established a number of poor-relief initiatives

---

48. Crowner and Christianson, "General Introduction," p. 27.

49. See Groh, *Nineteenth-Century German Protestantism*, pp. 110-12; Crowner and Christianson, "General Introduction," p. 27; and Hartmut Lehmann, "Pietism and Nationalism: The Relationship between Protestant Revivalism and National Renewal in Nineteenth-Century Germany," *Church History* 51, no. 1 (March 1982): 39-53.

50. See Crowner and Christianson, "August Tholuck: Introduction," in *The Spirituality of the German Awakening*, ed. Crowner and Christianson, pp. 45-46.

in Berlin in 1807.[51] It was in the small group that met in the residence of von Kottwitz that Tholuck was assimilated into the mores of neo-Pietism.

A "mediating theologian," Tholuck was a genial man who brought together different elements from a variety of theological perspectives in the service of revival. He was professor of theology in Berlin from 1821 until 1826, when he was appointed to the theological faculty at Halle, where he stayed for the remainder of his career. Here he impacted the lives of thousands of students, which, as Karl Barth noted, may have been his single greatest contribution to the Awakening movement.[52]

Tholuck's 1823 work, *The Lesson Learned about Sin and the Reconciler; or, The True Consecration of the Skeptic,* put him on the map as a major figure in the Awakening. The work was structured as a series of letters between two friends (Guido and Julius) who share their struggles to come to a true and living faith. Rejecting rationalist critique, conservative apologetics, and confessionalism as species of the same genus, Tholuck argued that knowledge of God was possible only through direct encounter with the living Christ: "It became clear to me that I had set out on a false path of salvation, taking things into my own hands, and had not yet understood reconciliation. I had neglected to turn my eyes to the certainty of my salvation, which lay outside and beyond me in his will."[53] Tholuck followed this approach in all of his writings and sermons, seeking to develop what might be called a "Christocentric theology of experience." Sharing convictions similar to those of Schleiermacher about the central place that the experience of faith plays in the Christian life and in Christian theology, Tholuck nevertheless differed in regard to the content of faith. It was not simply an experience of absolute dependence, but rather an encounter with the living Christ to which the whole of Christian life and piety was meant to lead: "God's Word proclaims that from eternity humanity has been **directed toward Christ**; that the creation of the world itself rests on

51. See Crowner and Christianson, "General Introduction," p. 18; and Arnd Götzelmann, "Die Soziale Frage," in *Geschichte des Pietismus*, vol. 3, ed. Gäbler, pp. 277-79.

52. See Karl Barth, *Protestant Theology in the Nineteenth Century* (Valley Forge, Pa.: Judson Press, 1973), p. 509.

53. August Tholuck, "The Lesson Learned about Sin and the Reconciler, or, The True Consecration of the Skeptic," in *The Spirituality of the German Awakening*, ed. Crowner and Christianson, p. 65.

him."[54] In addition to the older Pietist emphasis on the Bible and prayer, now nature, history, and conscience were all conduits through which God calls us to his Son Jesus Christ: "It is so universal **it pervades nature and the course of humankind. It pervades the spirit and heart of the human being.**"[55] In discerning the call of God, piety itself could become a cul-de-sac:

> Piety is supposed to be the **fountain** of life, but some will come along who make it the single **business** of life. Piety is supposed to be the **soul** of everything we do, but some will come along who make it the **object** of everything we do. Piety is supposed to be the **center** of life, but some will get the idea of making it the entire surroundings.[56]

What was necessary was a connection with the living Christ.[57] At the same time, however, this could never short-circuit the call to love others. In fact, real piety, and therefore real faith, was "faith expressing itself through love."[58]

Johann Hinrich Wichern and the Inner Mission

The greatest exemplar of the *Erweckungsbewegung* commitment to "faith expressing itself through love" was undoubtedly Johann Wichern (1808-1881). Although Wichern is relatively unknown in the English-speaking world, William O. Shanahan argues that Wichern was one of the most influential figures in nineteenth-century German Protestantism: "With

54. August Tholuck, "The Drawing of the Father to the Son," in *The Spirituality of the German Awakening*, ed. Crowner and Christianson, p. 102; emphasis in the original.

55. Tholuck, "The Drawing of the Father to the Son," p. 103; emphasis in the original.

56. August Tholuck, "Where the Spirit of the Lord Is, There Is Freedom," in *The Spirituality of the German Awakening*, ed. Crowner and Christianson, p. 113; emphasis in the original.

57. See Tholuck, "Where the Spirit of the Lord Is, There Is Freedom," p. 121.

58. See August Tholuck, "In Christ Jesus Neither Circumcision nor Uncircumcision Is of Any Consequence, but Faith Active through Love," in *The Spirituality of the German Awakening*, ed. Crowner and Christianson, pp. 122-29.

the possible exception of Schleiermacher and Hegel, whose influence was primarily theological, no other individual has exerted such a preponderant influence on the practical piety of German Protestants."[59] If Schleiermacher, Kierkegaard, and Tholuck all sought to respond to the challenges put forth by Enlightenment thought, Wichern sought to wrestle with the social and political challenges of industrialization and revolution.

Born in Hamburg in 1808, Wichern studied theology in Göttingen and in Berlin under August Neander (1789-1850), the eminent church historian and member of the Kottwitz circle. Although the depth of Kottwitz's influence on Wichern is not entirely clear, there can be little doubt that Wichern's later vision of social redemption owes something to the circle that met at the Kottwitz home.[60] As with Francke, who is associated above all with the Halle Institutions, Wichern is significant not so much because of his writings but because of his pioneering social initiatives.

His career effectively began in 1833 with the founding of the *Rauhe Haus* — "Rough House" — near Hamburg to serve orphaned poor children. A vocational training-school, boardinghouse, and religious institution all rolled into one, the Rough House was envisioned as a social-redemption endeavor. Wichern argued that removing children from the deleterious effects of a rapidly industrializing society would give them a path toward a more promising future. He proposed to work with small cohorts of boys (around twelve in each group) to connect them with a tradesman, provide religious instruction, help them develop personal responsibility through housework, and grant them leisure time for reading, writing, and singing.[61]

Almost from the inception of the Rough House, Wichern was working with an integrated vision of society.[62] Family, church, and society were conceived as having a symbiotic relationship; accordingly, through rescuing orphaned boys by giving them a legitimate chance at making a living

---

59. William O. Shanahan, *German Protestants Face the Social Question*, Volume I: *The Conservative Phase, 1815-1871* (Notre Dame: University of Notre Dame Press, 1954), p. 70.

60. Shanahan, *German Protestants Face the Social Question*, Volume I, p. 74.

61. See Gerald Christianson, "J. H. Wichern and the Rise of the Lutheran Social Institution," *Lutheran Quarterly* 19, no. 4 (November 1967): 360-61.

62. See Shanahan, *German Protestants Face the Social Question*, Volume I, pp. 76-77.

and having families of their own, the Rough House was contributing to the revitalization of German society and the German church. Wichern would eventually speak of this symbiotic organism as a *Volkskirche*, a term that simultaneously transcended and included the German state churches and was meant to convey not only the interconnection of church and society, but also a sense of national mission.[63] Undoubtedly nationalist and patriarchal, the pattern developed by Wichern at the Rough House was applied to a variety of other forms of mission: "missions to the poor, the alcoholic, the seaman, the inner city, and even folk-schools to distill learning and piety as a step toward the realization of a *Volkskirche*."[64] Eventually Wichern articulated a unified view for these different social initiatives and charities, which by 1841 he was calling the Inner Mission.[65]

Wichern faced criticism from clergy who believed that his charitable work was trespassing on the domain of the parish church. It didn't help that Wichern, in keeping with an Awakening and older radical Pietist tendency, was critical of the state church, refusing to identify it with the "true church": "In short, since the introduction and organization of state and national churches the true essence of the Christian church — its freedom, its truth, and its fellowship in Christ — has become less and less visible and increasingly something only to be hoped for and only to be realized in the next world."[66] Despite his reservations, Wichern was no sectarian. He espoused a "political ecclesiology" that used "Evangelical Catholicity as the principle in an associational mission reaching out to baptized Christians beyond the local parish. . . . A voluntary lay priesthood could help the divinely instituted clergy office, and so also overcome the fragmentation of Protestant Germany and its isolation from Europe."[67] Through the idea of the *Volkskirche*, Wichern sought both to overcome and include (i.e., *Aufhebung*) the structures of institutional

---

63. See Lehmann, "Pietism and Nationalism," pp. 47-48.

64. Christianson, "J. H. Wichern and the Rise of the Lutheran Social Institution," p. 361.

65. Crowner and Christianson, "Johann Hinrich Wichern: Introduction," in *The Spirituality of the German Awakening*, ed. Crowner and Christianson, p. 235.

66. Johann Hinrich Wichern, "The True Community of the Lord," in *The Spirituality of the German Awakening*, ed. Crowner and Christianson, p. 256.

67. Hope, *German and Scandinavian Protestantism*, p. 417.

Protestantism with the goal of national renewal and the realization of a fully Christianized society.

The Inner Mission was eventually melded into the apparatus of the state church in the wake of the Revolution of 1848. The revolution, which broke out in Paris in February of 1848 and quickly spread into Germany, revealed the democratic aspirations alive in German-speaking lands and across Europe.[68] Although Wichern viewed Friedrich Wilhelm IV's feigned cooperation with Berlin protestors with horror, he seized the opportunity that revolution offered. Speaking at the September *Kirchentag* (church conference), Wichern proposed the Inner Mission as a means by which to address the social ills — particularly the conditions of the working classes — that the revolution had revealed:

> The turning point in world history at which we currently find ourselves must become a turning point in the history of the Christian church as well, particularly of the German Evangelical Church, given that this church must enter into a new relationship with the people. . . . My friends, one thing is **necessary**, that the Evangelical Church as a whole acknowledge "The work of the inner mission is mine!" and that it set one great seal on the sum of this work: **love, as well as faith, belongs to me**. Saving love must become the great implement by which the church demonstrates the fact of its faith. This love must burn in the church like God's bright torch, revealing that Christ has taken shape in his people. Just as Christ reveals his entire self in the living **Word** of God, so, too, he must preach himself in the **deeds** of God, and the highest and purest of these deeds, and the one closest to the church's purpose, is saving love. If the message about the inner mission is accepted in this sense, then the first day of a new future will dawn in our church.[69]

In his appeal, Wichern referenced Spener and Francke as forerunners of the Inner Mission: "Two of our church's most gifted men of God, **Spener**

---

68. See Priscilla Robertson, *Revolutions of 1848: A Social History* (Princeton: Princeton University Press, 1952).

69. Johann Hinrich Wichern, "Wichern's Explanation, Address, and Speech at the Wittenberg *Kirchentag*, 1848," in *The Spirituality of the German Awakening*, ed. Crowner and Christianson, pp. 269, 285; emphasis in the original.

and **A. H. Francke,** were the foremost contributors, so it appears, to what has come: Spener by proclaiming the general priesthood, and Francke through his well-known work of mercy in Halle."[70] Connections to Halle notwithstanding, Wichern's social endeavors had already far surpassed the work of Francke: by 1848, there were some 1500 charitable organizations modeled on Wichern's Rough House.[71]

The response to Wichern's appeal was positive, and he was commissioned to form a steering committee which would develop a rationale for the Inner Mission and its place in the state church. As Gerald Christianson notes, in light of the memorandum produced by the committee, "the Inner Mission has both a negative and positive function: to denounce the revolution while assisting the state in preserving discipline, and to serve human need so that society can become a suitable place for man's redemption."[72] The first of these two purposes highlights an aspect of Wichern's program which would become more and more problematic as the nineteenth century wore on: the assimilation of the Inner Mission with conservative Prussian nationalism.

Although Wichern's analysis of the social problems facing Prussia was fundamentally moral — the result of the breakdown of traditional familial and ecclesial structures — the social project that the Inner Mission represented included an attempt to re-order society, though in a more decidedly conservative-nationalist direction.[73] The alliance between Wichern's Inner Mission and the state led progressives, liberals, socialists, those concerned with democratic reform, the workers movement, and the like to view such endeavors as cover for suppressing dissatisfaction and halting reforms before they could start. Rather than seeking to change the social, economic, and political conditions of the poor for the better through systemic reform, such endeavors offered little more than window-dressing, enabling the continued hegemony of conservative monarchist interests.

---

70. Wichern, "Wichern's Explanation, Address, and Speech at the Wittenberg *Kirchentag, 1848*," p. 281.

71. See Shanahan, *German Protestants Face the Social Question*, Volume I, pp. 81-82.

72. Christianson, "J. H. Wichern and the Rise of the Lutheran Social Institution," p. 368.

73. See Albert Wu, "'Unashamed of the Gospel': Johann Hinrich Wichern and the Battle for the Soul of Prussian Prisons," *Church History* 78, no. 2 (June 2009): 283-308.

After the unification of Germany in 1871, the widely held theological conception of Germany as a "chosen people," which Wichern shared and which his conception of the *Volkskirche* supported, produced an alliance between conservatives and liberals in their attempt to make the new Germany a Protestant-only nation.[74] In Wichern's eyes and in the eyes of many of the Awakened, Germany "was part of the sacred history of God's kingdom on earth. . . . The history of the Germans was tied into the history of the salvation of humankind. It was up to the Germans to live up to their mission, to meet the challenge and be blessed or to fail and be condemned."[75] Resistance to this sort of nationalist eschatology would have to wait until the end of the nineteenth century — though, as with Kierkegaard, it would come from figures within Pietism.

The Blumhardt Movement

Southwestern Germany boasted its own well-developed Awakening movement. The connections with the older Pietism in Württemberg were much stronger, owing to the fact that Pietism there had always been a predominantly grassroots phenomenon. At the same time, the founding of the *Christentumsgesellschaft* ("Christianity society") in Basel in 1780, ostensibly to fight the growing threat of rationalism, signaled a transition: this was a cooperative endeavor whose aim was the re-Christianization of society.[76] In 1803 the Basel Tract Society was founded, and in 1815 the Basel Missionary Society was created, the most influential missionary society in nineteenth-century German-speaking lands. The founding of these institutions marks the emergence of the early Awakening movement in

---

74. We are referring here to the so-called *Kulturkampf* ("Culture War") launched by Bismarck in an effort to curb the power of the Roman Catholic Church in Germany. See Wu, "'Unashamed of the Gospel,'" p. 307. See also Hartmut Lehmann, "'God Our Old Ally': The Chosen People Theme in Late Nineteenth- and Early Twentieth-Century German Nationalism," in *Many Are Chosen: Divine Election and Western Nationalism*, ed. William R. Hutchison and Hartmut Lehmann (Minneapolis: Fortress Press, 1994), pp. 85-107.

75. Lehmann, "Pietism and Nationalism," pp. 49-50.

76. See Lehmann, "Pietism and Nationalism," p. 44.

southwestern Germany, and figures like Philipp Matthäus Hahn (1739-1790), Johann Georg Rapp (1757-1847), Johann Michael Hahn (1758-1819), Christian Gottlieb Blumhardt (1779-1838), Ludwig Hofacker (1798-1828), Christian Gottlob Barth (1799-1862), and Sixt Karl von Kapff (1805-1879) — many of them lay theologians — all provided significant leadership for the movement.[77]

Johann Christoph Blumhardt

A figure of singular importance from this region was Johann Christoph Blumhardt (1805-1880). Although he was a product of the Awakening environment, Blumhardt's life and thought — and that of his son, Christoph Friedrich, whom we will discuss below — represented a significant alternative to the trajectory of the Awakening movement, and therefore deserve special attention as being among the novel re-inventions of the Pietist impulse in the nineteenth century. Blumhardt was born in Stuttgart, studied theology in Tübingen, and served as an instructor at the Basel Missionary Society from 1830 to 1837, where he taught Hebrew, chemistry, physics, mathematics, history, and dogmatics, among other subjects.[78]

Pastor in the village of Möttlingen (northwest of Stuttgart) from 1838 to 1852, Blumhardt became famous in certain circles both within Germany and beyond because of events that unfolded there from 1841 to 1843. According to church documents as well as eyewitnesses, Blumhardt found himself dealing with a purported case of demonic possession. One of his parishioners, Gottliebin Dittus (1815-1872), had approached him complaining of strange nocturnal events.[79] Initially repelled by her, Blumhardt agreed to become involved in her case and found himself confronted by troubling

---

77. See Benrath, "Die Erweckung innerhalb der deutschen Landeskirchen 1815-1888," pp. 230-37. See also Frank D. Macchia, *Spirituality and Social Liberation: The Message of the Blumhardts in the Light of Wuerttemberg Pietism* (Metuchen, N.J.: Scarecrow Press, 1993), pp. 21-42.

78. See Dieter Ising, *Johann Christoph Blumhardt: Life and Work: A New Biography* (Eugene, Ore.: Cascade Books, 2009), pp. 74-75.

79. See Friedrich Zündel, *Johann Christoph Blumhardt: An Account of His Life* (Eugene, Ore.: Cascade Books, 2010), p. 121.

theological and spiritual realities for which he was ill-equipped. After two years of prayer, fasting, Bible reading, and counseling, the struggle came to an end on December 28, 1843, with the confession of the alleged demonic power that "Jesus is the Victor."[80] This phrase would become a theological and spiritual watchword for Blumhardt, his son, and the circle of friends that eventually formed around the ministry of the Blumhardts.

Following the events described above, a regional revival centering on confession of sin, repentance, and absolution broke out in Möttlingen. Because of the sensational events involving Dittus and the subsequent revival, Blumhardt faced opposition from a variety of quarters, while would-be allies among the Awakened also kept their distance.[81] Eventually, in 1852, he moved his household to Bad Boll, taking up residence in a newly renovated health spa built to take advantage of the local hot springs. In sermons, letters, and especially the *Blätter aus Bad Boll* — a self-published devotional magazine — Blumhardt's ministry at Bad Boll, which centered on spiritual counsel, prayer for healing, and fellowship, was given a broader audience.[82] Even though he maintained cordial relations with many of the key leaders of the Awakening movement, Blumhardt labored to work through the implications of what had happened at Möttlingen, and he began to chart a new path, one that has come to be loosely identified as the "Blumhardt movement."[83]

In keeping with the common practice among the Awakened,[84] Blumhardt interpreted the events surrounding Dittus through an eschatological lens.[85] The events signaled that God was indeed breaking into the world — but rather than portending the end of "Christian society" or an event of doom for the world, as would have been more common among the Awakened,[86] Möttlingen marked something else, something more

---

80. See Zündel, *Johann Christoph Blumhardt*, pp. 150-52.

81. See Benrath, "Die Erweckung innerhalb der deutschen Landeskirchen 1815-1888," p. 235.

82. See Zündel, *Johann Christoph Blumhardt*, pp. 501-11.

83. See, for example, Jörg Ohlemacher, "Gemeinschaftschristentum in Deutschland im 19. und 20. Jahrhundert," in *Geschichte des Pietismus*, vol. 3, ed. Gäbler, p. 396.

84. See Groh, *Nineteenth-Century German Protestantism*, pp. 111-12.

85. See Ising, *Johann Christoph Blumhardt*, pp. 236-49.

86. See Ising, *Johann Christoph Blumhardt*, p. 407.

hopeful.[87] The events were more hopeful for Blumhardt in part because rather than becoming obsessed with the purported demonic power or the "spirit world," he was fixed on the event of liberation itself: Jesus Christ himself had come to liberate Dittus from the powers and principalities.[88] This was indeed a sign! But the sign was that God's work of transformation — or the sowing of a "new birth" in humanity — was not simply a spiritual reality meant for the individual, nor was it confined only to the Awakened. Rather, the event was to be both physical and spiritual, and would not be a respecter of persons, being cosmic in scope. Through a process of creatively reformulating Spener's "hope for better times," now the spiritual "new birth" was to be accompanied by God's healing work of transformation through "the miraculous" as signs of hope for the final transformation of all things.[89]

In dialogue with the pronounced eschatological expectations of Württemberg Pietism, especially that of Friedrich Christoph Oetinger and Johann Michael Hahn,[90] Blumhardt argued that the healing powers experienced at Möttlingen were meant for the whole cosmos, not just the "awakened."[91] This put him at odds with many in the Awakening movement on two counts. First, many of the Awakened were unconvinced or openly suspicious about whether or not charismatic gifts such as healing were to be expected from God in the present time.[92] But Blumhardt's experiences with Dittus and others compelled him to affirm and proclaim that God was indeed interested in intervening in direct and physical ways. Although his affirmations did not register among many of the German Awakened, his ideas did find a hearing in the transatlantic healing movement, as his ministry was mediated to the English-speaking world through figures like Charles Cullis (1833-1892) and A. J. Gordon (1836-1895).[93]

87. See Ising, *Johann Christoph Blumhardt*, pp. 228-36.

88. See Zündel, *Johann Christoph Blumhardt*, pp. 128-29.

89. See Christian T. Collins Winn, *"Jesus Is Victor!": The Significance of the Blumhardts for the Theology of Karl Barth* (Eugene, Ore.: Pickwick Publications, 2009), pp. 87-89.

90. See Friedhelm Groth, "Chiliasmus und Apokatastasishoffnung in der Reich-Gottes-Verkündigung der beiden Blumhardts," *Pietismus und Neuzeit* 9 (1983): 60-67.

91. See Collins Winn, *"Jesus Is Victor!"*, p. 88.

92. See Ising, *Johann Christoph Blumhardt*, pp. 413-14.

93. See Nancy A. Hardesty, *Faith Cure: Divine Healing in the Holiness and Pentecostal Movements* (Peabody, Mass.: Hendrickson Publishers, 2003), pp. 19-20.

The second distinction from the Awakening movement was Blumhardt's eschatological ecumenism. His downplaying of the categories of "converted" versus "unconverted"; his belief that the coming time of grace to which the eschatological events at Möttlingen pointed was meant for all of humanity; his rejection of the nationalism that many in the Awakening movement embraced — all these differences put him at odds with leading figures in the Awakening movement. In his counseling ministry, Blumhardt would constantly emphasize that one seeks healing not for immediate relief from suffering, but so that one might become a sign of hope that God's final restoration of all things was approaching — that one might become a sign that God intends to free the whole earth. And though he was politically inclined toward conservative politics, Blumhardt's radically inclusive eschatology — as well as the international flavor of his network of friends — helped to inoculate him against the nationalism that infected the vision of Wichern and others.[94] He refused to recognize the legitimacy or usefulness of categories like "converted" or "unconverted," and he was deeply critical when these categories were applied to whole groups of people like the French, as happened during the Franco-Prussian War (1870-1871).[95]

Christoph Friedrich Blumhardt

Blumhardt's son, Christoph Friedrich Blumhardt (1842-1919), pushed the "Blumhardt movement" even further. Possessed of an independent mind and fiery, charismatic personality, the younger Blumhardt was uncertain about following his father into ministry and far less sanguine about the Awakening movement, especially as it had developed in the late nineteenth century, owing partly to the treatment his father had received from its members. The "community movement" or *Gemeinschaftsbewegung* eventually displaced the Awakening movement as a new expression of Pietism

---

94. See Dieter Ising, "Eine 'Weckstimme durch alle Völker.' Die Revolution von 1848/1849 und die Anfänge der Inneren Mission in der Sicht Johann Christoph Blumhardts," *Pietismus und Neuzeit* 24 (1998): 286-308.

95. See Ising, *Johann Christoph Blumhardt*, p. 407.

in the latter half of the nineteenth century.[96] The movement, deeply influenced by the English and American "holiness movement," was sparked by the preaching of Robert Pearsall Smith (1827-1898), who was invited to preach in Germany in 1875.[97] From the very beginning, the elder Blumhardt was wary of this movement.[98]

After his father's death in 1880, Christoph assumed the mantle of leadership at Bad Boll. Although initially successful, by 1894 he had become so alienated from the churchly and pietistic culture that had developed at Bad Boll that he decided to no longer be identified as a pastor. He expressed great dissatisfaction that the message of hope for the kingdom that his father had developed had been turned into an excuse for people to seek a blessed life with no concern for the groaning of humanity. In keeping with his father's initial insights, Christoph believed that the true goal of the kingdom was the transformation of the whole world: "We do not first want to save ourselves and be satisfied with this, but we want to take to heart the sighing of all creation, the lamenting and groaning of countless human beings who are certainly not helped by our salvation, but who are helped a great deal if we cry out and pray: 'Thy Kingdom come!'"[99] Although inspired by the cosmic orientation of his father, Christoph turned even more resolutely toward the needs he discerned in society and the world.

Accompanying this turn was Christoph's reconsideration and recontextualization of his father's message and experience.[100] Christoph

96. See Ohlemacher, "Gemeinschaftschristentum in Deutschland im 19. und 20. Jahrhundert," pp. 393-464.

97. See Karl Heinz Voigt, *Die Heiligungsbewegung zwischen Methodistischer Kirche und Landeskirchlicher Gemeinschaft: die 'Triumphreise' von Robert Pearsall Smith im Jahre 1875 und ihre Auswirkungen auf die zwischenkirchlichen Beziehungen* (Wuppertal: R. Brockhaus Verlag, 1996); see also M. E. Dieter, "From Vineland and Manheim to Brighton and Berlin: The Holiness Movement in the Nineteenth Century," *Wesleyan Theological Journal* 9 (Spring 1974): 15-27.

98. See Ising, *Johann Christoph Blumhardt*, p. 350.

99. Christoph Blumhardt, *Eine Auswahl aus seinen Predigten, Andachten und Schriften*, vol. 2, 1888-1896, ed. R. Lejeune (Zurich: Rotapfel-Verlag, 1925), p. 89; translation by Collins Winn.

100. See Klaus-Jürgen Meier, *Christoph Blumhardt: Christ, Sozialist, Theologe* (Bern: Peter Lang, 1979), pp. 35-44.

argued that though his father had recovered a hope for the kingdom of God as made concrete in real physical transformation, he had not seen that the full extension of this hope must include a vision of the transformation of the social conditions of humanity. While for the elder Blumhardt, "Jesus is Victor!" had implied the healing of the body, for Christoph it implied the healing of the body politic.[101] Christoph began to envision the struggle with the powers and principalities in explicitly social and political terms. The powers against which Jesus struggled, and over which he would triumph, were now the structures that oppressed humanity and curtailed its flourishing.[102]

When a law suppressing the rights of workers was passed in 1898, Blumhardt was led by his new orientation to the unprecedented and highly controversial decision of publicly identifying himself with the Social Democratic Party (SPD) in 1899.[103] Blumhardt was universally attacked by the members of the "community movement" and labeled a traitor and a heretic, a fact that is not surprising given that this was one of the most intensely nationalistic movements in German Protestantism and would later provide some of the church support for the rise of Adolf Hitler.[104]

Blumhardt was also asked to resign his position as pastor by the state church consistory, so he lost his pension.[105] Nevertheless, he explained that his decision was in keeping with the deepest intentions of his father's ministry:

My appearance in workers' circles, and in particular my active support of Social Democracy, has caused concern among many of those whom I know. It is customary to connect Social Democracy with godlessness, and there is a fear that I am losing my faith. On the contrary: I believe,

101. For a fuller discussion of this, see Collins Winn, *"Jesus Is Victor!"*, pp. 110-54.

102. See Macchia, *Spirituality and Social Liberation*, p. 166.

103. See W. R. Ward, *Theology, Sociology, and Politics: The German Protestant Social Conscience, 1890-1933* (Bern: Peter Lang, 1979), p. 125.

104. See Dieter Lange, "Der Weg der Gemeinschaftsbewegung von 1918 bis 1933," *Pietismus und Neuzeit* 15 (1989): 114-31.

105. Lange, "Der Weg der Gemeinschaftsbewegung von 1918 bis 1933," pp. 114-31. Although Blumhardt had stopped functioning like a pastor, he hadn't renounced his orders; hence the loss of pension.

because of this, I must speak out. That which lives within me of Christ, that which I have believed and striven for all my life concerning the kingdom of God and his justice on earth, directs me in my association with the great struggle of the working classes — to them a struggle for survival![106]

Despite its formal godlessness (the SPD was officially an atheist party), Blumhardt saw in the socialist movement a parable of God's kingdom, a movement struggling to realize a more just and equitable society, one especially concerned for the poor. In the social-systemic critique of sin — the power that creates poverty through social systems that reward greed — the younger Blumhardt had indeed moved beyond earlier Pietist endeavors to serve the poor. Even so, this was a move that resonated deeply with the earlier Pietist conceptions of salvation and hope which had motivated Spener, Francke, and others, as was his criticism of the alliance of the church with the status quo.

Blumhardt's enthusiasm for socialist politics would eventually cool, in part because of party politics; he noted dryly, "At the end, it will finally be called the kingdom of God, not the Social Democratic kingdom."[107] Nevertheless, by reaching out to the workers' movement, the younger Blumhardt had found a way to make the Pietist themes of hope, "new birth," and transformation — all understood in his preaching in explicitly Christological terms — relevant to new challenges at the end of the nineteenth century. As a result, he was able to mediate the legacy of his father, and elements of the earlier Pietism, to a number of key figures in the German-speaking world in the twentieth century, including Karl Barth (1886-1968), Paul Tillich (1886-1965), Dietrich Bonhoeffer (1906-1945), and Jürgen Moltmann (b. 1926).

---

106. Christoph Blumhardt, *Eine Auswahl aus seinen Predigten, Andachten und Schriften*, vol. 3, ed. R. Lejeune (Zürich: Rotapfel, 1936), p. 472 (unpublished translation by Plough and the Brüderhof; used with permission).

107. Christoph Blumhardt, *Politik aus der Nachfölge. Der Briefwechsel zwischen Howard Eugster-Züst und Christoph Blumhardt, 1886-1919*, ed. Louis Speker (Zürich: Gotthelf Verlag, 1984), p. 173; translation by Collins Winn.

Conclusion

The nineteenth century presented challenges as well as opportunities to the Pietist impulse. As the eighteenth century came to a close, the older Pietism associated with figures like Spener and Francke needed to be re-thought and refitted to face those challenges. As we have seen, this resulted in multiple — sometimes conflicting — re-inventions of Pietism. Nevertheless, the concern for a living connection to Jesus, a commitment to serve the "least of these," and an irrepressible hope for the "breaking in" of God's future were hallmarks of some of the new expressions of Pietism in the nineteenth century. In our next chapter we offer four examples — in the church and in the theological academy — of attempts to appropriate Pietist themes to address the contemporary theological and spiritual challenges facing many Christian communities. As you will see, the examples — all twentieth-century and twenty-first-century figures — share in the impulse evident in the nineteenth century: an attempt to re-invent Pietism to address pressing challenges.

CHAPTER EIGHT

Contemporary Appropriations of the Pietist Impulse

Four Exemplars

Thus far we have examined misunderstandings of Pietism; Pietism's history as a movement; its living ethos, including its characteristic hallmarks; its influence on early American and British evangelicalism; its formative leaders, early and modern; and ways in which evangelical theology especially can benefit from rediscovering and re-appropriating its ethos. In this chapter we wish to demonstrate through four case studies of contemporary theologians how the Pietist ethos does actually live on and influence especially, but not only, evangelical Christianity.

The subject of each of our four case studies is someone (and in one instance also a movement) who has been widely recognized as a creative and influential Christian thinker and who has, at least partially, stood on the shoulders of or built on Pietism, incorporating significant aspects of its ethos into his theology. None of these men would wear the label "Pietist" on his forehead or his sleeve! But all have given credit to Pietism as a formative influence in their life and thought. All four are eclectic thinkers, but that does not nullify their underlying pietistic approaches to Christianity.

We hope these four exemplars will bring to light Pietism's enduring, dynamic character as a living impulse in at least some world-class evangelical (and other) theological projects. Many Christians who have been profoundly impacted by these four theologians have never become aware that, through them, they are being influenced by Pietism.

We chose our four exemplars carefully. All four have inspired us and give us, like others, much to feed on spiritually and intellectually. And we know that all four have broad and deep influence on evangelical theology (and, in some cases, theology beyond what would usually be considered evangelical).

The four are Donald G. Bloesch, Richard Foster (and the Renovaré Movement he helped found), Stanley J. Grenz, and Jürgen Moltmann. Anyone familiar with all four will recognize immediately how diverse they are. The first three are usually considered evangelicals. Moltmann is a German Protestant theologian who some evangelicals would consider evangelical in ethos, but he was never "an evangelical" in the sense of affiliation with the "evangelical movement." Bloesch stood within the broad Reformed tradition and taught throughout his whole career at a Presbyterian seminary. Foster is a Quaker, a member of the Evangelical Friends movement, who is known for his writing and speaking on spiritual renewal. Grenz was an evangelical Baptist, a progressive evangelical with postmodern leanings. Moltmann is German Reformed with both an evangelical side and a progressive side. We are aware that there are other theologians who have been strongly influenced by Pietism and who have incorporated aspects of its ethos into their theologies, but we chose these four because of their wide acceptance as influential Christian thinkers, their creativity and prolific writing and speaking careers, and their impact on us.

Donald G. Bloesch

Donald Bloesch (1928-2010) was one of the most prolific and influential evangelical theologians whose volumes inspired and informed numerous theologically minded Christians for four decades and continue to do so after his death. Many evangelical theologians and pastors, and some laypeople, testify that reading Bloesch helped them discover a path in theology between fundamentalism and liberalism. Some commentators called him a mediating theologian because he self-consciously sought a *via media* between extremes in theology. He was a member of the United Church of Christ, usually considered one of the most liberal Protestant denominations in the United States, but he was raised in its more conservative wing, the Evangelical and Reformed Synod (which merged with the larger and more liberal American Congregational Churches to form the UCC). However, for most of his career he taught systematic theology at the Presbyterian-related University of Dubuque Theological Seminary in Iowa.[1]

Bloesch graduated from UCC-related Chicago Theological Seminary, received ordination in his home denomination, and then embarked on Ph.D. studies in theology at the nearby University of Chicago Divinity School, where he earned his degree in 1956. Most of his theological teachers in both institutions were theologically liberal, but Bloesch found evangelical support in the InterVarsity Christian Fellowship group on the University of Chicago campus. This affiliation probably explains his life-long quest to remain an evangelical theologian within primarily more liberal contexts.

After earning his Ph.D., Bloesch conducted postdoctoral studies at Oxford University and in Basel, Switzerland, where he came into contact with Karl Barth, his lifelong theological conversation-partner. Bloesch probably did more than any other theologian to introduce Barth's theology to American evangelicals in a positive way (although he remained critical of some aspects of so-called neo-orthodoxy or dialectical theology).

Bloesch is best known for his books and his numerous articles in religious publications, but he was also an avid hymn-writer. Those who studied under him or just knew him personally found him to be a warm-hearted Christian, always irenic and constructive in theological conversations and debates, and possessed of a deep and infectious spirituality.

The Iowa theologian's best-known books include two sets of systematic theology: the two-volume *Essentials of Evangelical Theology* (1978, 1979) and his magnum opus, the multi-volume Christian Foundations series beginning with *A Theology of Word and Spirit* (1992) and ending with *The Last Things: Resurrection, Judgment, Glory* (2004). The Christian Foundations series included Bloesch's final published theological thoughts. However, his journey toward that massive system (if it can be called a system) began with three smaller books about theology, church

---

1. The biographical material here is taken from Roger Olson's research, which included several conversations with Bloesch. That research resulted in the publication of "Donald G. Bloesch" in *A New Handbook of Christian Theologians*, ed. Donald W. Musser and Joseph L. Price (Nashville: Abingdon Press, 1996), pp. 67-73.

renewal, and spirituality that were clearly influenced by Pietism. These included *The Crisis of Piety: Essays towards a Theology of the Christian Life* (1968), which echoed for twentieth-century Christians the Pietist message of Spener in *Pia Desideria*. Other influential Bloesch volumes include *The Ground of Certainty* (1971), *The Evangelical Renaissance* (1973), *The Future of Evangelical Christianity: A Call for Unity amid Diversity* (1983), and *The Struggle of Prayer* (1988) — perhaps his most pietistic book.

Bloesch's theology developed over time, but several themes remained constant. Between 1968 and 2004, for example, a careful reader can discern development in his thought — from cautious but definite emphasis on evangelical unity through renewal of both doctrine and spirituality to an increased emphasis on the rediscovery of confessional truth. In other words, as Bloesch observed his own denomination drifting further into doctrinal pluralism and away from concern for catholic continuity with ancient and Reformation sources, to say nothing of Scripture, he became more conservative in his thinking about doctrine. This turning point is nowhere more obvious than in his book *The Battle for the Trinity* (1985), where he irenically but firmly criticizes "inclusive language" for God and radical feminist theology. Still, throughout his career as a theologian, he identified his own orientation as "progressive evangelical." He did not believe, for example, in biblical inerrancy. And he insisted on a distinction between the Bible and the Word of God.[2] His constant and abiding concern was for church renewal through retrieval of basic Christian orthodoxy (his message mainly to liberal-leaning Christians) and the primacy of the gospel, the message of God's Word in Jesus Christ made alive by the Holy Spirit, over biblical literalism and dead orthodoxy (his message mainly to conservatives).

Our concern here is to point to Bloesch's emphasis on spiritual experience as another source for theological and church renewal. At any point where one dives into Bloesch's corpus, one will find some reference to inner experience of God as an essential part of authentic Christianity. But this goes beyond merely a typical evangelical emphasis on "devotional life" or "having a personal relationship with Jesus." In the Christian Founda-

---

2. Donald G. Bloesch, *A Theology of Word and Spirit: Authority and Method in Theology* (Downers Grove, Ill.: InterVarsity Press, 1992), p. 200.

tions series — the most mature expression of his theology, where Bloesch most emphasizes the catholicity of evangelical faith — he adds "the inner Word" to Karl Barth's "three forms of the Word of God": Jesus Christ, the Bible, and the church's proclamation. In true Pietist fashion, Bloesch adds "the inner Word" as a fourth form of the Word of God:

> In relation to Barth's typology, I would add a fourth form — the inner Word. . . . The written Word and the proclaimed Word have no efficacy unless Christ makes his abode within us by his Spirit. It is not only the light that comes to us from the Bible and the church but also the light that shines within us by the indwelling Spirit that convinces us of the truth. . . . Jesus Christ as the revealed Word of God in past history becomes the living Christ through the experience of being engrafted into his body by the Spirit.[3]

Bloesch makes his Pietist inclinations even clearer when he says a few pages later that this inner Word is not a universal God-consciousness (as in much liberal theology). Rather, the inner Word comes into an individual, and with it comes definite experience of God's grace. Of "Jesus Christ alone" as the "sure anchor and foundation of Christian faith," he says,

> Yet this is not Christ outside history or even Christ in past history but Christ alive in the church through his resurrection, Christ dwelling in our hearts by his Spirit. We come to know Christ as the power of creative transformation only through the experience of his cross and resurrection. We come to participate in the salvation that Christ offers only by being born from above by his Spirit.[4]

Bloesch made it absolutely clear that he did not consider this "inner Word" a source of truth apart from Scripture, but he spoke of a "perichoretic relationship" among the four forms of God's Word — including this inner Word.[5] In other words, they interpenetrate and interpret each other

---

3. Bloesch, *A Theology of Word and Spirit*, p. 191.
4. Bloesch, *A Theology of Word and Spirit*, p. 195.
5. Bloesch, *A Theology of Word and Spirit*, p. 191.

even though they stand in a hierarchical relationship with Jesus Christ above all. Doctrinal truth is judged by Scripture, not experience, but without the experience of being "born from above" by God's Spirit that brings participation in Christ, Scripture remains a dead letter, and doctrine is of no real value.

Nowhere did Bloesch lay out his Pietist leanings more clearly than in the little book mentioned above entitled *The Crisis of Piety*, which was his contemporary "Pia Desideria" — the latter's message brought up to date especially for twentieth-century American Protestants. Like Spener in 1675, Bloesch believed in 1968 that the church was experiencing a crisis of piety and stood in need of spiritual renewal. The book includes a section entitled "Learning from Pietism" (pp. 43-45) that is revealing about Bloesch's Pietist orientation.

According to Bloesch, "Whereas the [Protestant] Reformers place the accent upon *Christ for us* [Pietists] seek to give equal emphasis to *Christ with us* and *Christ in us.* . . . They concur in the judgment of the Reformers that God loves us as we are; but they go on to affirm that God wants us as He is."[6] He continues by pointing out five more contributions of Pietism to church renewal needed in his time (and, we add, in ours). First, there is the "rediscovery of evangelism" together with the reminder that "salvation consists in the conversion of the whole man to the living Christ."[7] In this connection, Bloesch quotes Zinzendorf. Second, he mentions spiritual warfare and uses Blumhardt as a model. Bloesch contends that "the demonic is to be viewed not as an empty negation but as a power that is at the same time creative and destructive."[8]

Third, Bloesch called on contemporary Christians to rediscover and use spiritual disciplines such as those promoted by "spiritual giants" such as Spener, John Wesley, Zinzendorf, and Richard Baxter. Among the disciplines he specifically mentions "prayer, devotional reading, and fasting," not as means to salvation but as "aids by which we continue in the salvation

---

6. Donald G. Bloesch, *The Crisis of Piety* (Grand Rapids: Wm. B. Eerdmans, 1968), p. 43.

7. Bloesch, *The Crisis of Piety*, p. 44.

8. Bloesch, *The Crisis of Piety*. Barth believed in Satan and the demonic as "Das Nichtige" — a power of negation — but not as a personal realm of destructive power with ontological being.

purchased for us by Jesus Christ."[9] Fourth, according to Bloesch, Pietism reminds us "that Jesus Christ is our pattern and example as well as our Saviour." In this case he cites Kierkegaard, "who strongly reacted against the objectivism in Lutheran orthodoxy" and "had a basic spiritual affinity with Pietism."[10] Finally, Bloesch affirms that "The Christian life cannot exist apart from a certain degree of separation and withdrawal from the world," by which he means "the spirit of the world, the idolatry and sin of the world," not "the lost and helpless of the world."[11]

Bloesch's whole theological career in the bosom of both evangelicalism and "mainstream Protestantism" was driven by a passion for the spiritual renewal of the church and the individual. And his debt to Pietism is both explicit, as in the above section of *The Crisis of Piety*, and implicit, as in his hundreds of quotations from and positive references to the historical prototypes of Pietism from Spener to Blumhardt.

Richard Foster

Richard Foster is sometimes hailed as "the world's most famous Quaker." But his lifelong affiliation with the Religious Society of Friends and Evangelical Friends (Quakers) has not hindered his ecumenical work for spiritual renewal and formation. His book *Celebration of Discipline: The Path to Spiritual Growth* (1978/1998) has sold over one million copies and is credited by *Christianity Today* magazine as one of the most influential Christian books of the twentieth century.

Foster was born into a Quaker family in 1942 in New Mexico. He went on to become a minister among the Evangelical Friends and eventually a teacher at Christian colleges and universities, including especially Friends University (his longest association) in Wichita, Kansas. He graduated from George Fox University in Oregon and earned his Ph.D. in theology from Fuller Theological Seminary in California. One of his most important legacies is and will be the Renovaré movement, which he founded in 1988. It

---

9. Bloesch, *The Crisis of Piety*, p. 44.
10. Bloesch, *The Crisis of Piety*, p. 45.
11. Bloesch, *The Crisis of Piety*, p. 45.

is a movement to promote inner spiritual formation among Christians of all denominations.

Foster is probably the best-known and most influential evangelical promoter of inward spiritual renewal and spiritual formation. Besides *Celebration of Discipline,* he has written numerous books dealing with Christian spirituality, including (with Kathryn Helmers) *Life with God: Reading the Bible for Spiritual Transformation* (2008), *The Challenge of the Disciplined Life: Christian Reflections on Money, Sex, and Power* (previously published as *Money, Sex, and Power* in 1985), and *Prayer: Finding the Heart's True Home* (1992). He has also edited a spiritual-formation study Bible and written books of prayers and collections of hymns. In addition, he speaks at churches, campuses, and conferences around the world.

Some readers might object that Foster is a Quaker, not a Pietist. However, as readers will know by now, we regard Pietism not as a denomination or an alternative to any denomination but as an ethos. Quakerism, the Friends movement, has been pervaded by a Pietist ethos for most of its existence. Its founder, George Fox (1624-1691), was deeply influenced by German Pietism as well as by radical, "spiritual" reformers such as Caspar Schwenkfeld (1490-1561). In our estimation at least, whether or not Foster would label himself a Pietist, he soaks in and exudes a Pietist ethos — virtually all the hallmarks of Pietism outlined in our previous chapter on them.

The January 2009 issue of *Christianity Today* contained an article by Foster entitled "Spiritual Formation Agenda" in which Foster outlines his priorities for the next thirty years. There, Foster speaks about the importance of congregational spiritual renewal via *ecclesiola in ecclesia* — the technical term for Pietism's "conventicles" or *collegia pietatis:*

> Let us do all we can to develop the *ecclesiola in ecclesia* — "the little church within the church." The *ecclesiola in ecclesia* is deeply committed to the life of the people of God and is not sectarian in any way. No separation. No splitting off. No setting up a new denomination or church. We stay within the given church structures and develop little centers of light within those structures. And then we let our light shine![12]

---

12. Richard Foster, "Spiritual Formation Agenda," *Christianity Today* 53, no. 1 (January 2009): 31.

Of course, "small group ministry" is not unique to Foster or Pietism, but the fact that he uses the term *ecclesiola in ecclesia* demonstrates an influence from historical Pietism.

What makes this connection between Pietism and Foster even clearer is that he goes on immediately after that to explain "three historical expressions" of the *ecclesiola in ecclesia* that "are particularly worthy of study."[13] The first one is Philipp Jakob Spener. The second is John Wesley. The third is Norwegian Pietist leader Hans Nielsen Hauge (1771-1824).[14] Foster concludes his case studies by saying,

> This *ecclesiola in ecclesia*, this spiritual formation work, produces a certain kind of fellowship, a certain kind of community. It produces a unity of heart and soul and mind, a bond that cannot be broken — a wonder-filled caring and sharing of life together that will carry us through the most difficult circumstances.[15]

Clearly, Foster is influenced by the Pietist tradition and ethos and highly recommends the contributions of some of its shining examples.

Further evidence of Foster's Pietism appears in his comments about the spiritual life. First, he emphasizes the transformation of the "inner life" over doctrine or activism without denigrating either one of them. For him, spiritual formation is crucial to being a fulfilled Christian; being a Christian is not just a matter of right belief or right worship or ethics. He even goes so far as to say that "all other matters" (than "heart work") "we gladly leave in the good hands of God."[16] What is this "heart work," this "spiritual formation" that Foster considers so crucial? It is a gift of God that must be accepted:

> Of primary significance [for the Christian life] is our vital union with God, our new creation in Christ, our immersion in the Holy Spirit. It is this life that purifies the heart. . . . When the heart is purified by the action of the Spirit, the most natural thing in the world is the virtu-

13. Foster, "Spiritual Formation Agenda," p. 31.
14. Foster, "Spiritual Formation Agenda," p. 32.
15. Foster, "Spiritual Formation Agenda," p. 32.
16. Foster, "Spiritual Formation Agenda," p. 30.

ous thing. To the pure in heart, vice is what is hard. . . . But God does not come uninvited. . . . It is a work known only to God. It is the work of heart purity, of soul conversion, of inward transformation, of life formation.[17]

This clearly correlates with Spener's concept of the transformation of the "inner man" in *Pia Desideria* and other writings.

What of conversion? Pietism always places a high premium on conversion. In true Pietist fashion, Foster allows that conversion is necessary but that there is no single formula for it. "Conversion" is simply another word for what begins in new birth and continues throughout the Christian life. In a passage that rings with Pietism, Foster says that conversion

> begins first by our turning to the light of Jesus. For some, this is an excruciatingly slow turning, turning until we turn round right. For others, it is instantaneous and glorious. In either case, we are coming to trust in Jesus, to accept Jesus as our Life. As we read about in John 3, we are born from above. But our being *born* from above, of necessity, includes our being *formed* from above. Being spiritually born is a beginning — a wonderful, glorious beginning. It is not an ending.[18]

This new birth, this inward transformation, according to Foster, is not necessarily ecstatic. Rather, it is a matter of receiving from God, inwardly, a new "heavenly orientation."[19] Its marks are "serenity, unshakeableness, and a firmness of life." But it does not come all at once, and its progress is "arduous and lifelong."[20]

What are the means of receiving this "heavenly orientation" of life? Anyone who has studied Foster's *Celebration of Discipline* knows that it focuses on "the spiritual disciplines." The "inward disciplines" include meditation, prayer, fasting, and study. The "outward disciplines" include

17. Foster, "Spiritual Formation Agenda," p. 30.
18. Foster, "Spiritual Formation Agenda," p. 30.
19. Foster, "Spiritual Formation Agenda," p. 31.
20. Foster, "Spiritual Formation Agenda," p. 31.

simplicity, solitude, submission, and service. The "corporate disciplines" include confession, worship, guidance, and celebration.[21]

Foster's Pietism appears in the *emphasis* he places on inward spiritual transformation, "heart work," and the goal of a "heavenly orientation" (without perfection). For him, as for Pietists, this is the center of Christianity. It also appears in the *manner* in which he promotes this — ecumenical, trans-denominational, and irenic. And it appears in the *Christocentricity* of his vision of spiritual formation. Contrary to some critics' claims, Foster does not promote a mysticism that violates the Creator-creature distinction. His mysticism, which we prefer to call his Pietism, is thoroughly Christ-centered. It is always bringing the person closer to Christ, to being conformed to Christ's image.

Foster's Renovaré movement can be seen as a revival of Pietism for American Christians. It centers on publications and conferences that promote spiritual formation as described above. Speakers and authors such as philosopher Dallas Willard (1935-2013) and pastor Roger Fredrickson (b. 1921) have been major leaders in Renovaré. It is a truly ecumenical movement for the spiritual renewal of individuals and congregations without boundaries. It tends to attract Christians with an intellectual "bent," but it does not put spiritual formation and renewal on a "high shelf," difficult to reach. Reading materials are taken from the church fathers, medieval mystics and theologians, Protestants of all traditions, and modern mystics and thinkers. The movement maintains a broad appeal and refuses to be pinned down by narrow doctrinal commitments even though its basic orientation is evangelical.

A major emphasis of Renovaré is small-group devotion and practice of the spiritual disciplines with the aims of encouragement and accountability. These *ecclesiola* are not necessarily *in ecclesia*, however, and that has drawn some criticism. While Foster and Renovaré do not discourage active participation in churches and denominations, they do countenance and even encourage active participation in character-transforming small groups outside of any formal church structure.

We find it ironic that many people who admire Foster, who drink

---

21. Richard Foster, *Celebration of Discipline: The Path to Spiritual Growth*, rev. ed. (San Francisco: Harper & Row, 1988), passim.

deeply at his wells, and who view Renovaré as a healthy movement would never associate him or it with Pietism because of misconceptions about Pietism. Foster's Renovaré program, however, contains within it a creative re-expression of Pietism's living ethos, one suited especially for the challenges of our late modern context. This is not to reduce Foster or Renovaré to Pietism one-dimensionally. There's more to them than Pietism, but they are, nevertheless, contemporary manifestations of Pietism's living ethos.

Stanley J. Grenz

Our next example of Pietism is Stanley J. Grenz (1950-2005), who was a key member of a new generation of evangelical theologians before his untimely death in 2005. The author of over twenty volumes, including the multi-volume project *The Matrix of Christian Theology*,[22] Grenz was concerned to revitalize not only evangelical theology but also the Christian church as a whole. Drawing on a variety of figures in an attempt to articulate a constructive evangelical theology from a free-church perspective, Grenz also appropriated Pietist themes and thinkers. This would come as no surprise to anyone who has read his essay "Concerns of a Pietist with a Ph.D."[23]

Son of a Baptist minister, Grenz was born in Michigan. Although he had a strong interest in the sciences, particularly physics, Grenz felt a call to ministry early in his undergraduate career. After graduating from the University of Colorado at Boulder (1973), he went on to study at Denver Seminary (1976) and was ordained in 1976. At the University of Munich, he wrote a dissertation titled "Isaac Backus — Puritan and Baptist" under the direction of Wolfhart Pannenberg and graduated in 1978. Grenz held pastoral positions from 1971 to 1976 and from 1979 to 1981, when he

---

22. Only two volumes of this series were published: *The Social God and the Relational Self: A Trinitarian Theology of the Imago Dei* (Louisville: Westminster John Knox Press, 2001), and the posthumously published *The Named God and the Question of Being: A Trinitarian Theo-Ontology* (Louisville: Westminster John Knox Press, 2005).

23. See Stanley J. Grenz, "Concerns of a Pietist with a Ph.D.," *Wesleyan Theological Journal* 37, no. 2 (Fall 2002): 58-76.

began a full-time teaching career at North American Baptist Theological Seminary in Sioux Falls, South Dakota (now Sioux Falls Seminary). From 1990 to 2002, Grenz taught at Carey Theological College in Vancouver, British Columbia; he also held a dual appointment at Regent College. After a brief one-year appointment at Baylor University in Waco, Texas, Grenz returned to Carey. His sudden death in 2005 was a shock to the Christian theological community, and many lamented not only that he had been taken too soon, but that the revitalized theological vision he was working to articulate would never be fully realized.

Grenz's debt to Pietism is especially evident in his later writings. This is owing to his friendship with Roger Olson, as well as to a sabbatical spent in Germany from 1987 to 1988. It was on this sabbatical that Grenz rediscovered the pietistic heritage of his youth:

> Since 1988, I have been seeking to integrate the rationalistic and pietistic dimensions of the Christian faith. In continuity with the training I received from my mentors, I acknowledge the crucial role of reason in the theological enterprise. At the same time, I am convinced that a personal faith commitment as nurtured in a community of faith — piety — is also significant in our attempt to understand and to pursue the constructive theological task. Thus, while theology may be an intellectual search for truth, this search must always be attached to the foundational, identity producing encounter with God in Christ. And it must issue forth in Christian living.[24]

As a result of this "rediscovery," Grenz began to argue that theology must emerge out of a living relationship with God and be expressed in holy Christian living, a matrix that Grenz would eventually appropriate to describe his own identity: "A Pietist with a Ph.D."

Grenz identified the "Pietist" side with the "convertive piety" of Pietism, which included an emphasis on the warm-hearted *experiential* aspect of the Christian faith, while the "Ph.D." descriptor referred to Grenz's commitment to rigorous theological reasoning focused on understanding

---

24. Stanley J. Grenz, *Theology for the Community of God*, 2nd ed. (Grand Rapids: Wm. B. Eerdmans, 2000), p. xxxii.

and articulating biblical doctrine. But Pietism was for Grenz far more than praxis added to doctrine, as the descriptor "Pietist with a Ph.D." would seem to imply. Indeed, Grenz utilized Pietist sources to articulate and develop theological doctrines themselves.

The most obvious place where Grenz draws on Pietist sources is in his doctrine of Scripture. In the Pietist doctrine of Scripture, Grenz saw a way of overcoming the rigid rationalism of Protestant Orthodoxy, which had been actively appropriated by the early figures of post-fundamentalist evangelicalism in North America. In his attempt to articulate a "post-conservative" evangelicalism,[25] Grenz sought to recapture the role of experience for evangelical theology, while simultaneously criticizing the individualism inherent in much evangelical theology and piety.

In *Theology for the Community of God*, Grenz departed from much of post-fundamentalist evangelical theology by relocating Scripture under the locus of pneumatology. He argued that the Bible is best understood as "the Spirit's book."[26] Scripture's power and authority lay in the fact that in and through it, the Spirit speaks here and now in the midst of the community. Spener had emphasized that "if we could separate the Holy Spirit from the Word (which we cannot do), the Scripture would no longer work."[27] Likewise for Grenz, as the Spirit illumined and inspired the authors in their writing of the text, so must the Spirit be present in the reading or hearing of Scripture so that a person might truly hear and be "sealed" by the Word of God.[28]

For Grenz, in much the same way as for the Pietists, Scripture plays

25. Roger E. Olson was the first to coin the term "post-conservative evangelicalism." See Roger E. Olson, "Postconservative Evangelicals Greet the Postmodern Age," *Christian Century* 112 (3 May 1995): 480-83. See also Olson's most recent reflections on "post-conservative" evangelical theology: *Reformed and Always Reforming: The Post-conservative Approach to Evangelical Theology* (Grand Rapids: Baker Academic, 2007); and the more popular *How to Be Evangelical without Being Conservative* (Grand Rapids: Zondervan, 2008).

26. Grenz, *Theology for the Community of God*, p. 379.

27. Spener, "On the Necessary and Useful Reading of the Holy Scriptures," in *The Pietists: Selected Writings*, ed. Emilie Griffin and Peter C. Erb (San Francisco: HarperSanFrancisco, 2006), p. 72.

28. See Martin Schmidt, "Philip Jakob Spener und die Bibel," in *Pietismus und Bibel*, ed. Kurt Aland (Witten: Luther-Verlag, 1970), pp. 19-20.

a central role in God's active and living self-communication. The various missions of the Spirit bring this instrument alive. These include revelation, inspiration, and illumination, but relative to Scripture, Grenz argued that it was the Spirit's work of illumination which was primary.[29] In Pietism, illumination was also the key category under which both the production and the reception of Scripture were understood. Spener, among others, spoke more of the Spirit's work of inspiring or illuminating the writers of Holy Scripture than he spoke of an "inspired text." At the same time, Spener argued that the same Spirit which had illumined the authors of the text was necessary for its understanding. Thus, in general, Spener did not make a qualitative distinction between the guidance of the Holy Spirit in the production of the text and the guidance of the Holy Spirit in its reception. This allowed him to speak of "inspired" writers *and* readers of Holy Scripture.[30]

For Grenz, following the lead of many Pietists, it is the *Spirit speaking contemporaneously* through the Bible rather than a pneumatologically produced but now static (though supernaturally endowed) *text* that is the basis of Protestant theological authority. In other words, the authority of Scripture derives not from a quality in the text per se, but from the presently speaking Spirit who takes that text up — which nonetheless still has its origin in divine inspiration — and breathes life into the community of hearers through it. The real purpose of the Bible is to create fellowship with God. Grenz, explicitly drawing on the Pietist heritage, argued that Scripture is the source of spiritual sustenance:

> Thinkers such as Philip Jakob Spener (1635-1705) — the "father of Pietism" — and August Hermann Francke (1663-1727) focused on the importance of the Bible reader's spiritual condition: Only the regenerate understand Scripture correctly, they asserted. For the Pietists, talk about the truth-claims of the Bible was less important than the fact that "truth claims," that Scripture lays hold of the life of the reader and calls

29. See Grenz, *Theology for the Community of God*, p. 397.

30. For a discussion of this, see Donald W. Dayton, "The Pietist Theological Critique of Biblical Inerrancy," in *From the Margins: A Celebration of the Theological Work of Donald W. Dayton*, ed. Christian T. Collins Winn (Eugene, Ore.: Pickwick Publications, 2007), pp. 193-205.

that life into divine service. For them, the ultimate goal of Bible study is spiritual formation. Consequently, the Pietist way of reading the Bible included both diligence in bringing all our hermeneutical skills to bear on a passage and patience in listening for God's voice speaking through that text.[31]

Pietism spoke of Scripture inspiring a godly life in response to God.[32] The critical point for Grenz was that the source of theological authority *and* spiritual renewal lies with the Holy Spirit speaking through Scripture, rather than with an inherent quality that resides in the text. In emphasizing this point, Grenz, following the Pietists, was able to highlight the relational matrix in which the knowledge of God occurs. That is, for Pietists, there was a distinction between knowing God and knowing about God. Knowing God was the same thing as being encountered by God.[33]

Grenz's account of illumination also emphasized the communal dimension of the interpretation of Scripture. In his judgment, the *church* is the locus for discerning what the Spirit is saying through the text of Scripture. The event of illumination should be seen as more properly occurring in an ecclesiological context rather than in the interiority of the isolated individual. Although Grenz understood his ecclesially based hermeneutic as a safeguard against deficiencies in Pietism,[34] it is in fact consonant with the key aims of Pietism. In Spener's *Pia Desideria*, the emphasis on

31. Grenz, *Theology for the Community of God*, p. 389. See also Grenz, *Renewing the Center: Evangelical Theology in a Post-Theological Era* (Grand Rapids: Baker Academic, 2006), pp. 62-64.

32. See also C. John Weborg, "Pietism: Theology in Service of Living toward God," in *The Variety of American Evangelicalism*, ed. Robert K. Johnston and Donald W. Dayton (Knoxville: University of Tennessee Press, 2001), pp. 161-83.

33. This pneumatologically focused biblical hermeneutic and theological epistemology reinforced the conception of theology as a "practical discipline." See Philip Jacob Spener, *Pia Desideria* (Philadelphia: Fortress Press, 1964), pp. 104-5. For a brief discussion of this and its impact on theological education, see Johannes Wischmeyer, "Continuity and Change: The Study of Protestant Theology in Germany between the Reformation and the Humboldtian University Ideal," *Communio Viatorum* 47, no. 3 (2005): 246-50. See also Harry Yeide Jr., *Studies in Classical Pietism: The Flowering of the Ecclesiola* (New York: Peter Lang Publishing, 1997), pp. 39-61.

34. See Grenz, *Renewing the Center*, p. 291.

"new birth" was closely connected to a hope for the renewal of the church at large.[35] Thus, though substantial emphasis was indeed placed on the "new birth" as personally experienced, the context in which this occurred was not that of the isolated individual but that of the ecclesia — or, more precisely, the *ecclesiola in ecclesia*.

The role of Pietist cell groups — that is, the *ecclesiola in ecclesia, collegia pietatis*, or conventicles — was first and foremost to renew the church.[36] Spener argued that the renewal of the whole church would occur through exposure to Scripture, exercise of the priesthood of all believers, praxis over against mere intellectual assent, theological irenicism in matters of controversy, and the general reform of the educational system.[37] Although the personal element of transformation was central to this, the scope of these reforms suggests a far more communal and ecclesiological aim than Grenz was willing to admit. Spener had emphasized that scriptural study, and therefore illumination, did *not* refer primarily to private devotional reading but rather to reading and discussion in the cell group, or in the presence of the community.[38] Thus, Grenz's move to situate illumination in the context of the church was in fact a deeply pietistic move.

Grenz's attempt to recover the experiential dimension of Christian existence led him to reconsider and reconstruct his doctrine of Scripture along the lines of Pietists, who emphasized that Scripture's function was to give life and bring the community of faith into a renewing encounter with the living God. Although Grenz was unable to bring his full vision to fruition, his maturing theological work leaves a rich legacy with potent possibilities for the renewal of evangelical theology and offers a model for how to appropriate and integrate the insights of Pietist theological themes into a constructive vision for the present and the future.

35. See Spener, *Pia Desideria*, pp. 76-86.

36. An excellent discussion of this can be found in Dale W. Brown, *Understanding Pietism* (Grand Rapids: Wm. B. Eerdmans, 1978). Harry Yeide Jr. has shown that the full implication of these conventicles was not worked out until the late eighteenth and early nineteenth centuries. See his *Studies in Classical Pietism: The Flowering of the Ecclesiola*.

37. See Spener, *Pia Desideria*, pp. 87-115.

38. Spener, *Pia Desideria*, pp. 89-90. "But how shall they occupy themselves with the Word of God? They shall use it for themselves and among or with others." See Philipp Jakob Spener, "The Spiritual Priesthood," in *The Pietists: Selected Writings*, ed. Griffin and Erb, p. 7.

Jürgen Moltmann

Our final case study of a contemporary theologian influenced by Pietism is one of the most important and widely read Protestant theologians of the latter half of the twentieth century. Jürgen Moltmann (b. 1926) was born in Hamburg, Germany. In 1943, Moltmann was conscripted into the auxiliary air force as an anti-aircraft gunner. That same year, he survived Operation Gomorrah, which resulted in the fire-bombing of Hamburg and the death of 40,000 civilians.[39] He was captured by the British army in 1945 and was a prisoner of war, being moved from camp to camp, until 1948. His experience as a POW, as well as the revelations of the Holocaust, which became known after the war, plummeted Moltmann into a deep depression, and he surrendered his long-held desire to study mathematics and science. "What was the point of it all?" he asked.[40]

It was during this time that Moltmann received a Bible, and through reading it and developing friendships with the Scottish camp guards and workers, he slowly found a new path and a new set of questions. Those questions centered on the reality of human suffering, the presence of the crucified Jesus in the midst of human suffering, and the power of God's future. Moltmann would later say that this was the beginning of his companionship with Jesus, whom one must decide to follow again and again.[41] After studying theology at Göttingen University, where he encountered the theology of Karl Barth, Moltmann served as pastor of a Reformed congregation in a village in the region of Bremen from 1953 to 1958. From 1958 to 1963, he was professor of theology at the *Kirchliche Hochschule* in Wuppertal; from 1963 to 1967, he was professor of systematic theology and ethics at the University of Bonn; and from 1967 until his retirement in 1994, he held the chair in Protestant systematic theology at the internationally renowned University of Tübingen.

Moltmann's contributions to theology have been considerable, especially in the field of eschatology. Highlights include his *Theology of Hope* (1964), *The Crucified God* (1972), *God in Creation* (1985), *The Spirit of Life*

39. Jürgen Moltmann, *A Broad Place: An Autobiography* (Minneapolis: Fortress Press, 2008), pp. 16-17.
40. Moltmann, *A Broad Place*, p. 26.
41. Moltmann, *A Broad Place*, pp. 30-31.

(1991), and *The Coming of God* (1995). All of Moltmann's work is marked by a deep commitment to think through the contemporary social and political challenges that confront society and Christian theology "after Auschwitz," and to attempt to do so from the position of those "on the underside of history" — that is, from the perspective of the marginalized, the oppressed, and the broken-hearted, who cry out for liberation from bondage to the death-dealing powers and principalities of this world.

With regard to the influence and appropriation of Pietist themes and figures, over the course of his long career Moltmann has been especially drawn to the eschatologically charged aspects of Württemberg Pietism.[42] This interest has manifested itself both in his eschatology proper and in his attempt to offer an eschatologically framed theology of creation.

In his 1985 volume *God in Creation*, Moltmann appropriated elements of Friedrich Oetinger's theology of nature. This is especially evident in chapter ten, the title of which is "Embodiment Is the End of All God's Works" (a well-known aphorism of Oetinger);[43] here Moltmann articulates a holistic theological anthropology in which a central theme is life. Critiquing the dualisms of body and soul, Moltmann argues for an organic conception in which neither soul nor body can be said to take primacy: "If 'embodiment' is the end of all God's works, then the human body cannot be viewed as a lower form of life, or as a means to an end — and certainly not as something that has to be overcome."[44] Rather, both body and soul mutually interpenetrate one another and are oriented in the direction of God's redemptive embodiment: the new creation. "We arrive at the theological perception of the truth of the human being in the arc that reaches from his physical creation to the resurrection of the body."[45] Moltmann's conception of an organic vision of human identity and nature in no sense slavishly follows Oetinger; indeed, it creatively goes beyond Oetinger by including the constitutive role that context or *Gestalt* plays in constituting the individual human being. In this, and in his emphasis on the new creation teleology that forms and moves human life, Moltmann's work shares

---

42. See Moltmann, *A Broad Place*, p. 155.

43. See Jürgen Moltmann, *God in Creation* (Minneapolis: Fortress Press, 1993), p. 244.

44. Moltmann, *God in Creation*, p. 245.

45. Moltmann, *God in Creation*, p. 246.

substantial similarities to Oetinger's theology of life, which we discussed earlier.[46]

Recently, Moltmann has turned more resolutely to the theology of Christoph Blumhardt as a source for articulating his theology of creation. Blumhardt's emphasis on the cosmic Christ, and especially his conviction that the resurrection of Jesus reveals to us the true end not only of humanity but of the earth itself, have been especially important to Moltmann. Blumhardt "understood the kingdom of God as the 'kingdom of the resurrection on earth,' and brought the realism of bodiliness and faithfulness to the earth into Protestant theology, which was, generally speaking, idealistic and individualistic."[47] "With Christ's resurrection the purification of the earth from 'sin and death' already begins now. God's new world is already beginning in the midst of the old one."[48] For Moltmann, Blumhardt embodied a radical, Christologically grounded faithfulness to the earth.[49]

The influence of Christoph Blumhardt can also be detected in Moltmann's theology of hope and eschatology. As Moltmann himself admitted, "My 'Theology of Hope' has two roots: Christoph Blumhardt and Ernst Bloch. I was not in Bad Boll; nor was I in Württemberg. But I was first influenced by Christoph Blumhardt before I read Ernst Bloch through my involvement with others in a 'Blumhardt circle.'"[50] What drew Moltmann to Blumhardt was the latter's orientation toward "the lost horizons of Christian faith: genuine worldliness, true humanness, simple naturalness, and the 'wide space' of the Spirit in the dawn of the Kingdom of

---

46. See also Martin Weyer-Menkhoff, "Friedrich Christoph Oetinger (1702-1782)," in *The Pietist Theologians*, ed. Carter Lindberg (Malden, Mass.: Blackwell Publishing, 2005), pp. 250-52. See also Jürgen Moltmann, *Theology of Hope: On the Ground and Implications of a Christian Eschatology* (Minneapolis: Fortress Press, 1993), p. 72.

47. Jürgen Moltmann, *Ethics of Hope* (Minneapolis: Fortress Press, 2012), p. 118.

48. Jürgen Moltmann, *Sun of Righteousness, Arise!: God's Future for Humanity and the Earth* (Minneapolis: Fortress Press, 2010), p. 81.

49. See Jürgen Moltmann, "The Hope for the Kingdom of God and Signs of Hope in the World: The Relevance of Blumhardt's Theology Today," *Pneuma* 26, no. 1 (Fall 2004): 4-16.

50. Moltmann, "The Hope for the Kingdom of God and Signs of Hope in the World," p. 4.

God."[51] Over the course of Moltmann's long career, the orientation about which he speaks has been translated into fundamental convictions, including these: Christianity is essentially eschatological in its orientation; the Christian ethic is shaped and driven by hope in God's future for the world; and God's future for the world leaves open a hope for a universal restoration of all things.[52]

Of particular importance was Blumhardt's insight that the resurrection generates hope and hopeful action in and for this age, and not simply for an age or time "outside of history." The resurrection of Jesus is God's protest in the here and now against the dominion of death — a protest that will eventuate in death's final defeat, because "the living God and death are irreconcilable antitheses."[53] Taking up Blumhardt's passionate cry that "No hell, no sin, no death counts, because Jesus is alive!",[54] Moltmann argues that God is at work overthrowing the powers of death in the here and now. In light of the divine revolution, God's act of resurrection enlists the Christian community, and they become a "protest people against death"[55] — a people who set aside their own ambitions in order to pray and struggle for the liberation of humanity and the earth from the powers of death.[56]

Furthermore, for Moltmann, as for Blumhardt, the resurrecting power of God knows no bounds, a fact which gives it a cosmic horizon and opens him to the temptation to universalism. Nevertheless, he denies that he is a universalist. Rather, he argues that he is compelled to contemplate and hope that God's grace is greater than can possibly be imagined: "If I examine myself seriously, I find that I have to say: I am not a universalist,

---

51. Moltmann, "The Hope for the Kingdom of God and Signs of Hope in the World," p. 5.

52. For a discussion of these, see Christian T. Collins Winn and Peter Goodwin Heltzel, "'Before Bloch, there was Blumhardt': A Thesis on the Origins of the Theology of Hope," *Scottish Journal of Theology* 62, no. 1 (2009): 32-35, 37-39.

53. Moltmann, *Sun of Righteousness, Arise!*, p. 81.

54. Christoph Friedrich Blumhardt, *Eine Auswahl aus seinen Predigten, Andachten und Schriften*, ed. R. Lejeune (Zürich: Rotapfel-Verlag, 1936), p. 17.

55. Moltmann, *Sun of Righteousness, Arise!*, p. 81.

56. See Jürgen Moltmann, *The Church in the Power of the Spirit: A Contribution to Messianic Ecclesiology* (Minneapolis: Fortress Press, 1993), p. 283.

but God may be one."[57] This approach bears a striking resemblance to the thinking of a number of key figures in Württemberg Pietism, a fact of which Moltmann is well aware.[58]

On Moltmann's seventy-fifth birthday in 2001, the Protestant Regional Bishop from Württemberg, Paul Dieterich, described Moltmann as a "Swabian Father" who ranked alongside Johann Albrecht Bengel, Friedrich Christoph Oetinger, and Christoph Blumhardt. In response, Moltmann noted that he struggled to find words of thanks for being included among those "beside whom I had never deemed myself worthy to stand."[59] In spite of his genuine humility, it is undeniable that although it draws from a wide variety of sources, Moltmann's theological vision is nevertheless in many ways a translation of some of the most important themes of Württemberg Pietism into the idioms and contexts of the twentieth- and twenty-first centuries. And thus his work helps present and future generations to see the genuine possibilities and promise of this remarkable strand of the Pietist tradition.

Conclusion

The Pietist ethos is alive and well in contemporary Christianity even if the word "Pietism" is often misunderstood and the concept misrepresented. Our four exemplars in this chapter confirm the continuing influence of true Pietism in scholarly Christian theology. None of the people described in this chapter could be considered anti-intellectual or legalistic or "holier-than-thou" super-spiritual people who were or are too heavenly-minded. They are all highly respected and influential Christian theologians who embodied (and, in Moltmann's case, still embody) the Pietist spirit and spread it to others even where "Pietism" is disdained (due to misunderstanding). We believe these four and other Pietist theologians have much to offer the renewal of contemporary Christianity.

57. Jürgen Moltmann, *Jesus Christ for Today's World* (Minneapolis: Fortress Press, 1994), p. 143.

58. See Jürgen Moltmann, *The Coming of God: Christian Eschatology* (Minneapolis: Fortress Press, 1996), pp. 238-39.

59. Moltmann, *A Broad Place*, p. 363.

Pietism as a Way of Doing Evangelical Theology

If we have been successful in this book, we have not only informed readers about Pietism, the movement and the ethos, but also convinced readers that Pietism offers valuable resources for contemporary, postmodern, evangelical Christianity. We make no claim that it is the only valuable resource — just that it is a much-neglected and often unfairly maligned one. On the other hand, we do believe that Pietism points toward a way of doing Christian theology that is more authentically evangelical than alternatives.

If evangelical Christianity is anything, it is orthodoxy on fire, "head belief" and "heart experience" brought together. Evangelicals believe these two dimensions — doctrine and devotion — belong together for holistic, authentic Christian life. Too often these dimensions are divorced from each other, if not pitted against each other. True Pietism urges that they be united, and that the heart experience of God in Jesus Christ through the Holy Spirit — which touches the emotions, the affections — informs belief.

That makes especially conservative evangelicals (and perhaps others) nervous. Their fear is that Pietism will allow subjective experience to guide doctrinal belief, with the end result that "anything goes." That's not true Pietism. Any good thing can be misused. The cure for abuse is not disuse but proper use. As we have shown throughout this book, churchly Pietism, as opposed to some radical Pietism, does not offend the authority of the Bible or reject orthodox doctrine. What Pietism opposes is not right belief but dead orthodoxy — right belief without right affections.

It would be wrong to suppose, however, that Pietism is simply an attempt to add feeling to correct doctrine — as if the former had nothing to say to or about the latter. Pietism asks whether dead orthodoxy ever *is* "correct doctrine." And it insists that without convertive piety, devotion that arises from and deepens the transforming personal relationship with God in the "inner man," doctrine and theology amount to little more than useless speculation. Pietism says that God's revelation to humanity in Jesus Christ and Scripture was not primarily for information but primarily for transformation. Pietism interprets Paul's exhortation to be transformed by the renewing of our minds (Rom. 12:2) to mean that right thinking about God comes only in and through the Holy Spirit's renewing activity. It is not something we do to ourselves merely by means of reading and studying.

Pietism does not wish to empty the cognitive dimension of Christian faith of its importance; it wants only to put it in its proper place — as servant of God's main purpose, which is to transform us into Christ-like persons. The most coherent and contemporary system of theology does not do that by itself; the most correct creed does not change anyone's life by itself. As important as these are, they too easily become substitutes for Christian commitment that arises only from devotion that is real only in personal relationship with God through Jesus Christ, the living and loving Savior who wants to be our friend as well as our master.

So, what does this mean for Christian theology? What does Christian theology informed by Pietism look like?

First, doctrine informed by Pietism should be ministerial rather than magisterial. Its aim should be inspiration and instruction, not mere propositional knowledge. And doctrine, as important as it is, should not be viewed as the "essence" of Christianity, which is transformation of the "inner man" into the image of Christ. However, just because correct doctrine is not the essence of Christianity does not mean it is unimportant; it serves an essential role in Christian life — guiding the church's witness and proclamation and inspiring Christians to glorify God and enjoy him because of who he is and what he has done.

Second, theology informed by Pietism avoids useless speculation and arguments over matters that do not touch the gospel or have nothing to do with God's transforming mission in individuals' lives and in the world. Of course, a certain amount of speculation is inevitable in theology, but it should be labeled as such and not elevated to the status of dogma. Pietism resists detailed systems of propositional truth claims that go beyond what Scripture warrants and Christian living requires in terms of logical coherence and detail. During the Middle Ages, so it is often reported, Christian theologians debated how many angels could dance on the head of a pin. Pietism turns away from that and similar questions to issues that matter to Christian life. Surely referring to the overly detailed, scholastic theological systems of his day, Zinzendorf quipped that as soon as one puts Christianity into a system, he kills it. That may be hyperbole, but Pietism is suspicious of closed and totalizing systems because they often become substitutes for the Bible itself and shut out new light from God's Word.

Third, theology informed by Pietism seeks to be irenic and ecumenical. Contrary to common misconceptions of Pietism, however, theology informed by it is not open to anything and everything. As we have shown throughout this book, historical, classical Pietism values doctrine and has been, for the most part, orthodox. However, a popular Pietist maxim, often quoted by people who have no appreciation for Pietism, is this: "In essentials, unity; in non-essentials, liberty; in all things, charity [love]."[1] That expresses irenicism — peaceful acceptance of non-essential differences in theology and love for all — even heretics! But what are essentials and non-essentials? Most Pietists, including the Pietist founders, would say the essentials are the core dogmas of historic, orthodox Christianity: the incarnation of God in Christ, the Trinity, and salvation through Christ's atoning death. Non-essentials would include doctrines about the "end things" (eschatology) and theories of the atonement.

Far too much conservative evangelical theology has been devoted to debating non-essentials, often using the rhetoric of exclusion against those who disagree with a particular "sacred cow" doctrine of a theologian or group. Pietism seeks unity around the essentials and love for persons in spite of disagreements about doctrines not tied to the gospel itself.

Pietism in theology also reaches across traditional boundaries and barriers to establish dialogue with "other" Christians. It does not neces-

---

1. The maxim is attributed to many individuals, and nobody knows who first uttered or wrote it. It was used as a principle by Moravians and other Pietists, but no claim is made here that Pietists coined it.

sarily seek the visible and institutional unity of churches, considering that less important than fellowship, cooperation, mutual understanding, and intercommunion. Pietism does not disdain proper preserving of particularities; it only seeks mutual acceptance as equally Christian among believers in Jesus Christ and the gospel who disagree about secondary matters. In an age of so-called Balkanization in which denominations and religious organizations continually divide and often cast aspersions at each other, such ecumenism of the Spirit is a much-needed corrective.

Fourth, according to Pietism, theology should be informed and guided (not governed) by prayer and devotion. Pietism believes that Christian theology should never be a merely academic exercise; it should be practiced and believed within the bosom of the worshiping community by individuals whose lives are committed to Christ by faith. This is not to say that theology is esoteric — a secret discipline understood only by initiates and adepts (as in Gnosticism). It means that, like every discipline, theology is best worked out in love for its object — God and God's special revelation in Jesus Christ and Scripture. Head and heart should operate in harmony and cooperation in the "doing" of theology. Pietists are rightly wary of Christian theologians who lack clear evidence of devotion to Christ in vibrant spirituality and for whom theology is an "objective science" divorced from life-transforming experience of God. To put it bluntly, a systematic theology or set of dogmas that does not evidence and evoke spiritual feelings of gratitude to God, sorrow for sin, and aspirations for holiness is worthless if not harmful. An Eastern Orthodox maxim is that prayer is the rule of theology. Pietists agree. In other words, theology that cannot be prayed or does not evoke prayer has gone off the rails.

None of this is to say that individual spiritual experience governs doctrine; for Pietism, doctrine is governed by revelation found especially in Scripture. It does mean, however, that profoundly spiritual experience that is Christ-centered and God-glorifying should guide theology into new paths of inquiry and reflection and away from doctrinal dead ends. Pietists have typically focused a great deal of attention not on the fine points of systematic theology but rather on the dynamics of faith, the meaning of repentance, and the process of sanctification, because these intersect with spiritual life and growth in transforming intimacy with God.

Fifth, theology and doctrine informed by Pietism should never be objects of devotion. Karl Barth declared that the lowest reaches of hell are reserved for those who are more interested in their thoughts about God than in God himself. Of course, that was hyperbole, but it points to a truth valued by Pietism. Doctrines and systems of theology (and Barth would include his own in this!) should never be put on a pedestal and venerated. Pietists believe that this is a common form of idolatry found especially among Christians who overemphasize orthodoxy to the neglect of orthopathy (right feeling) and orthopraxy (right living). This idolatry appears as a danger whenever Christians grant ultimacy to a doctrine or theological system. Instead, theology and doctrine informed by Pietism should always point away from themselves toward God. That means they must remain open to correction in the light of God's Word.

We are convinced that classical Christian Pietism, as we have reclaimed it here, offers contemporary evangelical Christianity a resource for its own renewal, and that holds true for evangelical theology as well as evangelical devotion and worship. Forgetfulness of evangelicalism's Pietist heritage can lead to dead orthodoxy, unnecessary and divisive disputes over secondary doctrines, polemics over spiritual enrichment and growth, and a focus on speculation about obscure portions of Scripture. Evangelicalism that remembers and learns from the Pietist heritage can only be spiritually stronger and theologically more balanced as a result of rediscovering its impulses.

General Index